Lecture Notes in Computer Science   9228

Commenced Publication in 1973
Founding and Former Series Editors:
Gerhard Goos, Juris Hartmanis, and Jan van Leeuwen

Editorial Board

More information about this series at http://www.springer.com/series/7409

Muhammad Younas · Irfan Awan
Massimo Mecella (Eds.)

Mobile Web and Intelligent Information Systems

12th International Conference, MobiWis 2015
Rome, Italy, August 24–26, 2015
Proceedings

 Springer

Editors
Muhammad Younas
Oxford Brookes University
Oxford
UK

Massimo Mecella
Sapienza University of Rome
Rome
Italy

Irfan Awan
School of Engineering and Informatics
University of Bradford
Bradford, West Yorkshire
UK

ISSN 0302-9743   ISSN 1611-3349   (electronic)
Lecture Notes in Computer Science
ISBN 978-3-319-23143-3   ISBN 978-3-319-23144-0   (eBook)
DOI 10.1007/978-3-319-23144-0

Library of Congress Control Number: 2015946572

LNCS Sublibrary: SL3 – Information Systems and Applications, incl. Internet/Web, and HCI

Springer Cham Heidelberg New York Dordrecht London

Printed on acid-free paper

Springer International Publishing AG Switzerland is part of Springer Science+Business Media (www.springer.com)

Preface

This volume includes a collection of research articles presented at the 12th International Conference on Mobile Web and Intelligent Information Systems (MobiWis 2015), held in Rome, Italy, August 24–26, 2015.

Mobile Web and technologies have now become part of everyday life. The number and use of mobile/smart phone users has been increasing at a rapid pace. People have now access to the Web at anytime and from anywhere in order to carry out various activities ranging from simple Web browsing through to social networking (Twitter, WhatsApp, Facebook) to online shopping. The surge of mobile apps has further contributed to the significant increase in the use and popularity of mobile Web. Google Play, Apple's App Store, and others provide a plethora of apps for different mobile devices and for different tasks. Examples include, FitBit, AEMC, GMaps+, Viber, and Uber, to name but a few.

The International Conference on Mobile Web and Intelligent Information Systems (MobiWis) aims to advance research on and practical applications of mobile Web, information systems, and related mobile technologies. It provides a forum for researchers, developers, and practitioners from academia and industry to share research ideas, knowledge, and experiences in the areas of mobile Web and information systems. MobiWis 2015 comprised a set of tracks that included new and emerging areas such as: smart and intelligent systems, mobile software systems, middleware/SOA for mobile systems, context- and location-aware services, data management in the mobile Web, mobile cloud services, mobile Web of things, mobile Web security, trust and privacy, mobile networks, protocols and applications, mobile commerce and business services, HCI in mobile applications, social media, and adaptive approaches for mobile computing.

MobiWis 2015 attracted 55 submissions from various countries across the world. All the papers were peer-reviewed by members of the Program Committee. Based on the reviews, 20 papers were accepted for the conference – 17 full and 3 short papers, with the acceptance rate of 36 %. The accepted papers covered a range of topics related to the theme of the conference. In addition to the research articles, MobiWis 2015 featured two invited talks by Riccardo Rosati, Sapienza Università di Roma, Italy, and Avigdor Gal, Technion - Israel Institute of Technology, Israel. These talks were delivered in conjunction with the co-located conferences of the Third International Conference on Future Internet of Things and Cloud (FiCloud 2015) and the International Conference on Open and Big Data (OBD 2015).

We would like to thank the invited speakers for delivering very interesting and visionary talks. We would also like to thank all authors for submitting their work to MobiWis 2015 and for contributing to this. We also thank all the Program Committee members who provided valuable and constructive feedback to the authors and to the program chairs. We would like to thank members of the Organizing Committee for their help and support in the organization of the conference.

We would like to thank the local organizing team of the Sapienza Università di Roma, Italy, for their great help and support, in particular Francesco Leotta and Andrea Marrella. Our sincere thanks also go to the Springer LNCS team, Alfred Hofmann, and Anna Kramer for their valuable support in the approval and production of the conference proceedings.

August 2015

Muhammad Younas
Irfan Awan
Massimo Mecella

Organization

MobiWis 2015 Organizing Committee

General Chair

Massimo Mecella   Sapienza Università di Roma, Italy

Program Co-chairs

Muhammad Younas   Oxford Brookes University, UK
Leonard Barolli   Fukuoka Institute of Technology, Japan

International Liaison Chair

Irfan Awan   University of Bradford, UK

Local Organizing Chair

Francesco Leotta   Sapienza Università di Roma, Italy

Track Chairs

Abdel Lisser   Université Paris Sud, France
Agnis Stibe   Massachusetts Institute of Technology (MIT), USA
Alberto Sillitti   Free University of Bolzano, Italy
Barbara Masucci   University of Salerno, Italy
Hadi Otrok   Khalifa University, UAE
George Ghinea   Brunel University, UK
Jian Yu   Auckland University of Technology, New Zealand
Markus Aleksy   ABB AG Corporate Research Center, Germany
Mirella M. Moro   Universidade Federal de Minas Gerais, Brazil
Rafidah Noor   University of Malaya, Malaysia
Sergio Ilarri   University of Zaragoza, Spain
Takahiro Hara   Osaka University, Japan
Tomoya Enokido   Rissho University, Japan
Vincenzo De Florio   University of Antwerp and iMinds Research Institute,
                                  Belgium
Weifeng Chen   California University of Pennsylvania, USA

Workshop Coordinator

Samia Loucif   ALHOSN University, UAE

Publicity Chair

Eiman Kanjo   Nottingham Trent University, UK
Andrea Marrella   Sapienza Università di Roma, Italy

Journal Special Issue Coordinator

Bernady O. Apduhan   Kyushu Sangyo University, Japan

Program Committee

Track: Smart and Intelligent Systems

Sergio Ilarri   University of Zaragoza, Spain (Track Chair)
Apostolos Papadopoulos   Aristotle University of Thessaloniki, Greece
Carlos Calafate   Technical University of Valencia, Spain
Cristian Borcea   University Heights, Newark, USA
Diego Lopez-de-Ipina   Deusto Institute of Technology, Spain
Florence Sedes   University Paul Sabatier Toulouse, France
Maria Luisa   Damiani Università degli Studi di Milano, Italy
Ouri Wolfson   University of Illinois at Chicago, USA
Philippe Roose   IUT de Bayonne, France
Raquel Trillo   University of Zaragoza, Spain
Riccardo Martoglia   University of Modena and Reggio Emilia, Italy

Track: Mobile Software Systems

Alberto Sillitti   Free University of Bolzano, Italy (Track Chair)
Ruth Breu   University of Innsbruck, Austria
Anton Georgiev   Free University of Bolzano, Italy
Francesco Di Cerbo   SAP, France
Grace Lewis   Canegie Mellon University, USA
Tommi Mikkonen   Tampere University of Technology, Finland
Davide Taibi   University of Kaiserslautern, Germany
Aaron Visaggio   University of Sannio, Italy
Tony Wasserman   Carnegie Mellon University Silicon Valley, USA
Grace Lewis   Carnegie Mellon Software Engineering Institute, USA

Track: Adaptive Approaches for Mobile Computing

Vincenzo De Florio   University of Antwerp and iMinds Research Institute,
                                     Belgium (Track Chair)
Maher Ben Jemaa   ReDCAD-ENIS, Tunisia

Andrea Clematis IMATI - CNR, Italy
Giovanna Di Marzo University of Geneva, Switzerland
  Serugendo
Flavio Lombardi Istituto per le Applicazioni del Calcolo, IAC-CNR,
  Italy
Henry Muccini University of L'Aquila, Italy
Eric Pardede La Trobe University, Australia
Patrizio Pelliccione Chalmers University of Technology and University of
  Gothenburg, Sweden
Philipp Reinecke Freie Universität Berlin, Germany
Francesca Saglietti University of Erlangen-Nuremberg, Germany

Track: Middleware/SOA for Mobile Systems

Tomoya Enokido Rissho University, Japan (Track Chair)
Aniello Castiglione University of Salerno, Italy
Makoto Ikeda Fukuoka Institute of Technology, Japan
Akio Koyama Yamagata University, Japan
Stephane Maag Telecom SudParis, France
Francesco Palmieri Second University of Naples, Italy
Vamsi Krishna Paruchuri University of Central Arkansas, USA
Fumiaki Sato Toho University, Japan
Noriki Uchida Saitama Institute of Technology, Japan
Minoru Uehara Toyo University, Japan
Isaac Woungang Ryerson University, Canada

Track: Context- and Location-Aware Services

Weifeng Chen California University of Pennsylvania, USA
  (Track Chair)
Rafael E. Banchs I2R, Singapore
Cyril Ray Naval Academy Research Institute (IRENav), France
Diego Lopez-de-Ipina Deusto Institute of Technology, Spain
Dragan Stojanovic University of Nis, Serbia
Florence Sedes Paul Sabatier University, France
Maria Luisa Damiani Università degli Studi di Milano, Italy
Ouri Wolfson University of Illinois at Chicago, USA
Philippe Pucheral University of Versailles Saint-Quentin en Yvelines,
  France
Thierry Delot University of Valenciennes and Inria Lille, France
Quanqing Xu Data Storage Institute, Singapore
Ying Yan Microsoft Search and Technology Center, China
Bin Yang Max Planck Institute for Informatics, Germany
Yongluan Zhou University of Southern Denmark, The Netherlands
Tingting Yang Dalian Maritime University, China
Costas Mourlas University of Athens, Greece

Andrea Omicini   University of Bologna, Italy
Viet-Duc Le   University of Twente, The Netherlands

Track: Pervasive and Ubiquitous Applications

Hadi Otrok   Khalifa University, UAE (Track Chair)
Azzam Mourad   Lebanese American University, Lebanon
Rabeb Mizouni   Khalifa University, UAE
Jamal Bentahar   Concordia University, Canada
Zbigniew Dziong   ETS University, Canada
Rebeca Estrada   Escuela Superior Politecnica del Litoral, Ecuador
Ahmad Al-Rubaie   British Telecommunication BT/EBTIC, UK
Anis Ouali   EBTIC, UAE
Jean Marc Robert   ETS University, Canada
Babak Khosravifar   McGill University, Canada
Noman Mohammed   University of Manitoba, Canada
Koralia Pappi   Aristotle University of Thessaloniki, Greece
Omar Abdel Wahab   Concordia University, Canada
Ehsan K. Asl   Concordia University, Canada
Katty Rohoden Jaramillo   Universidad Tecnica Particular de Loja, Ecuador

Track: Data Management in the Mobile Web

Mirella M. Moro   Universidade Federal de Minas Gerais, Brazil
                                (Track Chair)
Carina Dorneles   Universidade Federal de Santa Catarina, Brazil
Davide Taibi   University of Bolzano, Italy
Eli Cortez   Microsoft, USA
Francesco Di Cerbo   SAP, France
Francesco Guerra   Università degli Studi di Modena e Reggio Emilia, Italy
Georgios Chatzimilioudis   University of Cyprus, Cyprus
Harmidah Ibrahim   Universiti Putra Malaysia, Malaysia
Marcos Antonio Vaz Salles   University of Copenhagen, Denmark
Rafael E. Banchs   I2R, Singapore
Renata Galante   Universidade Federal do Rio Grande do Sul, Brazil
Ruth Breu   University of Innsbruck, Austria
Tommi Mikkonen   Tampere University of Technology, Finland
Vanessa Braganholo   Universidade Federal Fluminense, Brazil

Track: Mobile Cloud Services

Takahiro Hara   Osaka University, Japan (Track Chair)
Claudia Canali   Università di Modena e Reggio Emilia, Italy
Chi-Yin Chow   City University of Hong Kong, Hong Kong,
                                SAR China
Yuka Kato   Tokyo Woman's Christian University, Japan
Hiroaki Kikuchi   Meiji University, Japan
Sanjay Madria   Missouri University of Science and Technology, USA

Pedro Jose Marron	University of Duisburg-Essen, Germany
Ken Ohta	NTT DoCoMo, Japan
Masahiro Sasabe	NAIST, Japan
Hiroshi Shigeno	Keio University, Japan
Lei Shu Guangdong	University of Petrochemical Technology, China
Stephan Sigg	Technische Universität Braunschweig, Germany
Jorge Sa Silva	University of Coimbra, Portugal

Track: Mobile Web of Things

George Ghinea	Brunel University, UK (Track Chair)
Wu-Yuin Hwang	National Central University, Taiwan
Johnson Thomas	Oklahoma State University, USA
Daniel Rodriguez	Alcala University, Spain
David Bell	Brunel University, UK
Gabriel-Miro Muntean	Dublin City University, Ireland
Andre Hinkenjann	Bonn-Rhein-Sieg University, Germany
Dide Midekso	Addis Ababa University, Ethiopia
Ramona Trestian	Middlesex University, UK
Tacha Serif	Yeditepe University, Turkey
Tor-Morten Gronli	Westerdals - Oslo School of Arts, Communication and Technology, Norway
Rajkumar Kannan	King Faisal University, Saudi Arabia

Track: Mobile Web Security, Trust, and Privacy

Barbara Masucci	University of Salerno, Italy (Track Chair)
Karl Andersson	Lulea University of Technology, Sweden
Aniello Castiglione	University of Salerno, Italy
Thanh van Do	Telenor and Norwegian University of Science and Technology, Norway
Muslim Elkotob	MB TDF Group, Germany
Anna Lisa Ferrara	University of Surrey, UK
Ugo Fiore	University of Naples, Italy
Paolo Gasti	New York Institute of Technology, USA
Hiroaki Kikuchi	Meiji University, Japan
Shinsaku Kiyomoto	KDDI R&D Laboratories Inc., Japan
Fang-Yie Leu	TungHai University, Taiwan
Jin Li	Guangzhou University, China
Jingwei Li	The Chinese University of Hong Kong, Hong Kong, SAR China
Jeng-Wei Lin	TungHai University, Japan
John Lindstrom	Lulea University of Technology, Sweden
Jung-Chun Liu	TungHai University, Japan
Lidia Ogiela	AGH University of Science and Technology, Poland
Marek R. Ogiela	AGH University of Science and Technology, Poland
Emmanuela Orsini	University of Bristol, UK

Francesco Palmieri   Second University of Naples, Italy
Akira Yamada   KDDI R&D Laboratories Inc., Japan
Yinghui Zhang   Xi'an University of Posts and Communications, China
Florin Pop   University Politehnica of Bucharest, Romani
Massimo Cafaro   University of Salento, Italy

Track: Mobile Networks, Protocols, and Applications

Abdel Lisser   Université Paris Sud, France (Track Chair)
Paolo Nesi   University of Florence, Italy
Alexandre Caminada   University of Belfort Monbeliard, France
Jianqiang Cheng   University of Paris Sud, France
Janny Leung   Chinese University of Hong Kong, Hong Kong,
                            SAR China
Pablo Adasme   University of Santiago de Chile, Chile
Ignacio Soto Campos   University Carlos III de Madrid, Spain
Carlos A. Iglesias   Universidad Politecnica de Madrid, Spain
Andrea Cullen   University of Bradford, UK
Rafael Andrade   Federal University of Sierra, Brazil

Track: Mobile Commerce and Business Services

Jian Yu   Auckland University of Technology, New Zealand
                            (Track Chair)
Ding Chen   Ryerson University, Canada
Paolo Falcarin   University of East London, UK
Talal Noor   Taibah University, Saudi Arabia
Hong-Linh Truong   Vienna University of Technology, Austria
Guiling Wang   North China University of Technology, China
Lianghuai Yang   Zhejiang University of Technology, China
Lina Yao   The University of Adelaide, Australia
Sira Yongchareon   Unitec Institute of Technology, New Zealand
Zibing Zheng   The Chinese University of Hong Kong, SAR China

Track: HCI in Mobile Applications and Socially Influencing Systems

Agnis Stibe   Massachusetts Institute of Technology (MIT), USA
Lalit Garg   University of Malta, Malta
Anna Spagnolli   University of Padua, Italy
Jaap Ham   Eindhoven University of Technology, The Netherlands
Anssi Oorni   University of Oulu, Finland
Samir Chatterjee   Claremont Graduate University, USA
Filip Drozd   National Center for Infant Mental Health, Norway
Teppo Raisanen   Oulu University of Applied Sciences, Finland
Daryl Foy   University of Tasmania, Australia
Frank Verberne   Eindhoven University of Technology, The Netherlands
Rita Orji   Yale University, USA
Borja Gamecho   University of the Basque Country, Spain

Fabio Paterno   National Research Council (CNR), Italy
Joanna Lumsden   Aston University, UK
Jose Coelho   University of Lisbon, Portugal
Kari Kuutti   University of Oulu, Finland
Dan Lockton   Royal College of Art, UK
Saskia Kelders   University of Twente, The Netherlands

Track: Industry and Demo

Markus Aleksy   ABB AG Corporate Research Center, Germany
                           (Track Chair)
Giacomo Cabri   University of Modena and Reggio Emilia, Italy
Shakeel Mahate   ABB Corporate Research, USA
Thomas Preuss   University of Brandenburg, Germany
Mikko Rissanen   Improventions, Malaysia
Didier Stricker   DFKI, Germany

Track: General - Mobile Web and Intelligent Information Systems

Rafidah Noor   University of Malaya, Malaysia (Track Chair)
Artur Niewiadomski   Siedlce University, Poland
Chi (Harold) Liu   Beijing Institute of Technology, China
Christos Bouras   University of Patras, Greece
Fabio Crestani   University of Lugano (USI), Switzerland
Fatma Abdennadher   National School of Engineering of Sfax, Tunisia
Lina Yao   University of Adelaide, Australia
Lulwah AlSuwaidan   King Saud University, Saudi Arabia
Maizatul Akmar Ismail   University of Malaya, Malaysia
Michael Sheng   The University of Adelaide, Australia
Mohammad Reza   University of Malaya, Malaysia
  Jabbarpour
Mohd Hanafi Ahmad Hijazi UMS, Malaysia
Muhammad Shiraz   Federal Urdu University of Arts, Science and
                           Technology, Pakistan
Natalia Kryvinska   University of Vienna, Austria
Norazlina Khamis   Universiti Malaysia Sabah, Malaysia
Novia Admodisastro   Universiti Putra Malaysia, Malaysia
Oche Michael   University of Malaya, Malaysia
Olivier Le Goaer   University of Pau, France
Rashid H. Khokhar   Charles Sturt University, Australia
Sajad Khorsandroo   The University of Texas at San Antonio, USA
Seriel Rayene Boussalia Constantine 2 University, Algeria
Simon K.S. Cheung   The Open University of Hong Kong, Hong Kong,
                           SAR China
Suraya Hamid   University of Malaya, Malaysia

Contents

Mobile Services and Applications

Automatic Evacuation Guiding Scheme Using Trajectories of Mobile Nodes

Nobuhisa Komatsu$^{(\boxtimes)}$, Masahiro Sasabe, Jun Kawahara, and Shoji Kasahara

Graduate School of Information Science, Nara Institute of Science and Technology,
8916-5 Takayama-cho, Ikoma, Nara 630-0192, Japan
{komatsu.nobuhisa.kg1,sasabe,jkawahara,kasahara}@is.naist.jp
http://www-lsm.naist.jp/index.php/top-e

Abstract. When large-scale disasters occur, evacuees have to evacuate to safe places quickly. In this paper, we propose an automatic evacuation guiding scheme using mobile nodes of evacuees. Each node tries to navigate its evacuee by presenting an evacuation route. It can also trace the actual evacuation route of the evacuee as the trajectory by measuring his/her positions periodically. The proposed scheme automatically estimates blocked road segments from the difference between the presented evacuation route and the actual evacuation route, and then recalculates the alternative evacuation route. In addition, evacuees also share such information among them through direct wireless communication with other mobile nodes and that with a server via remaining communication infrastructures. Through simulation experiments, we show that 1) the effectiveness of the proposed scheme becomes high with the increase of degree of damage and 2) the effect of information sharing through communication infrastructures is higher than that through direct wireless communication.

Keywords: Automatic evacuation guiding · Mobile nodes · Trajectories

1 Introduction

In the 2011 Great East Japan Earthquake, both fixed and mobile communication networks had not been available for a long time and/or in wide areas, due to damage to communication infrastructures. As a result, it has been reported that disaster victims and rescuers could not smoothly collect and distribute important information, e.g., safety information, evacuation information, and government information, even though they carried their own mobile nodes, e.g., cellular phones and smart phones [9].

When disasters occur, disaster victims quickly have to evacuate to near safety places to keep their own safety. Under such situations, it is necessary to grasp the following information: safety places and safe routes to those places. Although they can acquire static information, e.g., map and locations of safety places, in usual time, they cannot grasp dynamic information, e.g., damage situations in disaster areas.

M. Younas et al. (Eds.): MobiWis 2015, LNCS 9228, pp. 3–14, 2015.
DOI: 10.1007/978-3-319-23144-0_1

Quickly grasping damage situations will help evacuees to determine actions for evacuation, but it is not necessarily easy to grasp the damage situations, e.g., outbreak of fire, collapse of buildings, flood, and cracks in the ground. It is possible to detect the damage situations by cameras and/or various types of sensors, but it has a potential drawback of restriction of coverage area and breakdown of both such devices and/or communication infrastructures. Therefore, the larger the disaster scale is, the more difficult it is for public institutions to quickly investigate damage situations and to distribute such emergency information to the evacuees.

Under the background, Fujihara and Miwa proposed an evacuation guiding scheme that relies on cooperation among evacuees [3]. They use a Delay Tolerant Networks (DTN) [2], which is constructed by mobile nodes of evacuees, for communication among evacuees. When evacuees discover blocked road segments during their evacuations, they record the information on their nodes. After that, if they encounter other evacuees, they share these information through direct wireless communication between their nodes, such as Bluetooth and Wi-Fi Direct. Thus, they can find out evacuation routes without blocked road segments that have been already discovered.

This scheme is useful because it utilizes mobile nodes that evacuees usually carry and can work without communication infrastructures. It, however, requires evacuees' operations to record damage situations. Evacuees cannot afford to operate their mobile nodes in disaster areas because they may not be safe near the areas. They have to give top priority to their safety and avoid actions except evacuation until they finish evacuating.

To solve the issue, we propose an automatic evacuation guiding scheme using evacuees' mobile nodes, which can automatically grasp damage situations and guide evacuees. Evacuees can obtain the surrounding map and locations of safety places by preinstalling applications for evacuation guiding in their mobile nodes. When disasters occur, the applications calculate evacuation routes with these local information and navigate the evacuees using the routes. In addition, the applications can also grasp the actual evacuation routes of the evacuees, i.e., their trajectories, by measuring their positions periodically. With the help of the interaction between evacuation guiding by mobile nodes and evacuees' actual evacuations, the applications can automatically estimate blocked road segments and recalculate evacuation routes by using the estimated information of the blocked road segments (See the details in section 3).

As in [3], evacuees share the information about blocked road segments among them through direct wireless communication with other mobile nodes and that with a server via remaining communication infrastructures. Note that we deploy the server on cloud systems to protect the server itself from disasters. Such shared information about blocked road segments will help evacuees who are late for evacuations.

Fig. 1 illustrates the overview of the proposed evacuation guiding system. The system consists of following three functions: 1) Mobile nodes of evacuees measure evacuees' trajectories, present evacuation routes, and estimate blocked

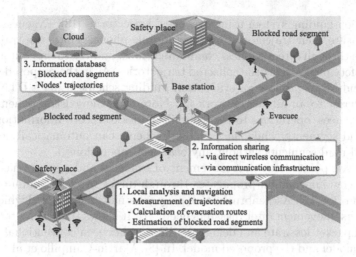

Fig. 1. Overview of evacuation guiding system

road segments; 2) They share these information through direct wireless communication with other nodes and communication infrastructures; 3) Cloud systems maintain the obtained information. We evaluate the effectiveness of the proposed scheme through simulation experiments.

The rest of this paper is organized as follows: Section 2 gives related work. Section 3 describes the proposed scheme. The simulation results are shown in Section 4. Finally, Section 5 provides conclusions and future work.

2   Related Work

ICT support for disaster evacuation can be classified into evacuation planning and evacuation guiding. Evacuation planning is suitable for disasters which are predictable at a certain level, e.g., flood, hurricane, and typhoon. On the other hand, for disasters whose extent of damage is not easy to predict, e.g., earthquake, evacuation guiding in response to damage situations becomes important.

There are several existing studies on evacuation planning [7,10]. Lim et al. formulate planning of evacuation routes in case of hurricane disasters as a network flow problem and proposes an algorithm that can derive optimal solutions [7]. Takizawa et al. propose a method to partition appropriately a region into small areas such that a unique evacuation center is located in each area [10]. Considering the difficulty in predicting damage situations caused by an earthquake, e.g., the outbreak of fire and collapse of buildings, they propose a method to enumerate all partitioning patterns.

On the other hand, evacuation guiding has also been studied [3,4,13]. Iizuka et al. propose an evacuation guiding system using an ad hoc network whose connectivity is almost always guaranteed [4]. It can present evacuees with both evacuation routes and timing to avoid crowds of evacuees. Winter et al. propose

an evacuation guiding system using evacuees' trajectories [13]. Evacuees continuously measure their trajectories by their mobile phones, share the trajectories
with others through direct wireless communications, and try to find out available
paths to safety places using the collected trajectories. As in the proposed scheme,
Fujihara and Miwa propose an evacuation guiding scheme using a DTN, which
is more inferior to an ad hoc network [3]. Note that the existing scheme in [3]
requires evacuees' operations to their mobile nodes to record information about
blocked road segments, while the proposed scheme can automatically estimate
the blocked road segments without any evacuees' operations.

It has been pointed out that movement of evacuees and rescuers has a great
impact on how information propagates through direct wireless communications
among them [1,8,11]. Aschenbruck et al. propose a movement model which simulates rescuers' movement after disasters occur [1]. It shows that characteristics of
end-to-end packet loss rate and delay are different between conventional random
way point model and the proposed model. In [8], Martín-Campillo et al. compare
the performance of various DTN routing methods under the movement model
proposed in [1]. Uddin et al. propose a crowd's movement model after hurricanes
occur and evaluates inter-meeting time between mobile nodes and the number of
neighboring nodes [11]. In this paper, we assume that evacuees try to evacuate
according to the evacuation routes presented by the evacuation guiding applications but autonomously avoid blocked road segments on the routes by their own
decisions.

There is a project that aims to construct a distributed regional network,
called NerveNet, for robust communication infrastructures [5]. NerveNet can
supply users with a local and stand-alone communication network, which consists of base stations that function as both wireless access points and servers.
The proposed scheme can effectively navigate evacuees by deploying the cloud
systems into this kind of regional networks.

3   Proposed Scheme

3.1   Preliminaries

$G = (\mathcal{V}, \mathcal{E})$ denotes a graph representing the internal structure of the target
region, where $\mathcal{V}$ is a set of vertices, i.e., intersections, and $\mathcal{E}$ is a set of edges, i.e.,
roads in the map. There are K $(K > 0)$ evacuees in the region and each of them
has a mobile node. $\mathcal{K} = \{1, 2, \ldots, K\}$ denotes a set of the nodes. Each node
$k \in \mathcal{K}$ measures its own locations by using Global Positioning System (GPS) at
a certain interval I_M $(I_M > 0)$.

3.2   Fundamental Scheme in Evacuation Guiding Using Trajectories

Fig. 2 illustrates the flow of guiding one evacuee to a safety place. Note that the
evacuee has to preinstall an application for evacuation guiding into his/her mobile
node before disasters occur. The application obtains the surrounding map of the

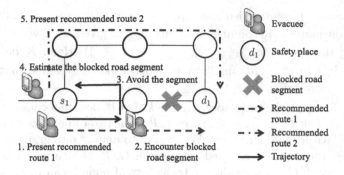

Fig. 2. Flow of evacuation guiding

target region and the location information of the safety places in usual time. When disasters occur, the evacuee initiates the applications on his/her node. The application first finds out the nearest safety place d_1 from the location s_1 of node k, which was recorded on startup. Next, it calculates an evacuation route $\widehat{p}^k_{s_1,d_1}$ and presents him/her the route as a recommended route (Step 1 in Fig. 2).

The evacuee tries to move along the recommended route. When the evacuee discovers a blocked road segment during his/her evacuation along the recommended route $\widehat{p}^k_{s_1,d_1}$ (Step 2 in Fig. 2), he/she will take another route by his/her own judgment (Step 3 in Fig. 2). The application can trace his/her actual evacuation route as the trajectory by measuring his/her positions periodically. Thus, the application can detect road e, which yields the difference between the recommended route and the actual evacuation route (See the details in Section 3.3). The application adds road e to the set of blocked road segments (Step 4 in Fig. 2). After that, the application recalculates the nearest safety place d_2 from the current location s_2. Next, it also recalculates a new evacuation route, which does not include blocked road segments ($\forall e \in \mathcal{E}^k_{NG}$), and presents him/her the route (Step 5 in Fig. 2). The succeeding flow is the same as that for the first recommended route $\widehat{p}^k_{s_1,d_1}$ (Noted that $s_2 = s_1, d_2 = d_1$ in Fig. 2). Evacuation guiding finishes when the evacuee reaches the safety place or the application cannot find out any evacuation route to any safety place.

In addition, the evacuee may encounter other evacuees and get a chance to communicate with infrastructures during his/her evacuation. Under these situations, the application will obtain new information about blocked road segments (See the details in Section 3.4). Then, it recalculates a new recommended route and present it to him/her.

3.3   Estimation of Blocked Road Segments

This section describes how the application estimates blocked road segments by using difference between the recommended route and the evacuee's actual evacuation route, i.e., his/her trajectory. Suppose that the application of node $k \in \mathcal{K}$

shows its evacuee recommended route $\widehat{p}_{s,d}^k$ between source $s \in \mathcal{V}$ and destination $d \in \mathcal{V}$ on map G. Recommended route $\widehat{p}_{s,d}^k$ is given by a vector of edges constructing the route, i.e., $(e_{s,m_1}^k, e_{m_1,m_2}^k, \ldots, e_{m_{H-1},d}^k)$. Here, H denotes the number of edges in $p_{s,d}^k$. For simplicity in description, we assume that $s = m_0$ and $d = m_H$. Noted that $m_h \in \mathcal{V}$, $e_{m_h,m_{h+1}}^k \in \mathcal{E}$ $(h = 1, \ldots, H-1)$.

Next, we focus on the trajectory of node k. Let l_i^k denote location that node k measures at i-th $(i = 1, 2, \ldots)$ interval. l_i^k is a two-dimensional coordinate composed of latitude and longitude. We require to map l_i^k into graph G, because recommended routes are calculated over graph G. l_i^k is located on one of the edges, e_i^k, in graph G. As a result, the trajectory of node k can be expressed by the vector $(e_1^k, e_2^k, \ldots)$.

The following phenomena may happen according to the value of measurement interval I_{M}. If I_{M} is extremely small, e_i^k and e_{i+1}^k may be identical for some i. In this case, the application can obtain trajectory p^k of node k by eliminating the duplicate edges. On the other hand, if I_{M} is extremely large, e_i^k and e_{i+1}^k may not be connected on graph G. In this case, the application has to interpolate the route between them. As a result, the appropriate value of I_{M} should be determined according to both the distribution of edges' lengths and evacuees' moving speed.

For simplicity in explanation, we assume that $e_{s,m_1}^k = e_1^k$ and the evacuee judges at the vertex m_{h-1} whether road e_{m_{h-1},m_h}^k $(h = 1, \ldots, H-1)$ on the recommended route is a blocked road segment. When the evacuee finds out that the h-th road e_{m_{h-1},m_h}^k on the recommended route $\widehat{p}_{s,d}^k$ is a blocked road segment, he/she selects another road $e_{m_{h-1},o}^k$ $(e_{m_{h-1},o}^k \in \mathcal{E} \setminus \mathcal{E}_{\mathrm{NG}}$, $o \neq m_h)$ rather than e_{m_{h-1},m_h}^k by his/her own decision. Here, the recommended route is given by

$$\widehat{p}_{s,d}^k = (\underline{e_{s,m_1}^k, \ldots, e_{m_{h-2},m_{h-1}}^k}, \overline{e_{m_{h-1},m_h}^k}, \ldots, e_{m_{H-1},d}^k)$$

and his/her trajectory is as follows:

$$p^k = (\underline{e_{s,m_1}^k, \ldots, e_{m_{h-2},m_{h-1}}^k}, \overline{e_{m_{h-1},o}^k}).$$

Thus, when the application compares the recommended route and the trajectory, it will obtain the list of consensus edges (dotted lines) followed by the different edge (solid lines). As a result, the application can estimate and record the edge e_{m_{h-1},m_h}^k on the recommended route as a blocked road segment.

3.4   Information Sharing

As mentioned above, the application of each node $k \in \mathcal{K}$ automatically obtains the information about trajectory p^k and blocked road segments $\mathcal{E}_{\mathrm{NG}}^k$ on the way to the safety place. If nodes can share these information among them, the information acquired by evacuees at the early stage of evacuation will help evacuees who delay in evacuating. There are two ways to share the information among nodes: direct wireless communication among nodes and communication with the server via remaining communication infrastructures.

Information Sharing Through Direct Wireless Communication Among Nodes: As in [3], information sharing through direct wireless communication can be achieved by existing DTN routings, e.g., epidemic routing [12]. When node k encounters node j $(k, j \in \mathcal{V}, k \neq j)$, they exchange the information about discovered blocked-road-segments and update their local databases with it. Note that the encountering applications need not exchange their trajectories, because they do not directly use the trajectories for evacuation guiding.

Information Sharing Through Communication Infrastructures: After disasters occur, communication infrastructures may be still available in the part of region. When the node can communicate with edge nodes of the communication infrastructures, e.g., access points of wireless LANs and base stations of cellular networks, it tries to access the cloud systems through the edge nodes. The cloud systems have databases to maintain information collected by mobile nodes, i.e., blocked road segments and trajectories. The application and cloud systems first exchange their own information of blocked road segments with each other.

In addition, the application can also upload the information about its own trajectory to the cloud systems because the transmission rate between the node and the communication infrastructures is sufficiently high. We plan to apply the trajectories collected in the cloud systems to global evacuation guiding, e.g., alleviation of congestion, as future work.

4 Simulation Results

Through simulation experiments, we evaluate the proposed scheme in terms of the following points: effectiveness of the proposed scheme, impact of degree of disaster, and effect of information sharing.

4.1 Simulation Model

We used the ONE simulator [6]. We also used the street map of Helsinki, which is included in the ONE. The size of the map is 4500 [m] × 3400 [m] and its internal graph structure is composed of 1578 vertices and 1986 edges. We assume that all of a hundred evacuees have their own mobile nodes and their initial positions are randomly chosen from the points on the streets of the map. In addition, we set one safety place near the center of the map, which has access to the Internet via communication infrastructures. We set the simulation time to be 7200 [s]. When the simulation starts, a disaster occurs and each of evacuees starts evacuating from their initial positions to the safety place at moving speed of 4 [km/h].

We set measurement interval I_{M} to be 10 [s], which is obtained at the preliminary experiments and small enough to avoid the trajectory disconnection problem as mentioned in Section 3.3. We assume that direct wireless communications among nodes are given by either BlueTooth or Wi-Fi Direct whose transmission ranges R_D are 10 [m] and 100 [m], respectively. We also assume that communications between nodes and servers are supported by Wireless LANs whose transmission ranges R_S are 100 [m]. Wireless LAN access points are located at $N \times N$ grids. We define *coverage* as the ratio of the area of roads included in the transmission ranges of the access points to the whole area of all roads. We can control the coverage by changing N.

We made damaged situations by randomly choosing a certain number of edges on graph G as blocked road segments. We evaluate the degree of disaster by *evacuation possibility*, δ $(0 \leq \delta \leq 1)$, which is defined by the probability that evacuation routes exist from arbitrary points to the safety place.

We use *evacuation time* and *evacuation ratio* as evaluation criteria. The evacuation time of an evacuee is the time interval from the evacuation start to the evacuation completion. We define the evacuation ratio as the ratio of evacuees have finished evacuating to all evacuees. The succeeding results are the average of 500 independent simulation experiments.

4.2   Evacuation Schemes for Comparison

We also evaluate the following two evacuation schemes, in addition to the proposed scheme.

- Evacuation guiding using successful routes
  In this scheme, nodes share the information about their trajectories instead of the information about blocked road segments with other nodes. On receiving new trajectories, they try to find out successful routes to the safety place under the constraint where only roads included in the trajectories are available for evacuation.
- Normal evacuation
  As normal evacuation where evacuees try to evacuate without the proposed scheme, we use the proposed scheme without information sharing. In this scheme, evacuees only use the map and the information about blocked road segments that are discovered during their own evacuation. Note that only 100σ $(0 \leq \sigma \leq 1)$ percent of the evacuees know the location of the safety place at the start of evacuation. If evacuees know the location of the safety place, they try to move to that place. Otherwise, they try to move to a place randomly chosen in the map. When evacuees meet other evacuees, they share their information about the location of the safety place, through conversation.

4.3   Effectiveness of The Proposed Scheme

Fig. 3 illustrates the transition of evacuation ratio for the three schemes: proposed scheme, evacuation guiding using successful routes, and normal evacuation. Note that we set σ to be 0.8 and 1.0 in case of normal evacuation. The values of the parameters for this scenario are given as follows. The evacuation possibility δ is

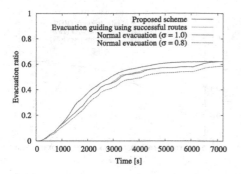
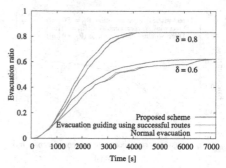

Fig. 3. Effectiveness of the proposed scheme

Fig. 4. Impact of degree of damage

0.6. The transmission range of direct wireless communication R_D is 100. The coverage of communication infrastructures is about 7 % where N is 5.

First, we observe that some evacuees without initial knowledge of the location of the safety place cannot complete their evacuations in case of normal evacuation with $\sigma = 0.8$. This is because they cannot meet other evacuees who know the location of the safety place during their evacuations. Next, we compare the results of proposed scheme, evacuation guiding using successful routes, and normal evacuation with $\sigma = 1.0$. The evacuation ratio of the proposed scheme increases faster than those of other two schemes. As a result, the average (resp. maximum) evacuation time of the proposed scheme is 1940 [s] (resp. 2288 [s]), which is about 15 % (resp. 21 %) shorter than that of the normal evacuation.

We also find that there is almost no difference between the result of evacuation guiding using successful routes and that of normal evacuation. The information about successful routes can be obtained only from the trajectories of evacuees who have finished their evacuations. On the other hand, nodes can share the information about blocked road segments with other nodes even if they are in evacuating.

4.4   Impact of Degree of Damage

Fig. 4 illustrates the transition of evacuation ratio for the three schemes when δ is set to be 0.6 and 0.8. The values of the parameters for this scenario are given as follows. We set σ to be 1.0. The transmission range of direct wireless communication R_D is 100. The coverage of communication infrastructures is about 7 % where N is 5. As in Section 4.3 where $\delta = 0.6$, the evacuation guiding using successful routes shows almost the same result as the normal evacuation, in case of $\delta = 0.8$. We also observe that the evacuation ratio of the proposed scheme increases faster than those of other schemes, regardless of the degree of damage. Both average and maximum evacuation times of the proposed scheme are about 7 % shorter than those of the normal evacuation when δ is 0.8. Comparing the results of $\delta = 0.6$ and those of $\delta = 0.8$, we find that the larger the degree of damage is, the higher the effectiveness of the proposed scheme becomes.

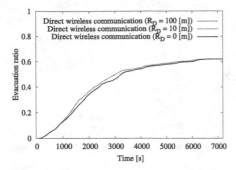 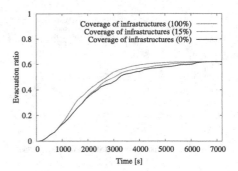

Fig. 5. Effect of direct wireless communication

Fig. 6. Effect of communication infrastructures

Because we randomly choose the blocked road segments in this scenario, evacuees can easily find alternative evacuation routes by themselves when they encounter blocked road segments. We expect that the proposed scheme will be more effective when the blocked road segments are not randomly scattered but spreads over a certain region in the form of lines, e.g., cracks in the ground, or circles, e.g., outbreak of fire. In such kinds of damage situations, it will be difficult for the evacuees to find out alternative evacuation routes without the proposed scheme and information sharing among nodes will become more important. We plan to evaluate this point as future work.

4.5 Effect of Information Sharing

The proposed scheme can share the information through direct wireless communication and communication infrastructures. Evacuees can improve their evacuations by using the information about blocked road segments acquired by other evacuees. In this section, we evaluate the effect of information sharing based on direct wireless communication and communication infrastructures.

Fig. 5 illustrates the transition of the evacuation ratio of the proposed scheme when the coverage of communication infrastructures is set to be 0 % and the transmission range R_D of direct wireless communication is set to be 0, 10, and 100 [m]. Note that the proposed scheme without communication infrastructures and direct wireless communication ($R_D = 0$) is equivalent to normal evacuation. We observe that the effect of direct wireless communication is slightly improved by the increase of R_D. Specifically, average (resp. maximum) evacuation times of the proposed scheme with $R_D = 100$ and $R_D = 10$ are 2054 [s] (resp. 5917 [s]) and 2184 [s] (resp. 6103 [s]), respectively, which are about 6 % (resp. 3 %) and 0.4 % (resp. 0.4 %) shorter than that of normal evacuation.

Although the increase of R_D leads to frequent meetings between nodes, the improvement of evacuation ratio is limited. This is because both the direction of evacuations and that of information propagation are identical due to the fact that the information is carried by the evacuees themselves. Evacuees can improve their evacuations only when they know whether the current evacuation routes include blocked road segments. This means that the direction of information propagation should be opposite to that of evacuations. The direction of evacuations will be reversed when evacuees have to retrace their evacuation routes due to blocked road segments.

Next, Fig. 6 illustrates the transition of the evacuation ratio of the proposed scheme when the coverage of communication infrastructures is set to be 0 %, 15 %, and 100 %, and the direct wireless communication is not used ($R_D = 0$). Average (resp. maximum) evacuation times with 100 % coverage and 15 % coverage are 1836 [s] (resp. 4866 [s]) and 2062 [s] (resp. 5917 [s]), respectively, which are about 16 % (resp. 20 %) and 6 % (resp. 3 %) shorter than that of the normal evacuation. Comparing Fig. 6 with Fig. 5, we observe that the increase of coverage has larger impact on the improvement of evacuation ratio than that of the transmission range R_D of direct wireless communication. This is because the use of communication infrastructures is one of the ways to achieve the information propagation with the opposite direction to evacuations.

5   Conclusions

In this paper, we proposed the automatic evacuation guiding scheme using evacuees' mobile nodes to achieve quick evacuation after disasters occur. With the help of the interaction between evacuation guiding by mobile nodes and evacuees' actual evacuation, the proposed scheme can automatically estimate blocked road segments. Evacuees try to improve their own evacuations by sharing the information about blocked road segments through both direct wireless communication and communication infrastructures.

Through simulation experiments, we evaluated the effectiveness of the proposed scheme, the impact of degree of damage, and the effect of information sharing. We observed that the larger the degree of damage is, the higher the effectiveness of the proposed scheme becomes. We also found that the direction of information propagation should be carefully considered to improve the evacuation guiding.

As future work, we will evaluate the proposed scheme in more realistic disaster situations. For example, cracks in the ground and outbreak of fire may cause blocked road segments in a continuous and/or expanding manner. We also plan to propose global evacuation guiding scheme to alleviate traffic congestion by using the trajectories collected in the cloud systems. Furthermore, we have been implementing the proposed scheme as a real mobile application. We will evaluate the practicality and effectiveness of the application in terms of evacuation ratio, evacuation time, and battery consumption.

Acknowledgement. This research was partly supported by Strategic Information and Communication R&D Promotion Programme (SCOPE) of Ministry of Internal Affairs and Communications, JSPS KAKENHI Grant Number 15H04008, and JSPS KAKENHI Grant Number 15K00126, Japan.

References

1. Aschenbruck, N., Gerhards-Padilla, E., Martini, P.: Modeling Mobility in Disaster Area Scenarios. Performance Evaluation **66**(12), 773–790 (2009)
2. Fall, K.: A delay-tolerant network architecture for challenged internets. In: Proc. of SIGCOMM 2003, pp. 27–34 (2003)
3. Fujihara, A., Miwa, H.: Disaster evacuation guidance using opportunistic communication: the potential for opportunity-based service. In: Bessis, N., Dobre, C. (eds.) Big Data and Internet of Things: A Roadmap for Smart Environments Studies in Computational Intelligence. SCI, vol. 546, pp. 425–446. Springer, Heildelberg (2014)
4. Iizuka, Y., Yoshida, K., Iizuka, K.: An effective disaster evacuation assist system utilized by an ad-hoc network. In: Stephanidis, C. (ed.) Posters, Part II, HCII 2011. CCIS, vol. 174, pp. 31–35. Springer, Heidelberg (2011)
5. Inoue, M., Ohnishi, M., Peng, C., Li, R., Owada, Y.: NerveNet: A Regional Platform Network for Context-Aware Services with Sensors and Actuators. IEICE Transactions on Communications **E94–B**(3), 618–629 (2011)
6. Keränen, A., Ott, J., Kärkkäinen, T.: The one simulator for DTN protocol evaluation. In: Proc. of the 2nd International Conference on Simulation Tools and Techniques, pp. 55:1–55:10 (2009)
7. Lim, G.J., Zangeneh, S., Baharnemati, M.R., Assavapokee, T.: A Capacitated Network Flow Optimization Approach for Short Notice Evacuation Planning. European Journal of Operational Research **223**(1), 234–245 (2012)
8. Martín-Campillo, A., Crowcroft, J., Yoneki, E., Martí, R.: Evaluating Opportunistic Networks in Disaster Scenarios. Journal of Network and Computer Applications **36**(2), 870–880 (2013)
9. Ministry of Internal Affairs and Communications: 2011 WHITE PAPER Information and Communications in Japan. http://www.soumu.go.jp/johotsusintokei/whitepaper/eng/WP2011/2011-index.html
10. Takizawa, A., Takechi, Y., Ohta, A., Katoh, N., Inoue, T., Horiyama, T., Kawahara, J., Minato, S.: Enumeration of region partitioning for evacuation planning based on ZDD. In: Proc. of of the International Symposium on Operations Research and its Applications, pp. 64–71 (2013)
11. Uddin, M.Y.S., Nicol, D.M., Abdelzaher, T.F., Kravets, R.H.: A post-disaster mobility model for delay tolerant networking. In: Proc. of the 2009 Winter Simulation Conference, pp. 2785–2796 (2009)
12. Vahdat, A., Becker, D.: Epidemic Routing for Partially Connected Ad Hoc Networks. Tech. Rep. CS-200006, Duke University (2000)
13. Winter, S., Richter, K.F., Shi, M., Gan, H.S.: Get me out of here: collaborative evacuation based on local knowledge. In: Proc. of Third International Workshop on Indoor Spatial Awareness, pp. 35–42 (2011)

TREKIE - Ubiquitous Indoor Localization with Trajectory REconstruction Based on Knowledge Inferred from Environment

Attila Török[1]($\boxtimes$), András Nagy[2], and Imre Kálomista[1]

[1] Bay Zoltán Nonprofit Ltd. for Applied Research,
Fehérvári út 130, Budapest 1116, Hungary
attila.torok@bayzoltan.hu

[2] University of Pannonia, Egyetem út 10, Veszprém 8200, Hungary

Abstract. The recent indoor localization techniques use inertial sensors for position estimations in order to obtain a certain degree of freedom from infrastructure based solutions. Unfortunately, this dependency cannot be completely eliminated due to the cumulative errors induced in the localization process. While many methods are designed to reduce the required number of reference points, completely infrastructure independent solutions are still missing. In this paper we extend the approach of DREAR, a mobile-based context-aware indoor localization framework. DREAR exploits the ability to recognize certain human motion patterns with a smartphone, representing activities related to walking, climbing stairs, taking escalators, etc. This allows the detection of corridors, staircases and escalators, knowledge which can be used to create building interior related reference points. Based on these a scenario specific context interpreter controls the localization process and provides position refinement for the elimination of the cumulated errors. However, due to the cumulated errors in the trajectory, in case of neighbouring reference points with similar characteristics an adequate distinction cannot made, based solely on the detected activities, which leads to wrong reference point associations and erroneous location refinements. Thus, we extended DREAR with a trajectory reconstruction algorithm, to cope with these errors and their effect on the outcome of reference point selection. The proposed solution is evaluated in a complex subway scenario, its performance is analysed focusing on path reconstructions and the benefits of using specific context-related information. The results are promising, the proposed algorithm presents further improvements relative to the performance of DREAR, providing an excellent localization and path reconstruction solution.

1 Introduction

To obtain a certain degree of freedom from localization infrastructures (e.g. radiofrequency - RF - reference points) novel indoor positioning solutions leverage smartphones' built-in sensors in dead-reckoning (DR) algorithms to reconstruct the movement path of the navigated person [1]. Considering conventional

© Springer International Publishing Switzerland 2015
M. Younas et al. (Eds.): MobiWis 2015, LNCS 9228, pp. 15–26, 2015.
DOI: 10.1007/978-3-319-23144-0_2

use cases (localization in shopping centres, office buildings) the current solutions [2] [3] can provide an adequate level of adaptability regarding the configuration changes of the RF reference points. Nevertheless, there are scenarios, certain premises (e.g. subway systems), where the placement of any kind of reference points is beyond possibility, due to legal or investment issues, exposure to vandalism, or else their usability is simply questionable because of the effect of crowd dynamics on the system's performance. It is also hard to build truly ubiquitous indoor Location Based Applications (LBA) if the used localization solution leads to vendor lock-in due to a specific technology (e.g. iBeacon). Therefore, localization infrastructure dependency must be further relaxed and completely infrastructure-free solutions have to be introduced for well-defined use cases to build future ubiquitous indoor LBAs.

In [4] a novel approach for mobile-based infrastructure-free indoor localization services was proposed (called DREAR), aimed to provide a context-aware solution for ubiquitous indoor LBAs. The goal of DREAR was to build a localization system, which does not require any kind of localization infrastructure (e.g. previously deployed RF, visual or acoustic beacons) and where the user's active involvement for finding certain reference points can be also omitted. Therefore, human movement behaviour analysis and activity recognition algorithms were employed in a context-aware middleware, to control the localization and position refinement process. A context recognition layer was designed to acquire information from user movement events (detected activities, trajectory), infer about the actual context (likeliness of events, filtering out false detections) and control the position refinement process based on the recognized environment.

Unfortunately, deterioration in DR trajectory quality can be expected during DREAR's usage, due to the cumulative nature of both the heading and stride length estimation errors. Due to the erroneous heading information a wrong reference point (e.g. an escalator/stair, called Topological Anchor Points - TAP) could be selected from a neighbouring set of TAPs with similar characteristics by the localization process (TAP association problem), or due to trajectory dilation/shrinkage a wrong turn could be proposed for the user (location refinement problem). Therefore, we enhanced DREAR to cope with heading errors and their effect on TAP's selection outcome. We propose a trajectory reconstruction algorithm, which extends the context interpreter and improves activity filtering with TAP selection and trajectory matching. We present a detailed analysis of the designed algorithm, considering different indoor scenarios from a complex subway system. As we will show the proposed algorithm presents several positive effects related to the quality of the constructed trajectory, and the proper selection of the specific indoor reference points (TAPs).

Besides the relief from infrastructure dependence the proposed solution will be especially helpful to build end-to-end navigation for multi-modal transportation services [5]. This way the new trend to provide public transit information services for subway systems (e.g. Embark) can be extended with navigation and real-time route guidance solutions.

The paper is structured as follows: the related work is presented in the next Section, followed by the main Section presenting the proposed solution. The performance evaluation of the solution is presented in Section 4. Finally, the paper is summarized in Section 5.

2 Related Work

Unsupervised localization [3] [6] [7] [8] [9] is a recent trend to create and maintain indoor localization infrastructures with minimal assumptions or maintenance costs. To reduce calibration efforts additional mechanisms are proposed for the unsupervised collection and maintenance of the wireless fingerprint space or to reduce the assumptions in modelling. Both Zee [6] and LiFS [7] leverages human mobility to build user paths and to fuse DR results with WiFi fingerprints. While in Zee the DR is matched against the map of the building by using a particle filtering algorithm, in LiFS multidimensional scaling is applied to obtain a higher dimension fingerprint space representation. The main problem with these methods is in their mapping and path reconstruction processes, since a longer trail has to be traversed to get enough information for the backward belief propagation algorithm (Zee), or only corridor and room recognition is currently possible (LiFS). This leads to their limited applicability for complex indoor spaces (e.g. subway systems) or to the requirement to have uniquely structured scenarios (e.g. corridors), because shorter or ambiguously shaped trails cannot be unequivocally recognized. UnLoc [3] introduces an unsupervised indoor localization scheme where virtual landmarks are created using the existing WiFi infrastructure. The smartphones are used to collect environment signatures (e.g. produced by an elevator) and associate these with a locally overheard WiFi AP. Later the DR algorithm can be corrected if the mobile senses the respective landmark. While this method can incorporate different type of landmarks the collection and clustering of these must be confined to a small geographical region. Therefore, all the landmarks are associated with WiFi areas, which lead to an infrastructure lock-in problem, just like in the case of the previous solutions.

FootPath [10] presents an infrastructure-free solution where only the accelerometer and compass are used to provide turn-by-turn instructions. The authors propose matching techniques to compare and project the detected steps onto the expected route. Unfortunately, the sequence alignment algorithm can work only for long and specially shaped corridors. Obviously, the drawback of FootPath is similar to Zee's: if the planned path and the traversed scenario is not specific enough the user's path cannot be reconstructed properly. A different solution is proposed in FTrack [11], where an infrastructure-free floor localization system is presented. The accelerometer data is used to detect walking, climbing stairs and taking the elevator. Then by capturing user encounters (using Bluetooth) and analysing user trails FTrack finds the mapping from the traveling time or the step counts. While FTrack achieves high accuracy in a huge, 10-floor office building, its methods are inappropriate to be directly applied in the context of subway systems, where the topology is much more complex and where the exact paths must be also reconstructed with a finer granularity. In [12] the authors propose a solution which uses the mobile's cameras to recognize store logos for providing indoor localization. While this solution provides an infrastructure-free localization it cannot be used in subway systems where there are no such logos or the texts (commercials) are changing frequently.

Body-attached IMU-based DR uses heuristic drift elimination methods [13] [14] to minimize the drifting errors. These solutions assume that the majority of buildings have dominant directions defined by the orientation of their corridors; consequently a person walks along straight-line paths parallel to these. However, if no dominant directions are available (larger premises, halls) or a crowded subway station has to be crossed (sidestep people in your way) similar methods cannot be applied confidently. The foot-mounted approach of these solutions is also not applicable for our case.

3   TREKIE: Trajectory REconstruction Based on Knowledge Inferred from Environment

3.1   Problem Statement

Our goal is to provide a truly infrastructure-free indoor localization solution precise enough to navigate pedestrians in complex scenarios, such as subway systems, using only conventional smartphones. Unfortunately, deterioration in DR trajectory quality can be expected due to the cumulative nature of both the heading and stride length estimation errors. Since in the targeted scenarios usually there is no localization infrastructure present (e.g., RF, visual or acoustic beacons) applicable for position refinements, we extended the sensing capabilities of smartphones to detect and recognize human motion patterns specific of traversing particular structures of the indoor places. These structures (e.g. stairs, elevators, escalators) characteristic of building interiors are used to provide the required reference points (called *Topological Anchor Points -TAPs*) for localization error cancellation. While previous efforts [4] managed to provide an infrastructure-free localization solution through the introduction of context-related filtering, there are still issues to be solved, in order to provide a fully functional ubiquitous localization service.

Considering, for example a subway system (Figure 1(a)), along its route the user have to pass through several TAPs (2 and 4) and make proper decisions, turns in intersections (Zone A, B) to reach its destination (D). However, due to the accumulated DR trajectory errors (bluish cones on figure), by the time the user reaches the respective decision points wrong navigation instructions could be provided for him/her. In the constructed trajectories (dashed lines on figure) one of these errors can be attributed to the difficulties to provide proper heading error compensations, since currently there are no steady solutions, especially for such extreme indoor scenarios, with unusual topologies and frequent magnetic perturbations. Due to the erroneous heading information a wrong association could happen (TAP 3 in Zone A), respectively due to trajectory dilation/shrinkage a wrong turn could be made (late turn in Zone B).

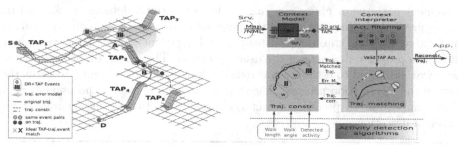

(a) Floor plan of a subway system   (b) The architecture of the context-aware
localization middleware

Fig. 1. Problem definition and building blocks for context-aware trajectory reconstruction

Even in cases when the users selects the proper escalator (and consequently the respective TAP events are detected) there will be no enough information for the localization middleware to decide about the outcome of the user's TAP selection (TAP 2 or 3), because the heading information of the DR is unreliable. In such cases a wrong turn could be interpreted as a correct route selection, and vice versa, following the planned path and choosing the proper TAP could be considered as taking the wrong direction.

Therefore, we shall employ a mechanism which helps the context interpreter to make correct associations (the factual TAP selection) in case of multiple TAPs, to confirm internally the outcome of the user's decision, and to act accordingly with localization error cancellation, respectively route guidance/re-planning. The trajectory dilation/shrinkage, attributed to stride length estimation errors for normal walking and walking on stairs/escalators, can be also compensated if the TAP event detections are properly fitted to the respective TAPs (by reducing the gap between the ideal and constructed trajectories' TAP events).

3.2 Concept of Trajectory Reconstruction Based on Context-Aware Middleware

The Context-Aware Localization Middleware. To enable the detection of TAPs DREAR [4] introduces feature detection algorithms used for human motion recognition, giving the ability to derive information for the error cancellation process. The activity recognition tasks were interpreted as a classification problem, aiming to recognize unique motion patterns in real-time with a fuzzy associative classifier. The activity and special TAP recognition (e.g. escalator) algorithms have been implemented as a separate layer in the middleware (see Figure 1(b)), producing the respective class labels and the DR information.

The location refinement is controlled by the detected TAP events provided by the activity detection algorithms. Unfortunately, due to the variance in user movement patterns or phone carrying habits the activity detections can lead to wrong predictions (on Figure 1(a) the false TAP events on traj. const.), providing false results (e.g. stair down instead of walking event). These false events will affect the proper refinement of the user's position. Therefore, a filtering mechanism was employed to estimate and remove unlikely or false events, to properly control the localization process. Since there can be long stairs and escalators it is also important to precisely detect their start/end to provide accurate zone traversal detections.

Algorithm 1. Trajectory Reconstruction Algorithm

Input: User position, heading ($U_{xy,h}$), Buffered trajectory ($Traj$), Error Model of $Traj$
($Err.M_{dist,head}$), Valid TAP Activity (TAP_{act}), Set of neighbouring TAPs
($TAP_{1:n}$)
Output: Reconstucted trajectory $Reconstr.Traj$
foreach $TAP_i \in TAP_{1:n}$ **do**
  if $(distance(U_{xy}, TAP_i) <= Err.M_{dist})$ && $(heading(TAP_i) \subseteq Err.M_{head})$ **then**
    Create temporary $Traj_i$ from $Traj$;
    Calculate $Traj.corr = heading(TAP_i) - U_h$;
    Calculate $heading\_diff = Traj_i[U_h[last]] - Traj_i[U_h[first]]$;
    foreach $U_{xy,h} \in Traj_i$ **do**
      Calculate $Matched.Traj_i = Correction(Traj.corr, heading\_diff)$ applied on
      $Traj_i[U_{xy,h}]$

    Estimate reconstruction quality of $Matched.Traj_i$ {
    Select $TAP_{act}[1:k]$ from $Matched.Traj_i[TAP[last : last - k]]$;
    Apply **TAP Association**(TAP Model(TAP_i), $TAP_{act}[1 : k]$);
    Calculate $Recon.Quality(Matched.Traj_i)$ from **TAP Association**;
    }
    Rank $Recon.Quality_{1:i}$;

$Reconstr.Traj = Traj_{Recon.Quality_1}$;
Apply **Viterbi Decoding** on $Reconstr.Traj$;

The role of the context-aware localization middleware is to provide the required functionality by making assumptions about the user's actual situation, namely to acquire, match and understand the perceived sensory information relative to the current belief about the ambient environment. Then the localization refinement can be influenced based on the recognized context and proper actions can be triggered during the navigation.

The context interpreter of DREAR is used to fuse and process the different levels of information, in order to understand the active context in its entirety. Its core is formed from a Hidden Markov Model (HMM), which is built, managed by the Context Model, and it will directly influence the constructed trajectory, respectively the evolution and control of the DR error. Viterbi decoding is effectuated on the model to find the maximum likely sequence of traversed zones which led to the detected TAP, if there is any TAP event.

Extending the Middleware Architecture. In order to provide solution for the problems mentioned in Section 3.1 we enhanced DREAR to cope with heading errors and their effect on TAP's selection outcome. One solution would be to increase the number of hidden states of the planar 2D grid zones and TAP models to represent the transition probabilities related to the evolution of the trajectory's heading. However, this decision would introduce a substantial increase in the system state dimensions, hindering the middleware's deployment on mobiles. The advantage of such a detailed representation is also questionable due to the aforementioned difficulties in heading error compensations, which possibly would result in infrequent heading corrections.

Therefore, we decided to employ a separation of concerns in the Context Interpreter (Figure 1(b)), treating separately the tasks related to recognition and understanding the detected TAP events considering the actual context. The first stage is provided by the *Activity Filtering* process, with the goal of finding and affirming valid TAP events from a noisy stream of detected activities and a distorted trajectory. When a valid TAP activity is detected the *Trajectory Matching* process can be triggered, where the reconstruction of the real trajectory can be effectuated, based on the characteristics of the recognized TAP and the knowledge derived from the actual context.

From the neighbouring TAPs' information delivered by the Context Model the TAP orientations can be used to calculate the hypothetical trajectory headings, which would occur if the respective, "virtual" TAP, was crossed by the user. Then a correction factor is applied on the heading and position elements of the original, buffered trajectory for each of these hypothetical TAP orientations. The matching process will search for an optimally fitted event sequence (the best match) between the detected TAP events along the traversed path and the structure of the neighbouring, physical TAPs. Its outcome is the TAP selection with the best match (the associated TAP), for which the trajectory reconstruction provides the most viable explanation considering the actual context.

Thus, in the trajectory reconstruction process we combine past and present sensory and context related information. The process is triggered by the occurrence of certain events, such as a confirmed TAP detection or acknowledged heading information. These will provide additional knowledge regarding the evolution of the trajectory by that time the respective event occurred, this information can be exploited to provide insights about the errors acting on sensor measurements and DR calculations (the trajectory).

Obviously, besides the utilization of these "virtual" TAP headings, the concept of trajectory reconstruction can also cope with the occasionally acknowledged heading information, coming from a fingerprint database or an orientation filtering algorithm.

3.3   The Trajectory Reconstruction Algorithm

As we presented above the algorithm starts when a valid TAP activity is detected by the Activity Filtering process, which is the positive outcome of the Viterbi decoding algorithm (a certain number of TAP events - parameter k - are detected and the model's state converges to a TAP zone). Then from the set of neighbouring TAPs (provided by the Context Model) the trajectory reconstruction process is triggered for those, where the distance between the user's position and the inspected TAP is inside, respectively the TAP orientation is within the bounds of the error model ($Err.M$). For such TAPs we calculate the correction factor ($Traj.corr$), the difference between the "virtual" TAP and user's heading, and the heading difference (*heading_diff*) accumulated along the user's path (trajectory construction phase). Using these values a *Correction* algorithm can be applied on a copy of the original trajectory, by using different heading/position alteration strategies on atomic/aggregated trajectory sections. Currently we use a linear and atomic correction algorithm. After this, for each trajectory reconstruction's outcome we have to estimate its quality. This will be effectuated by applying the *TAP Model* of the respective "virtual" TAP on the TAP events (1:k) which triggered the reconstruction process. A "virtual" TAP is more preferable than the others if its position, orientation and other physical characteristics (e.g. length, shape) provide better matching, a more viable explanation (the *TAP Association*), for the detected TAP events. Finally, based on the quality ranking (*Recon.Quality*) the best match will be selected (the reconstructed trajectory: *Reconstr.Traj*), which will be used in the Context Interpreter for Viterbi decoding, together with the newly arriving DR and TAP events; thus, continuing the localization and position refinement process.

4 Evaluation

We evaluated the performance of TREKIE focusing on certain aspects of the localization middleware by designating different walking paths (trails) in the most complex subway station of Budapest. To validate our solution four users performed several measurements for each of these trails, by using the escalators in different ways (e.g. walking and/or standing on it). The localization middleware was implemented on the Android mobile OS platform; the measurements were made with Samsung Galaxy S3 and S4 phones, mounted on belt. Two DR algorithms were implemented, based on step counting and different, personalized step lengths calculations [15], both tested with and without heading error compensations [16]. Due to space limits we present the evaluation only for a couple of trails; however, we should mention that for over 80% of the measurements TREKIE provided proper localization performance (enough precision to find the proper upcoming turning points). The scenarios are presented through a graphic representation of the world model using R, specifically designed for analysis and visualization purposes. In this model the planar 2D grid zones are constructed from grid maps, while the TAPs are represented by a series of consecutive zone elements, with length and direction conform to their actual dimensions.

Figure 2(a) presents the evaluation of a single scenario, where the user walked from the upper stairs (middle white TAP), crossed through the hall (2D grid) and reached the first escalator (TAP at bottom left). We can observe that when the TAP events are recognized (stairs down activities), due to the heading drift of the trajectory construction, the plain DREAR algorithm (blue line) selects the wrong TAP (blue striped stairs at the bottom centre). This would lead to an erroneous position cancellation and a confused navigation process, which in this case would be the conclusion that the user missed the correct TAP; thus, a replanning process is triggered. Such TAP association problems can happen if the neighbouring TAPs have similar types, or the activity detection algorithms

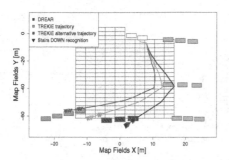 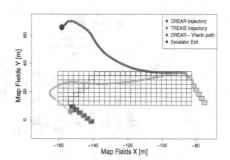

(a) Trajectory reconstruction in case of multiple TAPs (green: correct TAP, red/blue: wrong TAP)

(b) The effect of trajectory reconstruction on path and TAP event alignments (escalator exit detection)

Fig. 2. The effect of trajectory reconstruction considering different TAP scenarios

cannot distinguish TAP directions (e.g. up or down stair/escalator was taken). Fortunately, by applying TREKIE two derived, hypothetical trajectories (red and green lines) are built for these neighbouring TAPs, from which the best fit (green line) will help to select the TAP used in reality. While on the figure the other reconstruction (red line) could seem as a better fit, we must mention that its reconstruction quality will be much worse, due to its distance to the corresponding (striped, bottom centre) TAP.

Other aspects of the trajectory reconstruction algorithm are presented on Figure 2(b), where a plain DREAR trajectory (blue line) and its reconstructed TREKIE trajectory (green line) are represented. Here the user traversed a long corridor, which connects two escalators. The outcome of the Viterbi decoding (Viterbi path) is also represented on the figure. Since TREKIE approximates better the real path we will get an optimally fitted event sequence between the detected TAP events (escalator exit event) and the structure of the physical TAP. This helps to artificially effectuate a dilation on the final, reconstructed trajectory (green line between trajectory and TAP event), helping to cope with the different stride length estimations, necessary to properly consider walking on a longer escalator. Therefore, TREKIE's error cancellation is more efficient than DREAR's.

The effects of the TAP association on the final trajectory selection can be observed on Figure 3, where trajectory reconstruction in effectuated for three neighbouring TAPs (red dashed TAPs), resulting in wrong path reconstruction qualities (red dashed lines), while the original trajectory represents a better result (blue line). Fortunately, due to the TAP association step TREKIE selects the original trajectory instead of the other options, which besides of a more accurate alignment (TAP events get closer to the actual TAP) it will also provide a more concise, smaller DR error.

Figure 4 presents a scenario where the walking path starts outdoors and crosses through two escalators to reach the destination metro platform. There are two decision points along this path, one at the end of the first hall

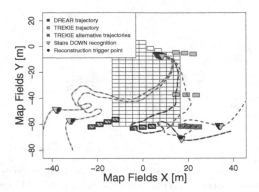

Fig. 3. The effect of TAP association on trajectory selection (blue: original, green: selected, red: alternatives)

(to find the first escalator), and one after the first escalator, to make a proper turn, in an intersection, to reach the second escalator, which leads to the destination platform (left panel on Figure 4). Without position refinements the DR error would grow unbounded, leading to inaccurate localization; thus, wrong navigation instructions would be provided. The question is if the localization is accurate enough to guide the user to the respective platform and how the different algorithms are performing in this context. During the measurements we recorded at specific points a predestined set of positions as ground truth; all positions on the graphs are related to these points. Thus, we are able to present the effect of TAPs on the evolution of the localization error. From these measurements we selected three different cases: the users stand still on the first, and acted differently (walking, standing, mixed movement patterns) on the second escalator.

On the left figure it can be observed how the trajectory reconstructions of TREKIE (green lines) and the plain DREAR trajectories (red lines) are related to each other. In this case the DREAR algorithm also finds the destination platform, since there is no possibility of TAP confusions, thanks to their type differences (escalators: grey, stairs: orange). The effect of trajectory reconstructions on localization error's evolution can be observer on the right figure. As we can see, the localization error for the reconstructed trajectories (red lines) is far below the ones presented by the DREAR algorithm. While at the end of the first escalator the localization error is reduced consistently to 2 metres, in case of the second escalator the error cancellation will vary between 1 and 6 metres.

Despite the eventuality to produce huge errors in position refinements (up to 40 metres for the second escalator) all the cases ended with a controlled and suppressed positioning error. Without this the raw DR (without DREAR+TR) would mess up the trajectory, leading to wrong navigation instructions. While in this case we did not profit directly from the TAP association and event alignment

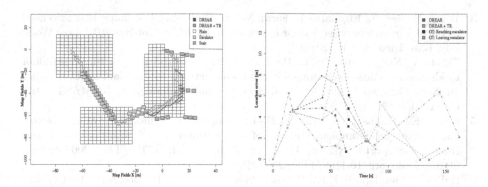

Fig. 4. The effect of trajectory reconstruction on trajectory matching

characteristics of TREKIE, since the first escalator was precisely recognized, and the distance to the second escalator was too short to produce significant DR errors, it became obvious that trajectory reconstruction can be also helpful for cases when tracking or map building functionalities must be provided. For such applications we can guarantee a more precise and realistic user path construction with less error than in case of a simple DR or even the DREAR algorithm.

5 Conclusions

In this paper we enhanced the approach of DREAR, a mobile-based localization middleware, which allows to exclude the infrastructural reference points (RF or visual), hence to provide a completely infrastructure-free localization system. Our goal was to further improve the context interpretation process, the detection of user movement activities (e.g. walking, taking stairs, using escalators) and the selection, association of position refinement points (TAPs) along the users' trajectories. The proposed solution was thoroughly evaluated in a complex subway system, focusing on different aspects of the trajectory reconstruction and localization process. TREKIE presents clear improvements related to the performance of DREAR, with promising results and a great potential for real-world scenarios (e.g. subway stations). As future work we want to consider also the inclusion of acknowledged heading information in the trajectory reconstruction process.

References

1. Jin, Y., Motani, M., Soh, W.-S., Zhang, J.: Sparsetrack: enhancing indoor pedestrian tracking with sparse infrastructure support. In: IEEE Infocom 2010, San Diego, California, USA (2010)
2. Youssef, M., Agrawala, A.: The horus wlan location determination system. In: ACM MobiSys 2005, Seattle, Washington (2005). doi:10.1145/1067170.1067193

3. Wang, H., Sen, S., Elgohary, A., Farid, M., Youssef, M., Choudhury, R.R.: No need to war-drive: unsupervised indoor localization. In: ACM MobiSys 2012, Low Wood Bay, Lake District, UK (2012)
4. Török, A., Nagy, A., Kováts, L., Pach, P.: Drear - towards infrastructure-free indoor localization via dead-reckoning enhanced with activity recognition. In: Conference on Next Generation Mobile Apps, Services and Technologies, NGMAST 2014, Oxford, UK (2014)
5. Rehrl, K., Bruntsch, S., Mentz, H.-J.: Assisting multimodal travelers: Design and prototypical implementation of a personal travel companion. Trans. Intell. Transport. Sys. 8(1), 31–42 (2007). doi:10.1109/TITS.2006.890077. http://dx.doi.org/10.1109/TITS.2006.890077
6. Rai, A., Chintalapudi, K.K., Padmanabhan, V.N., Sen, R.: Zee: zero-effort crowdsourcing for indoor localization. In: ACM Mobicom 2012, Istanbul, Turkey, (2012). doi:10.1145/2348543.2348580
7. Yang, Z., Wu, C., Liu, Y.: Locating in fingerprint space: wireless indoor localization with little human intervention. In: ACM Mobicom 2012, Istanbul, Turkey, (2012). doi10.1145/2348543.2348578
8. Liu, J., Chen, R., Pei, L., Guinness, R., Kuusniemi, H.: A Hybrid Smartphone Indoor Positioning Solution for Mobile LBS. Sensors 2012(12), 17208–17233 (2012). doi:10.3390/s121217208
9. Liu, K., Liu, X., Xiaolin, L.: Guoguo: Enabling Fine-grained Indoor Localization via Smartphone. In: ACM MobiSys 2013, Taipei, Taiwan, June 25–28 (2013)
10. Link, J.A., Smith, P., Wehrle, K.: Footpath: accurate map-based indoor navigation using smartphones. In: Indoor Positioning and Indoor Navigation (IPIN) Conference, Guimaraes, Portugal (2011)
11. Ye, H., Gu, T., Zhu, X., Xu, J., Tao, X., Lu, J., Jin, N.: Ftrack: Infrastructure-free floor localization via mobile phone sensing, pp. 2–10. IEEE PerCom, Lugano, Switzerland (2012)
12. Tian, Y., et al.: Towards ubiquitous indoor localization service leveraging environmental physical features. In: IEEE Infocom 2014
13. Jimenez, A., Seco, F., Zampella, F., Prieto, J., Guevara, J.: Improved heuristic drift elimination (ihde) for pedestrian navigation in complex buildings. In: Indoor Positioning and Indoor Navigation (IPIN) Conference, Guimaraes, Portugal (2011). doi:10.1109/IPIN.2011.6071923
14. Angermann, M., Robertson, P.: Footslam: pedestrian simultaneous localization and mapping without exteroceptive sensors - hitchhiking on human perception and cognition, In: Proceedings of the IEEE, Vol. 100, May 13, 2012
15. Weinberg, H.: Using the adxl202 in pedometer and personal navigation applications. Analog Devices AN-602 application note (2002)
16. Madgwick, S.O.H.: An efficient orientation filter for inertial and inertial/magnetic sensor arrays. Technical report, Univ. of Bristol, UK (2010)

Strong Authentication for Web Services with Mobile Universal Identity

Do van Thanhe[1(✉)], Ivar Jørstad[2], and Do van Thuan[3]

[1] Telenor and Norwegian University of Science and Technology, Snarøyveien 30 1331,
Fornebu, Norway
Thanh-van.do@telenor.com
[2] New Generation Communication, Rådhusgaten 9 0151, Oslo, Norway
ivar.jorstad@newgencom.com
[3] Linus, Martin Linges Vei 15 1364, Fornebu, Norway
t.do@linus.no

Abstract. To access services on the Web, users need quite often to have accounts, i.e. user names and passwords. This becomes a problem when the number of accounts keeps increasing at the same time password is a very weak form of authentication exposing the users to fraud and abuses. To address both mentioned issues we propose a Mobile Universal identity, which by combining Internet identifiers with mobile identifiers is capable of delivering strong authentication for Internet services. By introducing an identity provider, the solution enables the user to employ the Mobile Universal identity for multiple service providers. By federation with other identities, Mobile Universal identity can be used with service providers worldwide.

Keywords: Identity management · Strong authentication · Identity federation ·
Mobile identity · Mobile ID

1 Introduction

In the current digital age the Internet or more precisely the World Wide Web, is playing a central role in most individual's life. The preponderant position is probably due the immense number of fancy and diverse services that everyone can access and enjoy. However, in order to get granted access to services users are quite often required to create an account with an identity, i.e. to define a user name and a password at the service provider. As the number of identities, i.e. user names and passwords is increasing it is more and more challenging for users to remember them. Most critical is the weakness of passwords as authentication scheme. Indeed, passwords are exposed to cracking, sniffing, phishing, spoofing, etc. which can lead to identity theft and other serious economic consequences both for the user and the service provider. Stronger authentication is urgently required.

Contrastingly, in the mobile network, mobile users enjoy of the great protection all over the world thanks to by the SIM (Subscriber Identity Module), a tamper resistant

© Springer International Publishing Switzerland 2015
M. Younas et al. (Eds.): MobiWis 2015, LNCS 9228, pp. 27–36, 2015.
DOI: 10.1007/978-3-319-23144-0_3

device which hosts the International Mobile Subscriber Identity (IMSI) and is equipped with advanced cryptographic functions, is capable of carrying strong authentication towards the mobile network. In this paper we propose a new user identity, called Mobile Universal identity, which combines mobile identity and Internet identity to provide a strong and uniform authentication for access of both mobile and Internet services. The paper starts with a brief review of related works. Next is the investigation of identities and authentication in the Internet. The strong authentication used in the mobile network is examined thoroughly. The main part of the paper is the description of the proposed Mobile Universal identity.

1.1   Related Works

There were previously proposed some solutions which make use of the SIM card to provide stronger authentication to Internet applications and services. The 3GPP GBA (Generic Bootstrapping Architecture) [1] authentication enables the usage of the USIM/ISIM (IMS SIM) authentication for other Internet application clients than the IMS client such as email client, IM client, presence client, etc. Basically, the GBA provides a mechanism for establishing a short-term authentication key between a client on the user equipment and a service provider. Unfortunately GBA only applies to USIM/ISIM and not the regular SIM. The second and probably the most serious limitation lies on the fact that GBA requires the presence of the GBA client on the mobile phone, which is quite difficult because handset manufacturers do not have incentive to implement it. To remedy the situation the Eureka Mobicome project proposed a few solutions called SIM strong authentication that provides strong authentication from a regular browser on a regular mobile phone carrying a regular GSM SIM [2][3]. Unfortunately, as their names suggest, the described solutions are focusing only on providing stronger authentications and do not constitute a complete identity system offering strong and user-friendly authentication to the users.

2   Identities and Authentication on the Internet

In the Internet or more correctly the World Wide Web users can access a lot of information but to receive really useful and validated documents and services they usually need to have an account at the service provider. Such an account is tied to an identity, characterized by a user name and a password locally defined at the service provider Web site. As the number of identities increases the burden to remember the passwords is getting heavier for users. To address this problem Identity Providers (IDP) such as Facebook connect [4], Google ID [5], Twitter [6], etc. start to emerge and offer the usage of their identities at other Web sites. This makes it easier for both the users and Web sites. Unfortunately there still is a big problem. Passwords are still too weak authentication and the risk to be abused is still there.

To improve security some players like Google, Apple, etc. introduced two step authentication or more precisely two factor authentication in which the first factor password i.e. something you know is complemented with a second factor, the mobile phone, i.e. something you have. Upon sign on the user receives a one-time code in an SMS (Short Message Service) that he/she has to type in. This authentication, although stronger, could be challenging when the user is accessing through his mobile phone with smaller screen and keyboard. Lately, there are emerging software security tokens i.e. software application capable of carrying out strong authentication functions e.g. RSA SecurID Software authenticator [7] which can be downloaded to smartphone and provide a two factor authentication. Unfortunately, these software tokens as any software application are subject to duplication and one can only be sure that the claimant does have the token but not that he/she is the only one.

3   Mobile Identity and Strong Authentication in the Mobile Network

When subscribing to mobile services, i.e. voice and Short Message Service (SMS) the user receives a mobile identity consisting of two identifiers. The phone number, also called MSISDN (Mobile Subscriber Integrated Services Digital Network-Number) is a public identifier is used by the user to make and receive phone calls. The other one, IMSI (International Mobile Subscriber Identity) is a private identifier standardised to be recognized by every network in the world and used in the authentication of the subscriber. The IMSI is not confidential but should not be diffused too much because it reveals the identity of the subscriber and may pose privacy problem. The responsibility of authenticating the subscriber is assigned to a software application called SIM (Subscriber Identity Module) [8]. For protection, the SIM application together with the IMSI, credentials such as secret key Ki, personal identification number (PIN) for ordinary use, personal unblocking code (PUK) for PIN unlocking and cryptographic functions securely stored in a tamper-resistant integrated circuit called UICC (Universal Integrated Circuit Card), which is actually the physical module, commonly known as SIM card.

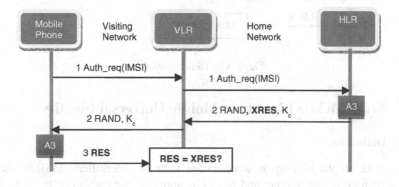

Fig. 1. GSM authentication

The SIM application combined with the UICC can provide strong two factor authentication with the PIN code as "something you know" factor and the UICC as "something you have" factor. As shown in Fig. 1 the strength of the GSM authentication is ensured by the use of a challenge-response mechanism. Upon power on the handset sends an authentication request with its IMSI to the Visitor Location Register (VLR) which forwards it to the Home Location Register. The Home Location Register (HLR) computes the 32-bit signed response (SRES) based on the encryption of a 128 bit random number (RAND) with the authentication algorithm (A3) using the individual subscriber authentication key (Ki) and send the triplet to the VLR. The VLR passes the random number RAND and the ciphering key Kc to the mobile phone which delivers them the SIM. The SIM computes the result RES using RAND and Ki, and submits it to the VLR. If RES = XRES the mobile phone is authenticated and Kc is used for the encryption of the air channel.

Although rather sophisticated at its invention time the GSM authentication scheme does not provide authentication of the mobile network by the mobile phone and exposes the mobile phone for man-in-the-middle attack by rogue base stations. To address this weakness, UMTS employs a mutual authentication allowing also the authentication of the 3G network by the handset. As shown in Fig. 2, the additional parameter AUTN enables the verification of the authenticity of the mobile network and also the expiration of the response.

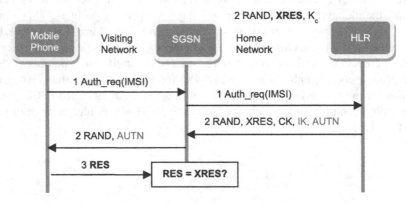

Fig. 2. UMTS authentication

4   From Mobile Identity to Mobile Universal Identity

4.1   Definition

The current Mobile identity as standardised with two identifiers: MSIDN and IMSI cannot be used in the Internet and has to be supplemented with one or more Internet identifiers. It could be a user name or a uniform resource identifier (URI) such an email, e.g.user@telenor.com that can be used for the authentication and authorisation of Internet services offered both by the mobile operator and third party service providers. Another major limitation of the Mobile identity lies in the fact that it is a subscriber identity and not really a user identity. There are many cases where the subscriber is not the user as follows:

- One subscriber may have multiple subscriptions distributed to multiple users: Typical example is a company or head of family that pays for a series of subscriptions which are distributed for use by employees or family members.
- One user can have multiple subscriptions and appear like multiple subscribers: This is the case of a user having multiple subscriptions for multiple devices: mobile phone, tablet, laptop, home alarm systems, etc.

We propose to introduce a Mobile Universal identity which is uniquely assigned to a user as a human being and lasts as long as the user likes. It must be sufficiently flexible to allow the inclusion, modification or removal of any mobile identifier or any Internet identifier that the user wants.

These identifiers can have different levels of assurance [9] from level 1 with full anonymity to level 4 with registration of user's name, address, nationality, picture and biometrics and the user is given the freedom to decide which identifier for each situation.

Since mobile identity, i.e. phone number and IMSI will be used in the authentication of the user and the user may have more than one it is necessary to have an enrolment process which registers the mobile identity for authentication. The user can run the enrolment process whenever he/she wants to change the phone number.

4.2   Mobile Phone Enrolment Process

The enrolment process although sufficiently secure is rather simple as follows:

1. The user signs on at the Mobile Universal identity provider (which could be the mobile operator) Web site using password
2. He/she enters the number of the mobile phone to be used in the authentication.
3. Mobile Universal identity provider verifies that the number is legitimate, i.e. in operation and not reported as lost or stolen.
4. If it is the case the mobile phone can be used and an SMS containing a one-time password is sent to the user's mobile phone.
5. By entering this one-time password at the Mobile Universal identity provider Web site the mobile phone is enrolled as authentication token.

4.3   User's Requirements

To be really useful and accepted by the users the Mobile Universal identity must fulfil the following requirements:

1. The user must experience a seamless authentication, i.e. no sign-in required when accessing from his/her mobile phone Internet services that do not require high level of security, e.g. social networks, net shops, etc.

2. For Web sites federated with the Mobile Universal identity service provider the user must be able to use his/her Internet identifier for sign in.
3. For Web sites having their own account, i.e. own user identity the user must be able to use strong authentication provided by his/her mobile identity.
4. The user will be asked to enter pin or select yes when accessing from his/her mobile phone Internet services requiring higher level of security, e.g. governmental services, health services, net banks, etc.
5. The user will be asked to enter pin or select yes when accessing from another device than his/her mobile phone all Internet services.
6. The user must be able to use his/her identity at service providers worldwide.

4.4   Overall Architecture

To realise the Mobile Universal identity fulfilling all the requirements mentioned in previous section, the mobile network has to be complemented with additional network element as shown in Fig. 3

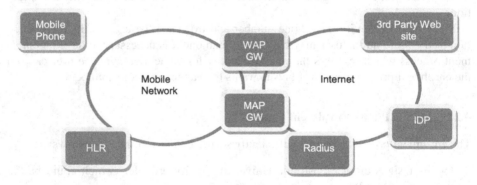

Fig. 3. The Mobile Universal identity overall architecture

- **Identity Provider (IDP):** is in charge of authentication and authorization for Internet services. In order to offer services to a wide range of 3rd party service providers the IDP supports several technologies and can act as a Liberty Alliance IDP [10], OpenID IDP [11], OAuth Authorization server [12]. It is communicating with the Radius server to request SIM or AKA authentication. This IDP can federate with other IDP including the ones of other operators to enlarge the usage of the user's Internet
- **Radius server:** This is a standard server that supports the EAP-SIM [13] and EAP-AKA [14] protocols. It can be used in the authentication of IP devices such as PC, Laptop, tablets, etc.
- **MAP gateway:** has on one side IP interface and on other side an SS7 interface allowing it to communicates with the HLR using the MAP (Mobile Application Part) protocol [15]. In fact it is viewed by the HLR as a VLR that sends authentication requests.

- **WAP gateway**: When offering Internet access Most of operators do have a WAP (Wireless Application Protocol) [16] gateway that translates Web pages onto adequate formats for mobile phones. For our solution, modifications have to be done to make the WAP gateway intercepting all the http requests and redirect to the IDP.

4.5   Typical Use Cases

To clarify how the Mobile Universal identity is working let us now consider a few typical use cases.

Use case 1: Sign on from mobile phone

1. The user browses on his/her mobile phone and visits a 3rd party Web site
2. The WAP Gateway intercepts http request and insert the mobile ID (MSISDN) in the header
3. The operator's WAP gateway redirects browser to Mobile Universal IDP
4. The Mobile Universal IDP sends an authentication request containing mobile ID to the MAP Gateway
5. The MAP Gateway forwards the authentication request to the HLR
6. The HLR returns an authentication vector to the operator's MAP Gateway
7. The MAP Gateway forwards authentication vector to operator's IDP
8. The Mobile Universal IDP sends authentication request with challenge to the user's mobile phone
9. The user's mobile phone sends challenge to SIM card and gets back response
10. The user's mobile phone sends response to the Mobile Universal IDP
11. The Mobile Universal IDP checks the response. If correct the Mobile Universal IDP inserts a security assertion in the browser and redirects it back to the 3rd Party Web server.
12. The user gets granted access to 3rd Party Web site without having to type anything.

Use case 2: Sign on from PC.

1. The user browses on his/her PC and visits a 3rd party Web site. A sign in page is presented.
2. The user enters his/her username at 3rd Party Web site and clicks on sign on.
3. The browser on the user's PC is redirected to the Mobile Universal IDP
4. The Mobile Universal IDP translates username to mobile ID sends an authentication request containing mobile ID (MSISDN) to the MAP Gateway
5. The MAP Gateway forwards the authentication request to the HLR
6. The operator's HLR returns an authentication vector to the MAP Gateway
7. The MAP Gateway forwards authentication vector to the Mobile Universal IDP

8. The Mobile Universal IDP communicates with the Short Message Service Center (SMS-C) to send an SMS to the user's mobile phone. The headers of this SMS ensure that the SMS is terminated on the SIM-card on the user's mobile phone.

9. On the SIM-card, a SIM Toolkit Application is triggered and a pop up appears in the display of the user's mobile phone. It asks the user if he wants to proceed with the authentication.

10. If the user accepts, an SMS is returned to the Mobile Universal IDP,

11. The Mobile Universal IDP inserts a security assertion in the browser and redirects it back to the 3rd Party Web site.

12. The user gets granted access to the 3rd Party Web site.

4.6   Making the Identity Really Universal

The Mobile Universal identity as described so far can only be used with service providers that trust the Identity Provider and are hence willing to use the Mobile Universal identity provided by this IDP. This is typically the case of local service providers in one country that build alliance with a national IDP. The IDP together with its service providers form a circle of trust in which the user can employ the same identity. Unfortunately, such a circle of trust has boundaries and there are certainly service providers that belong to other circles of trust. The user cannot use his/her Mobile Universal identity with these service providers.

To enable the usage of the Mobile Universal identity of one circle of trust in another one, federation of the two circles of trust has to be done as shown in Fig. 4. Federation is the exchange of metadata necessary for the mapping of one identity to the other.

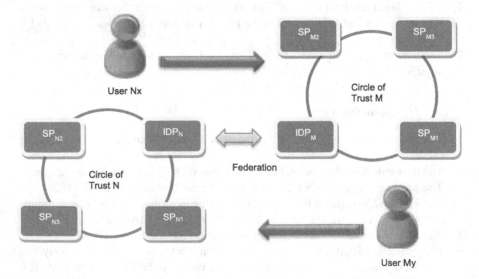

Fig. 4. Federation of identities

There are two federation methods and to explain them let us consider two circles of trust N and M with respectively IDP_N and IDP_M.

- **Federated identifier:** When user Nx of Circle of trust N visits a service provider SP_{M2} in Circle of trust M. IDP_M acts as a service provider in the Circle of trust N. For user Nx an account at IDP_N is created and federated both with SP_{M2} and IdP_N.
- **One Time identifier:** The visited SP_{M2} does not store any local account for the user. After being authenticated by the home IDP_N user Nx will be authorized by the SP_{M2} A new one-time identifier must be generated at access and the user can use her IDP_N identity.

For the travelling user accessing from mobile phone the sign-on is seamless as indicated previously in Use case 1. When the user is browsing from her laptop it is a little bit more challenging because the Internet identifier might not be recognizable for the visited SP. There are two solutions as follows:

- **Universal unambiguous Internet identifier:** IDP and SP have to agree on a common naming convention for identity that enables the identification of the home IDP.
- **User's assistance:** On the visited Web site there should be facility allowing users to indicate their origin.

5   Conclusion

In this paper, we propose an identity called Mobile Universal identity which can be used everywhere in the mobile networks and the Internet. The Mobile Universal identity is realised by including both mobile identifiers and Internet identifiers. Strong authentication is provided by using the mobile identity and the SIM. A proof-of-concept of the proposed solution has been implemented and tested to ensure feasibility. Some usability tests have been performed and the sign-on both mobile phones and PC are in the range of few seconds which is quite negligible for users. However, to really prove the usability of the Universal mobile identity it is necessary to carry field trials with real users. A federation trial between multiple circles of trust has also to be carried out for validation. Last but not least, to ensure the success and adoption by the market it is important to elaborate a sound business model such as for international roaming.

References

1. 3rd Generation Partnership Project: 3GPP TS 33.220 V8.2.0 (2007-12) Technical Specification Group Services and System Aspects; Generic Authentication Architecture (GAA) Generic bootstrapping architecture (Release 8)
2. Van Thanh, D., Jønvik, T., Van Thuan, D., Jørstad, I.: Enhancing internet service security using GSM SIM authentication. In: Proceedings of the IEEE Globecom 2006 Conference, San Francisco, USA, November 27, December 1, 2006. ISBN 1-4244-0357-X

3. Van Thanh, D., Jønvik, T., Feng, B., Van Thuan, D., Jørstad, I.: Simple strong authentication for internet applications using mobile phones. In: Proceedings of IEEE Global Communications Conference (IEEE GLOBECOM 2008), New Orleans, LA, USA, November 30, December 4, 2008. ISBN 978-1-4244-2324-8
4. Facebook Inc.: Facebook login. https://developers.facebook.com/docs/facebook-login/
5. Google: Google account. https://developers.google.com/+/features/sign-in
6. Twitter. https://twitter.com/
7. EMC[2.] http://www.emc.com/security/rsa-securid/rsa-securid-software-authenticators.htm
8. 3rd Generation Partnership Project: 3GPP TS 11.11 V6.0.0 (1998-04); Specification of the Subscriber Identity Module - Mobile Equipment (SIM-ME) Interface (Release 97)
9. NIST: National Institute of Standards and Technology. Special Publication 800-63 Version 1.0.2 Electronic Authentication Guideline, April 2006
10. T. Wason, et al., Liberty ID-FF Architecture Overview: Version: 1.2-errata-v1.0. Liberty Alliance Project (2005)
11. OpenId. http://openid.net/
12. oAuth. http://oauth.net/
13. The Internet Engineering Task Force: Network Working Group, Haverinen, H., Salowey, J.: EAP-SIM Authentication. RFC 4186, IETF, January 2006
14. The Internet Engineering Task Force: Network Working Group. RFC 4187 Extensible Authentication Protocol Method for 3rd Generation Authentication and Key Agreement (EAP-AKA)
15. ETSI TS 100 974 V7.15.0 (2004-03). Digital cellular telecommunications system (Phase 2+); Mobile Application Part (MAP) specification - (3GPP TS 09.02 version 7.15.0 Release 1998
16. Open Mobile Alliance (OMA): Wireless Application Protocol Architecture Specification - WAP Architecture Version, April 30, 1998

Optimization of 3D Rendering in Mobile Devices

Tomas Marek and Ondrej Krejcar[✉]

University of Hradec Kralove Faculty of Informatics and Management Center for Basic and
Applied Research, Rokitanskeho 62, 500 03 Hradec Kralove, Czech Republic
Tomas.Marek.5@uhk.cz, ondrej@krejcar.org

Abstract. Computer graphics in combination with mobile devices find much
use in the fields of entertainment, education and data displaying. The amount
of information that is possible to provide to the user depends greatly on the
optimization of graphic chain in the development of given application. The important element is simplification of the scene by removing objects that are not
currently visible or degrading the complexity of the models from the distance
of the observer. This paper describes implementation of the frustum culling
method on the Android platform as a solution for these problems.

Keywords: Mobile device · Engine · Graphics · Culling · Optimization

1 Introduction

Nowadays, the mobile devices replace every time more computers and laptops [11,
12]. Their constantly increasing output enables development of application environment in which it is possible to find tools for solution of many tasks. Moreover, these
devices are constantly available and ready to be used. This wide accessibility and
output increases demand for better and smarter applications in many branches [25].
Consequently, the computer graphics comes in with the employment of interface
Open Graphics Library (OpenGL) for Android and new Metal API (application programming interface) introduced with IOS8 [14]. The extent of employment is very
wide, from the effects during the video recording and taking photographs, for example, in the article [1] described depth of field effect, to 3D talking avatar [2] presented
in the conference APSIPA [13]. Significantly the most profitable and the most favour-
ite category across the applications are games, nevertheless 2D and 3D graphics are
finding application in other popular categories such as education or tools. In general,
we talk about modules for professional programmes, data displaying or augmented
reality. Even cheap mobile devices can display large medical data using volumetric
rendering [3]. With this trend the mobile versions of big graphic engines, such as
Unity, CryEngine or Unreal engine are beginning to appear. For the developers and
studies a questions comes to mind and that is: How should we start creating graphic
content?

Freely available engines have some disadvantages that have to be considered. The
first is the whole quality and speed of actualization. The developer does not have the

© Springer International Publishing Switzerland 2015
M. Younas et al. (Eds.): MobiWis 2015, LNCS 9228, pp. 37–48, 2015.
DOI: 10.1007/978-3-319-23144-0_4

full control over the engine and has to rely on the fact that errors will be corrected in time. Moreover, some modules can be written unsuitably for specific demanded solution. The advantage is the verified multiplatform solution. Another problem is speed of learning. Engines come with their own developers' tools and their full mastering can take the same time as creating a new engine. In many cases, it is more suitable to create own smaller solution [16].

2   Problem Definition

The basic characteristic in PC graphics is that better optimization enables displaying more content. The right idea about complicatedness of 3D scene can be acquired by using an example from gaming environment [4]. It can be thought about 3D as a world with dozens of rooms where each room contains other models and details. The complicatedness of the scene exceeds the possibility of the device for processing the whole content. There are animated models of figures moving between the rooms and some of them can be controlled by the user. Certain objects can be moved and destroyed, which is arranged using physical simulations. Everything is accompanied with sound effects to illustrate the atmosphere. In order to realize a vision like this it is convenient to prepare a tool that will facilitate and accelerate the work with the scene design. This kind of tool is called engine (Fig. 1).

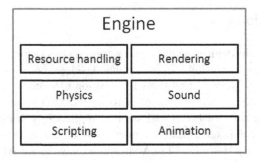

Fig. 1. Graphic engine

In general, 2D and 3D engines are tools for effective displaying and for work with graphics in order to display content to users [7]. Engines can also contain other tools, for example, for work with particles or for work on scene modelling. This work is dedicated to the basic parts of engine for rendering and those are resource handling and rendering.

The important parts of programme plotting are shaders. Those are short programmes that affect process of rendering. They can be divided into vertex and fragment shaders [5] according to their focus. The entire rendered data goes through them. The vertexes of the rendered objects are transformed using vertex shader. The data for these operations can be delivered to the shaders in the process of plotting using uniform variable. Opposed to uniform, that contains the same data for the whole model, the characteristics of the model (position, normal, colour, etc. for each vertex) are transmitted using attribute variable. Here it concerns matrixes needed for the right turn and deformation of the scene. The result from vertex shader is later processed and used in fragment shader that serves for performing operations on the level of individual pixels. Transmitted data are labeled in the shaders as varying.

It is almost impossible to display graphic content without use of textures. The texture is a 2D image, mostly defining a colour using RGB (a way to mix colours), that is mapped on the surface of the unit. The textures are used for a wide array of effects, for example for defining of wrinkled surface, for saving of shades or lights, for reflection or for directly mirrored images [17, 18]. Only rarely it is possible to map the texture to the object in a ratio of 1:1. Opengl in other cases uses the setting for texture filtering that can be used to define the way of acquiring data from the texture. Different settings bring various results and they have different impact on the speed of rendering.

The optimization of loaded data [20] means minimization of their size, alternatively preliminary preparation for simplification of following rendering. Fitting the colour mode to the really required number of colours, consideration a need for anti-aliasing effect, or minimise of interlaced images may be relevant tips for improvement of graphic compression results [21]. Shaders, together with complex models and textures, present the main load of the engine. With the growing scene other difficult calculations for physics, collisions, animations and others can accumulate. Actual rendering can be described as a data transmission to a graphic card and their passing through the graphic chain that contains shaders. In order to reduce the demanding nature of it, it is convenient to think about the data types, also about the use of compressed textures, textures of atlases, optimization of model data, the way of plotting etc.

Manner of rendering is processing of the data in the process of sending them to the graphic card. That is using calling glDrawArrays for non-indexed data and glDrawElements for indexed data [6]. The indexes for data lead to reducing the duplicity and many times to the increase of speed of rendering. With the parameter mode the type of graphic primitives that will be rendered can be adjusted. The aim is again acceleration of rendering and reduction of the size of data. The graphic primitives are POINTS, LINES, TRIANGLES, special kinds of connection of triangles – TRIANGLE_STRIP, TRIANGLE_FAN and others. Even before calling for rendering, it is necessary to load the data and send them to the graphic card. For different types of scenes there are different ways of data transmission. The basis is vertex arrays object (VAO), where the data are saved in RAM memory. A better solution is using vertex buffer object (VBO) and saving rendered data in video memory.

3   New Solution

For identification of places where it is possible to apply further optimization it is convenient to understand the process of graphic content rendering [6]. OpenGL ES API is a tool for creating an image from 2D and 3D objects. The result of rendering is saved to framebuffer of the graphic card (visual output device). Objects are composed of graphic primitives that are the foundation of rendering OpenGL and they are set during calling glDraw. In order to define such a basic shape it is necessary to have a set of vertices where each vertex is a point in the space. Every vertex is connected to its characteristics that are transmitted with it and connection of these vertices defines the whole model. In picture number 2 there is demonstrated a simplified process of graphic chain.

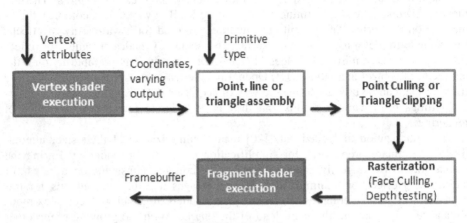

Fig. 2. Graphic chain

The results of vertex shader, which is run for every vertex, are the coordinates of vertex after transformations and possible varying variable. The next step, except for the automatic conversions for the following processes, is a creation of graphic primitives and cropping by viewing frustum. The next is rasterization (conversion to 2D image), activation of fragment shader and saving the figure to framebuffer. In case of triangle being partly out of the screen, some of his vertices are removed and for shape preservation new points are added on the edge of the viewing frustum. In the processing of the fragment (colour, depth, and varying data) it is sometimes necessary to read again the result of the previous record from framebuffer, for example when trying to resolve transparency. Before launching the fragment shader the testing of the depth happens and fragments that are lying behind other fragments are not processed.

These problems can be solved by differently complicated methods and recommendations [16]. For example, with the sampling system it is better to use the shape composed of more vertices. That means that instead of using ordinary triangle or square for a picture of circle, it is better to triangulate the resulting shape in a way so that it would correspond with the texture. Saving the output on fragment shader, where it is not necessary to solve the difference of the real and requested shape of transparency, is significantly higher than the price of bigger amount of vertices. An interesting possibility is to let the user to reduce the resolution where the calculations are being run. Some devices have exorbitant number of pixels per inch (DPI). The rendered scene cannot always reach such a detail and reducing the resolution can mean a significant improvement of the output. Another problem, excessive number of processed vertices, can be solved by using method level of detail, frustum and occlusion culling.

Fig. 3. Level of detail [8].

Level of detail (LOD) does not solve a problem that is directly visible in the graphic chain but it is perceptible in the complex scene. This method does not work directly to remove the unnecessary geometry but to simplify it. The object that is being rendered further from the camera takes up smaller area of the image because of the perspective transformation than the same object rendered closer [24]. That means that such model is displayed using a lower number of pixels. The consequence is that the object loses the level of detail but it is still difficult to render it. So with the increasing distance LOD changes the detailed model for its simplified version. The change of the level of details is almost undetectable even when using significantly simpler geometry. The scene can contain many distant objects thanks to LOD. The problem is the change of models that can cause a big leap. This leap is undesirable so it is convenient that LOD has as identical shapes as possible. Another possibility is using blending and let different levels of the model to blend. This method is mostly used for bigger objects such as trees and buildings. The lower level of the model for a tree can be simplified even to a mere 2D image of the original tree rendered using bill boarding (pivoting the surface always towards the camera). LOD can be used also for animations where apart from simplifying the model, the simplification of a skeleton can also happen. For example, with the figures it is not necessary to animate fingers for the large distance. If the distant object is too small it is even useless to render it. As exceptions can be dominant objects such as buildings and trees. Apart from the substitution of differently detailed models it is also possible to actively recalculate the models. The demand on the computing power [19] is higher but the memory demands are reduced and the scene has always a suitable level of detail. An illustration of LOD is depicted in figure (Fig. 3) [8].

In the 3D world not only do the changes of detail with the distance happen but they also overlap. Apart from sequencing the objects from the closest for the minimization of activation fragment shader, it is also practical to remove models from the scene that are completely hidden behind another objects. One possible solution is the method occlusion culling [9]. The techniques of occlusion culling can be divided into several methods. The first group is unit based occlusion culling that contains BSP (Binary Space Partitioning) and portal methods. During BSP the content of the scene is divided into hierarchically arranged units and those can be tested on overlapping and their position in relation to the camera. With this method it is necessary to undergo an extensive pre-processing of the scene, for example determination of the visibility of one unit among the others. Afterwards, it can be determined which units can the camera see from its actual position. The method of the portals completes BSP with hatches to other places. The units are considered as closed spaces and if the portal is not visible, the whole content of the unit is not visible. The visible portals delineate with their shape the viewing frustum to other units where the objects on the inside can be rendered. The disadvantage is the necessity of the preparation of the environment and the employment mostly in static scene. The characteristics of the methods imply that the most convenient use will be found in the closed scenes (buildings, rooms).

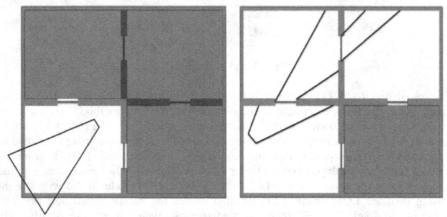

Fig. 4. Occlusion culling

The figure (Fig. 4) implies a scene of four rooms and a camera located in one of them. In the first part of the picture, the camera does not look at any of the portals so only one room is rendered. In the second part of the picture, there are two portals in the viewing frustum of the camera. From the first visible portal a viewing frustum with another portal is calculated. In case of division of the rooms into other units it is possible to continue limiting the content that is not visible and does not have to be processed. Other methods of occlusion culling applicable for dynamic and open scenes work in image space. The best-known method is hierarchical occlusion mapping (HOM). With this method we can define overshadowing solids (occluders) and overshadowed solids (occludees). The depth of occluders is rendered into texture and an occlusion map is created. This kind of map can subsequently test occludee solids. These techniques can be found in libraries that can be connected to engine. However, most of the time those are paid and for mobile devices demanding solutions. Another possibility is creating frustum shape defined by suitable objects formed from the models close to the camera. These objects can be called antiportales or occluders. All objects in this frustum can be subsequently removed. This method can be called antiportal because it inverts the so far described use of portals.

The mentioned methods are not dealing with the problem alone if the model or portal is in the viewing frustum of the camera. This problem is dealt with by a method frustum culling. The viewing frustum of the camera is defined using six surfaces. These surfaces create a shape of pyramid and each object in the scene is tested with these surfaces. However, this way is not optimal because it would be necessary to test all the vertices of the model. For the increase of effectivity the objects are wrapped in another simpler shape that is called bounding volume. This shape should depict the shape of a wrapped solid with the greatest precision possible. It is possible to use a sphere, a cuboid or a simplified version of the model. The calculation of the viewing frustum and the testing takes place in the processor. In case of the object being away from the pyramid, it is not rendered (Fig. 5). When it comes to more voluminous scenes, even after the simplification using bounding volume, testing can still be very demanding. The optimization is possible by assembling the models into a hierarchically ordered tree. The big covers then contain smaller ones until the level of individual models. It the big cover is not in the scene, the test of its whole content is skipped. This method can be further improved by combining it with occlusion culling or by using another system of scene division, for example octree. The objects that are in the viewing frustum only partially can be cropped and only the visible part can be rendered [9].

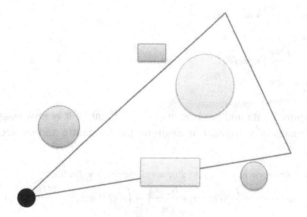

Fig. 5. Frustum culling

4 Implementation

The foundation needed for implementation of frustum culling is acquisition of the very viewing frustum of the camera. This information can be calculated from the matrixes necessary for rendering. These matrixes are view and projection. View matrix defines position of the observer, where he looks and where he is up (up vector). It is defined by the position of the camera (px,py,pz), by the direction of the view (dx,dy,dz) and by up vector (ux,uy,uz). The perspective matrix (projection) sets the perspective deformation of the world. Data from these matrixes can be used for acquisition of the shape that defines the edges of the visible scene. The parameters of the perspective matrix are field of view (fov), ratio (aspect ratio) and distance of the close and distant surface [10].

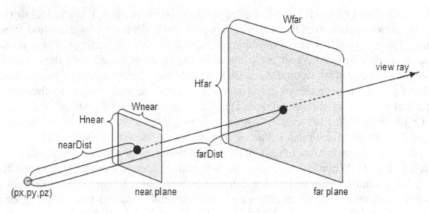

Fig. 6. Frustum planes [10].

In picture number 6 [10], there are data of the pyramid shape of viewing frustum. The height and width of the planes can be calculated from the present data.

$$Hnear = 2 * \tan\left(\frac{fov}{2}\right) * nearDist)$$

$$Wnear = Hnear * ratio$$

$$Hfar = 2 * \tan\left(\frac{fov}{2}\right) * farDist$$

$$Wfar = Hfar * ratio$$

From the acquired data and parameters of view matrix it is now possible to define the exact coordinates of vertices. For example the far centre and subsequently far top left.

$$farCenter = p\ (camera\ position) + d\ (view\ direction) * farDist$$

$$farTopLeft = farCenter + \left(upVector * \frac{Hfar}{2}\right) - \left(rightVector * \frac{Wfar}{2}\right)$$

The calculation of all the vertices will be done in a similar way. It is possible to use three points and a surface normal as a definition of each plane of the viewing frustum. This last datum can be acquired using cross product. Its result is perpendicular to both original vectors. One of the vectors can be up vector of the camera. The second one we can acquire as:

$$a = \left(nearCenter + rightVector * \frac{Wnear}{2}\right) - p$$

$$a = normalize\,(a)$$

$$normalRight = cross\,(up, a)$$

This way a normal vector of right plane of viewing frustum is acquired. All normals should be directed towards the inside of the shape to ease further processing. Apart from the stated geometrical process it is possible to calculate necessary data even in the space defined by the resulting matrix (VP) from view and projection (calculated in clip space). An arbitrary vertex p = (x,y,z,1) after multiplication of VP matrix will be in clip space as pc = (xc yc,zc,wc). This point is situated in homogeneous coordinates. After normalization (dividing by the wc figure) the result is pcn = (nx,ny,nz). In this normalized space, the viewing frustum is defined using axes with the centre in the origin. Those create the volume of the shape of cube located from -1 to 1 on all axes. So that the point pcn is visible, all of its coordinates have to be between -1 and 1. In homogeneous coordinates the delimitations for the point pc are – wc and wc. From this data we can ascertain the location of the vertex with respect to the previously mentioned plane. Therefore, the vertex is on the right side of the left plane if $-wc < xc$. View projection matrix can be written as:

$$\begin{pmatrix} A_{11} & A_{21} & A_{31} & A_{41} \\ A_{12} & A_{22} & A_{32} & A_{42} \\ A_{13} & A_{23} & A_{33} & A_{43} \\ A_{14} & A_{24} & A_{34} & A_{44} \end{pmatrix}$$

By using the point p = (x,y,z,1) transformed by its model matrix, it is possible to acquire wc and xc:

$$xc = x * A_{11} + y * A_{12} + z * A_{13} + A_{14}$$
$$wc = x * A_{41} + y * A_{42} + z * A_{43} + A_{44}$$

By editing this equation it is possible to get a general equation for the left plane (Ax + By + Cz + D = 0) such as:

$$-(x * A_{41} + y * A_{42} + z * A_{43} + A_{44}) < (x * A_{11} + y * A_{12} + z * A_{13} + A_{14})$$

$$(x * A_{41} + y * A_{42} + z * A_{43} + A_{44}) + (x * A_{11} + y * A_{12} + z * A_{13} + A_{14}) > 0$$

$$(x * A_{11} + y * A_{12} + z * A_{13} + A_{14}) + (x * A_{41} + y * A_{42} + z * A_{43} + A_{44}) > 0$$

$$x * (A_{11} + A_{41}) + y * (A_{12} + A_{42}) + z * (A_{13} + A_{43}) + A_{14} + A_{44} > 0$$

After normalization (A,B,C) corresponds with the normal vector of the plane and after the insertion of tested vertex, the result is positive or negative. The figure expresses at the same time distance from the plane. Positive result means that the point is located in a direction from the plane in which the normal vector is directed. That means towards the inside of the viewing frustum and it is possible to continue in testing with other planes. In the opposite case, the vertex is away from the viewing frustum. Inserting every vertex of a tested solid would not be very effective so the object is covered in a simpler shape and this one is tested against all six planes. For example, for a sphere it is enough to interchange a condition < 0, that describes an object beyond the viewing frustum, for < - radius. In case that the calculated distance < + radius, the object is only partially away from the viewing frustum. The value on the left side of the condition also corresponds with the distance from the tested plane. aIt is possible to test another shapes this way but those require a calculations for more vertices.

5   Testing of Developed Application

The method frustum culling should bring a visible increase in the output in the situations where the camera monitors only a part of the whole scene. The testing is unfolded from this prerequisite and it should bring a clear evidence of the advantages of this method. The first part of testing constitutes of setting up the 3D scene that will be sufficiently demanding. The demands of the scene mean that for the usual rendering the process speed would be negatively influenced. By using frustum culling a higher speed can be subsequently achieved. A sample application is composed of a landscape that forms a basis for rendered objects. The landscape is formed from 4096 vertices and it is covered in an ordinary skybox. This part of the scene is not influenced by cropping using viewing frustum. The influence of used method is tested on a model of a tree that has 1648 vertices. Part of this model is particle system for rendering details of branches with leaves. Each of the 99 trees is matched with a cover in a shape of a sphere. The location of the covers is visualized using a cube with a size of the diameter of the sphere. In figure (Fig. 7), there is a view from the camera located towards the centre of the scene.

Fig. 7. Sample scene with vegetation and illustration of covers from the observer's view

The main measured data is frame per second (FPS) where the value of 100 FPS means that one rendering lasts 0,001 s. Table (Table 1) shows a difference between the changes of 10 FPS deterioration when it has different starting FPS. The consequence is that a different load is needed for the 10 FPS change. When measuring the output, for that reason, we will also present data about the speed of rendering [16].

Table 1. Comparison of the speed change of image re-rendering entered in FPS in contrast to seconds

Initial speed [FPS]	Speed deterioration [FPS]	Initial speed [s]	Speed after deterioration [s]	Difference / deterioration in speed [s]
100	10	0,01	0,0111	0,001
20	10	0,05	0,1	0,05

6   Conclusions

It was practically verified that using methods for rendering optimization allows to increase the detail of the scene and to reduce the load on the computing power even when using mobile devices. The applied frustum culling method successfully removes uselessly processed scene content and using this method has, in the end, an influence on user's experience. Due to the increasing output and users' base it represents a necessity for competitiveness and profitability of graphic applications [15, 22, 23].

Acknowledgment. This work and the contribution were supported by project "SP-103-2015 - Smart Solutions for Ubiquitous Computing Environments" Faculty of Informatics and Management, University of Hradec Kralove, Czech Republic. Last but not least, we acknowledge the technical language assistance provided by Jirina Cancikova.

References

1. Wang, Q.S., Yu. Z, Rasmussen, C, Yu, J.Y.: Stereo vision-based depth of field rendering on a mobile device. Journal of Electronic Imaging **23**(2) (2014)
2. Lin, H.j., Jia. J, Wu, X.J, Cai, L.H.: stereo talking android: an interactive, multimodal and real-time talking avatar application on mobile phones, In: 2013 Asia-Pacific Signal and Information Processing Association Annual Summit and Conference (APSIPA) (2013)
3. Hachaj, T.: Real time exploration and management of large medical volumetric datasets on small mobile devices-Evaluation of remote volume rendering approach. International Journal of Information Management **34**, 336–343 (2014)
4. Eberly, H.: 3D game engine architecture: engineering real-time applications with wild magic, Ver. 1, p. 735. Morgan Kaufmann Publishers, Boston (2005)
5. Brothaler, K.: OpenGL ES 2 for Android: A Quick-Start Guide. The Pragmatic Programmers, Raleigh (2013)
6. KHRONOS GROUP: OpenGL ES Common Profile Specification Version 2.0.25 (Full Specification). (2010). [cit. 2014-11-14]. https://www.khronos.org/registry/gles/specs/2.0/es_full_spec_2.0.25.pdf
7. Behan, M., Krejcar, O.: Adaptive graphical user interface solution for modern user devices. In: Pan, J.-S., Chen, S.-M., Nguyen, N.T. (eds.) ACIIDS 2012, Part II. LNCS, vol. 7197, pp. 411–420. Springer, Heidelberg (2012)
8. Level-of-detail representation. In: New York University Computer Science. New York University (2001) [cit. 2014-11-16]. http://cs.nyu.edu/~yap/classes/visual/01f/lect/l4/
9. Gamedev.com. PIETARI, Laurila. Geometry Culling in 3D Engines (2000) [cit. 2014-11-16]. http://www.gamedev.net/page/resources/_/technical/graphics-programming-and-theory/geometry-culling-in-3d-engines-r1212
10. Lighthouse3d.com [cit. 2014-12-06]. http://www.lighthouse3d.com
11. Behan, M., Krejcar, O.: Modern Smart Device-Based Concept of Sensoric Networks. EURASIP Journal on Wireless Communications and Networking **2013**(155), 1 (2013). doi:10.1186/1687-1499-2013-155
12. Krejcar, O., Jirka, J., Janckulik, D.: Use of Mobile Phone as Intelligent Sensor for Sound Input Analysis and Sleep State Detection. Sensors **11**(6), 6037–6055 (2011)
13. Asia-Pacific Signal and Information Processing Association (2014). [cit. 2014-12-18]. http://www.apsipa.org/

14. IOS8. APPLE INC. Apple [cit. 2014-12-18]. https://www.apple.com/cz/ios/
15. Krejcar, O.: Threading possibilities of smart devices platforms for future user adaptive systems. In: Pan, J.-S., Chen, S.-M., Nguyen, N.T. (eds.) ACIIDS 2012, Part II. LNCS, vol. 7197, pp. 458–467. Springer, Heidelberg (2012)
16. Marek, T., Krejcar, O.: Optimization of 3d rendering by simplification of complicated scene for mobile clients of web systems In: 7th International Conference on Computational Collective Intelligence Technologies and Applications, September 21-23, 2015, Madrid, Spain, 10 p., Lecture Notes in Computer Science, (2015)
17. Machacek, Z., Slaby, R., Hercik, R., Koziorek, J.: Advanced system for consumption meters with recognition of video camera signal. Elektronika Ir Elektrotechnika 18(10), 57–60 (2012). 1392-1215
18. Ozana, S., Pies, M., Hajovsky, R., Koziorek, J., Horacek, O.: Application of PIL approach for automated transportation center. In: Saeed, K., Snášel, V. (eds.) CISIM 2014. LNCS, vol. 8838, pp. 501–513. Springer, Heidelberg (2014)
19. Maresova, P., Halek, V.: Deployment of Cloud Computing in Small and Medium Sized Enterprises in the Czech Republic. E & M Ekonomie a Management 17(4), 159–174 (2014)
20. Gantulga, E., Krejcar, O.: Smart access to big data storage – android multi-language offline dictionary application. In: Nguyen, N.-T., Hoang, K., Jędrzejowicz, P. (eds.) ICCCI 2012, Part I. LNCS, vol. 7653, pp. 375–384. Springer, Heidelberg (2012)
21. Horák, J., Růžička, J., Novák, J., Ardielli, J., Szturcová, D.: Influence of the number and pattern of geometrical entities in the image upon PNG format image size. In: Pan, J.-S., Chen, S.-M., Nguyen, N.T. (eds.) ACIIDS 2012, Part II. LNCS, vol. 7197, pp. 448–457. Springer, Heidelberg (2012)
22. Kasik, V., Penhaker, M., Novák, V., Bridzik, R., Krawiec, J.: User interactive biomedical data web services application. In: Yonazi, J.J., Sedoyeka, E., Ariwa, E., El-Qawasmeh, E. (eds.) ICeND 2011. CCIS, vol. 171, pp. 223–237. Springer, Heidelberg (2011)
23. Penhaker, M., Kasik, V., Snasel, V.: Biomedical distributed signal processing and analysis. In: Saeed, K., Chaki, R., Cortesi, A., Wierzchoń, S. (eds.) CISIM 2013. LNCS, vol. 8104, pp. 88–95. Springer, Heidelberg (2013)
24. Kasik, V., Cerny, M., Penhaker, M., Snášel, V., Novak, V., Pustkova, R.: Advanced CT and MR image processing with FPGA. In: Yin, H., Costa, J.A., Barreto, G. (eds.) IDEAL 2012. LNCS, vol. 7435, pp. 787–793. Springer, Heidelberg (2012)
25. Penhaker, M., et al.: Smart communication adviser for remote users. In: 1st International Conference on Context-Aware Systems and Applications, ICCASA 2012, Ho Chi Minh City, pp. 141–150 (2013)

Usability and Visualization

Principles of Usability in Human-Computer Interaction Driven by an Evaluation Framework of User Actions

Tomas Hustak[1], Ondrej Krejcar[1(✉)], Ali Selamat[1,2],
Reza Mashinchi[2], and Kamil Kuca[1]

[1] Center for Basic and Applied Research, Faculty of Informatics and Management,
University of Hradec Kralove, Rokitanskeho 62, Hradec Kralove 500 03, Czech Republic
{Tomas.Hustak,Kamil.Kuca}@uhk.cz, Ondrej@Krejcar.org
[2] Faculty of Computing, Universiti Teknologi Malaysia, 81310, Johor Baharu, Johor, Malaysia
aselamat@utm.my, r_mashinchi@yahoo.coms

Abstract. This paper tries to address problems that come out when designing a web page and how these problems affect people who use it. We will try to find the way to make our web pages easy to use and to give our user as little obstacles in his efforts as possible. He has to feel that every time he comes back to our web site, everything is on places where it should be and that everything acts as it should. One could say he has to see that everything looks normal. In this paper our aim will be to address web users, their needs and ways to improve their overall efficiency with achieving their tasks. We go through all main parts of usability issues according HCI as well as the current state of the art based on the most cited or specialised literature. In second part we introduce a development of a software platform that will sends user clicks to the server and allows us to go through these data in the web application for administrators. Design and development of this framework along with concrete computation of websites evolution index is also presented.

Keywords: Usability · Websites evaluation · Human-computer interaction · Framework

1 Introduction

Many web designers develop their projects without any feedback from the target audience and mainly focus to meet the contract requirements [5],[12-13]. They probably think users do not have adequate technical knowledge to understand such a complex field which web designing undoubtedly is. This is mostly true, on the other hand users know exactly what they need and that is something web designers cannot ignore. For even the most experienced web designers it is impossible to design a highly usable web site on their first attempt. This is because nothing like an average user [9] exists, every single user is different thus it is very hard to say what is good for all of them (or at least most of them).

© Springer International Publishing Switzerland 2015
M. Younas et al. (Eds.): MobiWis 2015, LNCS 9228, pp. 51–62, 2015.
DOI: 10.1007/978-3-319-23144-0_5

So if we want to create a good web site we need to listen to our users and communicate with them. The best thing we can do is to discuss with our potential users from the very beginning when we start prototyping [5], [3], [14].

Throughout all sections we will explain them in the detail, starting with the user-centered design. In the first part of this paper, we will answer the question "What is usability" and what impact usability has on users. The second part discusses HCI standards and their suitability for practical use. And lastly we will talk about interfaces between machines and humans in terms of usability [25].

2   What Is Usability?

Every web page creator or any program developer wants his web as usable as possible so naturally making UI intuitive, easy-to-use and consistent is the top priority. However, there are certain problems with making such UI, mainly because different web sites offer different things, thus it is very hard to make an ideal pattern for all sites. Another thing is to be original, to look not like a competition. That is why we need some methods that could tell us if we present our data to users in the right way [14, 23].

Usability is very important for web pages since it brings clear rules on how to make them easy to use without worries that people leave before finishing their tasks. The goal is not to make a user confused, information must not be hard to read and also it should answer users' questions (in other words users should get what they came for). Users should be always given the fewest possible answers because if we provide them too many answers even though all are correct, we might confuse our users to the point they just give up. Same applies to options, fewer options does not require that much thinking from users therefore they can concentrate on getting answers quicker. Users also prefer quick and straight responses, we do not want them to wait for unnecessarily long time, since they might get frustrated and leave. Any designer must take precautions to prevent his users wait for an unjustified period of time by for example removing all unnecessary big images from the page causing a long loading time on slow connections. Some web applications, however, need longer time to load the content, because there can be either some computations running on the background or some very important data are required to be downloaded. The most sensitive issues may be to utilise the 3rd party's services like web services which are out of our control. In such cases the preceding testing of external service quality is necessary [15, 16]. Either way, we want our user to wait until it is done, thus we should let him know something is going on and that he should wait before the application is ready.

What is quite disturbing and surprising at the same time, the users act differently and do things that a web developer would find hard to believe [14]. With this gained knowledge designers usually change the design a bit and conduct the same experiment again [5][6][3][10].

According to usability experts [6] who have already conducted some testings, searching for information is very frustrating and answering even simple questions can be challenging for users. What can be quite surprising is that graphic design does not have any significant impact on how usable a UI is. This, however, does not mean graphics is not important at all. For example to attract new users, increase site's credibility or sell products it can make a difference, but here we are talking whether it helps to find desired information.

So as we can see one of the very useful methods for testing usability is user testing. It involves obtaining representative users which means people who would probably enter the site of their own will. Observing what they do with an interface, listening what they think about it and noting their successes and fails significantly helps to address the potential interface usability issues.

2.1 Scanning

Many think users read on the web. According to [10] the reality is that users seldom actually read all the text on a web page. Users tend to scan the document until they find what catches their eyes [14]. For people it is impossible to disregard something they already learned, because they cannot go back to the state when they knew nothing [3].

When we say about some product that it is intuitive what it actually means is that it is well-learned. We could even say the more conventions involved the more intuitive product seems to be. Nobody would like driving cars without control elements everybody is used to, such as a steering wheel, pedals and a gear shifter. If a car manufacturer switched functions for two of these components, for example pedals would serve for steering and a steering wheel would make car accelerate and decelerate, then it could have fatal consequences. This example is a bit extreme, but illustrates how important conventions are in terms of usability.

Web designers in general assume that the first thing any visitor sees is a home page, while nothing could be further from the truth, since an average web user literally skips from page to page, not to mention almost everybody gets to a page by using web search engines such as Google, Yahoo! or Bing. Everybody should be able to recognize the main navigation, site logo, search option and something that tells us where we are in the current navigation tree.

2.2 Hard to Use

Unfortunately there is no way to safely design a usable website on first attempt, there are simply so many aspects that make it impossible to create a website based only on your best guess [14]. If it was difficult to use, good, for early internet users it was a challenge to muddle through. Nowadays however, the audience is more casual and unforgiving, for them technology is not another hobby, it is a tool they want to successfully use [3][5].

3   Human-Computer Interaction Standards from Usability View

Standards mean consistency and as already mentioned consistency is good for users, because they can transfer skill from one system to another which leads to decreasing the time needed to learn, thus enhancing their productivity and lowering costs for training them [3]. Human-Computer Interaction (HCI) Standards have been developed over the last 25 years most of them containing general principles for building applicable user interfaces [11].

However, various industry standards are platform dependent therefore quite diverse. Those who switch from one standard to another should always learn differences when developing for another platform [3], [14].

Apart from those listed, there is one more standard type we might encounter quite frequently. In-house standards are established by our organization mostly to meet its specific needs. Such standard should aim to be produced with respect to developers and their needs so they can apply and understand all parts of the standard easily. Rather than providing them an exhaustive body text developers appreciate involving examples, recommendations and a list of approved terms [3]. In-house standards can be significantly helpful and with combination with other standards (for example ISO) they can provide a high degree of usability.

Unfortunately there are risks and disadvantages involved when following standards. Having a product solely based on a standard can prevent further enhancements with regards to reduced flexibility and lesser motivation among developers, because they might feel that they do not share ownership of the user interface. Developers are often under the impression that following the standard automatically means they are designing a good user interface and might overlook serious design issues [3].

4   User Interface

When speaking about human-computer interaction, a user interface provides ways for communication between a human and a computer. Usually information is stored on various types of media, but mostly on hard disk drives of either personal computers or servers. Data are presented to users via user interface that describes what kind of data a user will see on a screen. In fact the user interface is where all communication between a human and a machine takes place [1-3][9].

4.1   GUI Design vs. Web Design

In connection with web applications we mostly talk about a graphical user interface (GUI) or a web user interface (WUI). There are also no restrictions in GUI creation, depending on an operating system you have the option to use predefined system components or you can create and use your own [2]. Each web site contains some navigation, where a user can move to another section of a website, it mostly also contains an actual content that user comes for. A web page however contains much more, for example blank areas where there is no text, no picture it can be just a background area or just an empty space between paragraphs. A web application has many limitations compared to desktop applications. A developer cannot affect the look of all elements on a page. Most probably the design will look different depending on used device and installed software [7]. The buttons might look different, each device has its own set of fonts and not to mention various screen resolutions. When creating a web design we have to keep in mind our pages will be displayed on more than just one platform [2].

4.2   Guidelines and Recommendations for Building a Usable User Interface

Everything begins when a decision about creating a new web site is made, at that point, people involved such as managers, designers, programmers etc. should take a great care and think about the target audience as the key, inseparable part of the system. Basically we can do simple tests even before a single line of code has been written, showing mock-up navigation to users or giving them paper cards and asking them questions. If we skip this part we may save costs for hiring initial test users but we might as well end up paying more money for a problem that is hard to find in the later phase of development because we omitted initial testing, which can be mostly very cheap. However, these methods work best if combined with user testing [5][3][16].

4.2.1   Guidelines
The first method that can help us with designing the UI are expert-made recommendations that we also known as the guidelines. Those are in fact best practices based on research, experience and there is a high probability that if you follow them your UI will be indeed easier to use. Let us mention the most important rules every designer should follow. Our user should always know where he is in context of the site navigation. That will be achieved by following several details that might help him to realize his location. Navigation should be consistent through all pages, no way would we let our users to get on a page without navigation. We might consider using breadcrumbs, it is an indicator how deep we are in the site's structure. Nowadays, breadcrumbs are very popular mainly on forum boards, but of course can be used on every web site, designers just need to make sure it is a supportive element, because it cannot entirely replace the classic navigation. According to [12], there has been a research that indicated daily users actually finish their tasks more effectively when a breadcrumb navigation is present.

Name links properly, try to avoid image-only links, since a graphical representation varies from country to country. Make obvious what is clickable [11], this has lots to do with conventions, users know how links look like from already visited sites, do not make them get used to another link style. Try to be consistent across your whole web site, give headers and titles same names as the links pointing at them.

4.2.2   Heuristic Evaluation
The second method is called a heuristic analysis, which means you will show your web site to an expert, who, depending on his skills may or may not find most of potential threats in your web [8, 24, 25]. As for the expert, you need to be trained well

and you need to practice a lot to be able to analyse any given web page with acceptable results [5][3][11]. However, you may try to analyse your own web site, you just have to switch and start thinking like a user. If you already read previous sections you may be familiar with many of the best practices, these might help you in finding possible problems. This involves noticing broken navigation, unclear links, chaotic forms, expendable graphic elements etc. With this approach you might be able to eliminate a lot of problems by just sitting in front of a computer and writing down every finding. Any web developer or a usability expert should never forget that details do matter [3].

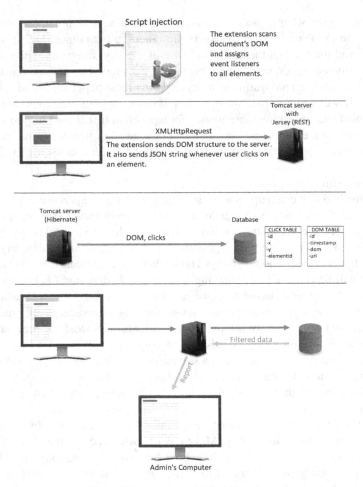

Fig. 1. Design of application structure

5   Designing of Evaluation Framework of User Actions

In this section we will be designing the user tracking software platform. We will describe the whole architecture and then we will take a closer look on all layers. This section contains only little implementation details.

Since there are several layers on which data flow, designing a software for tracking users' activities involves employment of many technologies (Fig. 1). The first layer starts on a tracked computer that is where our script will be capturing page events and sending them out. The second layer is our application server to which all data from the first layer are sent. It processes the data and after that sends them to the third layer, which is our database server where all the data are stored. The last layer brings the data to life by presenting them to the site administrator.

5.1   Architecture of Developed Solution

This is in fact a typical client-server architecture with a database server. In our case the client is the content script of our extension that runs in a user's browser context. So the main part of this architecture is the server and the client, both communicating via HTTP protocol following the REST paradigm. Once the extension is installed, the application can start with sending data to the server. Right after DOM is loaded, the content script sends this DOM snapshot to the server. Now the page is waiting and listening if there is any click event invoked. This captured click is going to be represented as a JSON object. It is very important to set a correct HTTP pattern in the extension's manifest.json file, since we will probably not need to check everything, just a web site or sites we want to analyze. Anything that is sent to the server is being persisted to the database, be it a snapshot or click entity. The server provides an administration interface that allows a web site administrator to generate reports for any site that is supported by the extension. The whole architecture is depicted in (Fig. 1).

5.2   Google Chrome Extension of Framework

A Chrome extension is added functionality to the Google Chrome browser. It can either provide ways of integrating extension's interface to the browser window or even inject scripts into visited pages. This injected script is called a content script and allows us to access the page's DOM elements and do whatever we wish to. There are certain limitations of what such scripts can do though. They cannot for example use chrome.* API (at least not directly) and are isolated from page scripts, thus cannot access their variables or functions. However, there is a way to communicate with the rest of the extension called message passing, because content scripts might need to exchange some data from time to time. Message passing is a very powerful way of sharing data between content scripts and all other resources that extension's background page has access to. Each extension has to have at minimum one file describing extension's purpose, name, permissions, files that will be used by the extension etc. This file is called manifest.json which is nothing more than a standard key-value pair JSON file. Extensions usually consist of the background page (which can be just a script file or a html file, it depends), manifest, and other files like images, sounds, scripts (including content scripts) and so forth. Developing Chrome extensions requires a good knowledge of web technologies such as HTML, CSS and JavaScript.

There is one favoured way of distributing extensions. Google itself launched an online store for applications called the Chrome Web Store where anybody with a developer account can upload and publish his extensions. Currently you have to pay an entry fee if you want to make a developer account from your regular google account. Any extension placed on the Chrome Web Store has a huge advantage being placed among other extensions, thus there is a greater chance that a user randomly roaming through the Web Store will notice your extension. It can be also rated by users who use it which adds credibility to your product. Nonetheless, nobody forces you to upload your extension there. Except of losing all the advantages listed above you can safely host your extension on your own server and offer visitors to download it. Unfortunately users would have to install it manually, since Google policy has changed recently and newer versions of Google Chrome browser does not allow auto-install from unverified sites (all sites except of the Web Store). Google rationalizes this decision by pointing out all the security loopholes and threats, coming from possibly malicious websites. There is no doubt that an unaware user could with best intentions install for example a nicely looking Clock extension that sends data from all input fields to an unauthorized person [17-22].

5.3   Listening Server and a Database

Probably the most crucial part of this design is an application server that stores logged clicks in a database. This server receives a snapshot of the DOM structure of a tracked web page which has been sent in a predefined format through a common HTTP protocol. It also waits for clicks to be sent from the originating extension script. Anything sent to this server, be it a click or a DOM snapshot, is validated and then dispatched to the database. Both the application server and the database server have to be compatible with each other to ensure the data being stored properly.

6   Discussion of Results

The results are nowhere near to reality [13], these are still laboratory values, because we would need many more users and thousands of clicks from longer period of time to obtain relevant statistics. Definitely more extensive tests should be made before going into production. As we open the web admin application, we have to fill in login and password. This action leads us to the main view, its appearance is depicted in the (Fig. 2).

If we press the button Report, the report view appear, where there is the table with records at the top and two charts at the bottom (Fig. 3). Closer look at the report indicates that participants were clicking on form elements to a high extent, those are namely FORM, SELECT and INPUT elements.

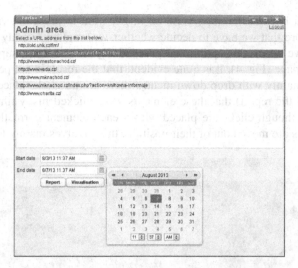

Fig. 2. Screenshot of admin area of developed solution

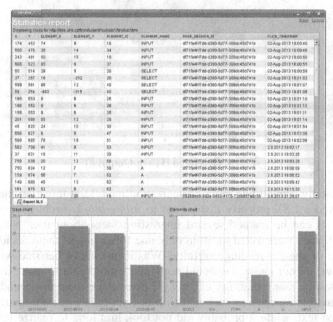

Fig. 3. The statistic report

There are also strange values for x and y coordinates, for example one line contains x = 59, y = 254, element x = -462, element y = -315 for an element with ID 40. This might indicate a problem with the drop down menu, the client script apparently have problems with mouse coordinates of the items in the menu and cannot read them properly. Apart from that, records seem to be consistent and none are missing. From the chart we can learn that the participants were accessing the page during four days (Fig. 3).

When we get back to the main view we might want to press the visualization [4] button, but before that we have to decide whether we want an overlay over a page or not, this time we check this option and proceed. By now, we are supposed to see a generated web page (Fig. 4). It is quite evident, that the result is not perfect, there are several issues mainly with drop down menus, there are no clicks placed even though we know (from the report) that these elements were clicked many times by our participants. Even though clicks are placed within each element correctly, some of the clicked elements are moved out of their position, this involves mainly form elements.

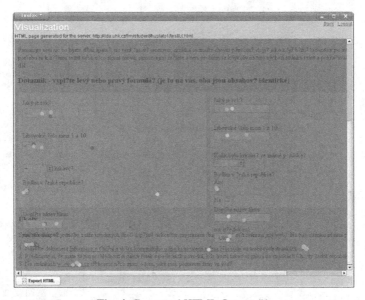

Fig. 4. Generated HTML Output #1

This is actually a small bug in the visualization module, it turns out that surrounding divs lacked a CSS property *display* set to *inline-block*. From generated HTML output (Fig. 4) can be learned several interesting facts about user behavior. Even though participants were asked to fill in only one form, one of them decided to fill in both. Was he or she not reading carefully? Was it just his or her free will to do so? The truth is we do not know, we would need much more data to make it statistically important. Despite many usability experts [3] discourage from using underlined text to prevent possible misreading such text as links, yet only one participant clicked on the underlined text, while it probably did not took him long to realize the right link. What we cannot say, however, whether the participants hesitated and hovered over the text to see if the cursor changes its shape from a pointer to a hand. Unfortunately we are not able to track this characteristic yet.

There is obviously a problem in a heat colour computation, also this chosen representation is adverse because human's eye hardly find it intuitive and natural. Choosing more insistent look, for example making each clicked element with a thick red border and replacing one colour background with a gradient would probably grab users' attention.

7 Conclusions

The purpose of this work was to introduce guidelines, practices and methods to increase users' satisfaction and making users more effective while interacting with our web pages. To support aforementioned we developed a software platform that sends user clicks to the server and allows us to go through these data in the web application for administrators. The data can be exported to XLS table format and even visualized as HTML. The Vaadin framework proved to be a good choice for this kind of web application, facilitating rapid development thus making a developer's life easier. The testing was unable to cover all possible variants, for example no pages with frames were involved. The future research in this area could focus on testing pages that have frames, fluid layout, embedded objects like Flash etc.

Acknowledgement. This work and the contribution were supported by project "SP-103-2015 - Smart Solutions for Ubiquitous Computing Environments" Faculty of Informatics and Management, University of Hradec Kralove, Czech Republic. The Universiti Teknologi Malaysia (UTM) and Ministry of Education Malaysia under Research University grants 02G31, and 4F550 are hereby acknowledged for some of the facilities that were utilized during the course of this research work.

References

1. Bartuskova, A., Krejcar, O., Kuca, K.: Evolutionary Approach of General System Theory Applied on Web Applications Analysis. In: ICOCOE 2014, Malacca, Malaysia, May 20–21 (2014), In Advanced Computer and Communication Engineering Technology. LNEE, vol. 315, part 2, pp 411–422 (2015)
2. Behan, M., Krejcar, O.: Adaptive Graphical User Interface Solution for Modern User Devices. In: Pan, J.-S., Chen, S.-M., Nguyen, N.T. (eds.) ACIIDS 2012, Part II. LNCS, vol. 7197, pp. 411–420. Springer, Heidelberg (2012)
3. Nielsen, J.: Usability Engineering. Morgan Kaufmann (1993) ISBN: 1-12-518406-9
4. Hajovsky, R., Pies, M.: Complex Measuring System for Longtime Monitoring and Visualization of Temperature and Toxic Gases Concentration. Elektronika ir Elektrotechnika **122**(6), 129–132 (2012)
5. Rubin, J., Chisnell, D.: Handbook of Usability Testing. Wiley Publishing, Inc. (2008) ISBN: 978-0-470-18548-3
6. Cimler, R., Matyska, J., Balík, L., Horalek, J., Sobeslav, V.: Security Issues of Mobile Application Using Cloud Computing. In: Abraham, A., Krömer, P., Snasel, V. (eds.) Afro-European Conf. for Ind. Advancement. AISC, vol. 334, pp. 347–358. Springer, Heidelberg (2015)
7. Behan, M., Krejcar, O.: Modern Smart Device-Based Concept of Sensoric Networks. EURASIP Journal on Wireless Communications and Networking (155) (2013)
8. Krejcar, O., Penhaker, M., Janckulik, D., Motalova, L.: Performance Test of Multiplatform Real Time Processing of Biomedical Signals. In: Proceedings of 8th IEEE International Conference on Industrial Informatics, INDIN 2010, July 13–16, Osaka, Japan, pp. 825–839 (2010). doi:10.1109/INDIN.2010.5549635
9. Krug, S.: Don't Make Me Think! A Common Sense Approach to Web Usability, 2nd edn. New Riders Publishing (2006) ISBN: 0-321-34475-8

10. U.S. Dept. of Health and Human Services. The Research-Based Web Design & Usability Guidelines, Enlarged/Expanded edition. Washington: U.S. Government Printing Office (2006)
11. Penhaker, M., Darebnikova, M., Cerny, M.: Sensor Network for Measurement and Analysis on Medical Devices Quality Control. In: Yonazi, J.J., Sedoyeka, E., Ariwa, E., El-Qawasmeh, E. (eds.) ICeND 2011. CCIS, vol. 171, pp. 182–196. Springer, Heidelberg (2011)
12. Machacek, Z., Slaby, R., Hercik, R., Koziorek, J.: Advanced system for consumption meters with recognition of video camera signal. Elektronika Ir Elektrotechnika. 18(10), 57–60 (2012)
13. Jancikova, Z., Kostial, P., Bakosova, D., Ruziak, I., Frydrysek, K., Valicek, J., Farakasova, M., Puchky, R.: The Study of Electrical Transport in Rubber Blends Filled by Single Wall Carbon Nanotubes. Journal of Nano Research 21(16), 1–6 (2013)
14. Hustak, T., Krejcar, O.: Principles of Usability in Human-Computer Interaction. In: Proceedings of the Advanced Multimedia and Ubiquitous Engineering, Future Information Technology. LNEE, Hanoi, Vietnam, May 18–1, 6 pages. Springer (2015)
15. Ardielli, J., Horak, J., Ruzicka, J.: View service quality testing according to INSPIRE implementing rules. Elektronika ir Elektrotechnika. (3), 69–74 (2012) ISSN: 13921215
16. Horák, J., Ardielli, J., Růžička, J.: Performance Testing of Web Map Services. In: Nguyen, N.T., Trawiński, B., Jung, J.J. (eds.) New Challenges for Intelligent Information and Database Systems. SCI, vol. 351, pp. 257–266. Springer, Heidelberg (2011)
17. Cerny, M., Penhaker, M.: Wireless body sensor network in Health Maintenance systems. Elektronika ir Elektrotechnika 9, 113–116 (2011)
18. Kasik, V., Penhaker, M., Novák, V., Bridzik, R., Krawiec, J.: User Interactive Biomedical Data Web Services Application. In: Yonazi, J.J., Sedoyeka, E., Ariwa, E., El-Qawasmeh, E. (eds.) ICeND 2011. CCIS, vol. 171, pp. 223–237. Springer, Heidelberg (2011)
19. Kasik, V., Penhaker, M., Novák, V., Bridzik, R., Krawiec, J.: User Interactive Biomedical Data Web Services Application. In: Yonazi, J.J., Sedoyeka, E., Ariwa, E., El-Qawasmeh, E. (eds.) ICeND 2011. CCIS, vol. 171, pp. 223–237. Springer, Heidelberg (2011)
20. Penhaker, M., Krejcar, O., Kasik, V., Snášel, V.: Cloud Computing Environments for Biomedical Data Services. In: Yin, H., Costa, J.A., Barreto, G. (eds.) IDEAL 2012. LNCS, vol. 7435, pp. 336–343. Springer, Heidelberg (2012)
21. Maresova, P., Halek, V.: Deployment of Cloud Computing in Small and Medium Sized Enterprises in the Czech Republic. E & M Ekonomie a Management 17(4), 159–174 (2014)
22. Ozana, S., Pies, M., Hajovsky, R., Koziorek, J., Horacek, O.: Application of PIL Approach for Automated Transportation Center. In: Saeed, K., Snášel, V. (eds.) CISIM 2014. LNCS, vol. 8838, pp. 501–513. Springer, Heidelberg (2014)
23. Mashinchi, R., Selamat, A., Ibrahim, S., Krejcar, O.: Granular-Rule Extraction to Simplify Data. In: Nguyen, N.T., Trawiński, B., Kosala, R. (eds.) ACIIDS 2015. LNCS, vol. 9012, pp. 421–429. Springer, Heidelberg (2015)
24. Bartuskova, A., Krejcar, O.: Evaluation Framework for User Preference Research Implemented as Web Application. In: Bădică, C., Nguyen, N.T., Brezovan, M. (eds.) ICCCI 2013. LNCS, vol. 8083, pp. 537–548. Springer, Heidelberg (2013)
25. Bartuskova, A., Krejcar, O.: Design Requirements of Usability and Aesthetics for e-Learning Purposes. In: Sobecki, J., Boonjing, V., Chittayasothorn, S. (eds.) Advanced Approaches to Intelligent Information and Database Systems. SCI, vol. 551, pp. 235–245. Springer, Heidelberg (2014)

A Study on User Perception of Mobile Commerce for Android and iOS Device Users

Perin Ünal[✉], Tuğba Taşkaya Temizel, and P. Erhan Eren

Middle East Technical University, Graduate School of Informatics, Ankara, Turkey
perinunal@gmail.com, {ttemizel,ereren}@metu.edu.tr

Abstract. Customer profiling in the mobile commerce (m-commerce) domain has recently gained importance due to the increased proliferation of smartphones and tablets. One of the major challenges confronting m-commerce developers is the need to know user perceptions of m-commerce applications in order to better design and deliver m-commerce services. In this paper, user perceptions of mobile commerce applications is analyzed based on their gender and the operating system (OS) of the devices in use, which are important factors for user profiling in mobile business models. The results show that there is a significant difference between Android and iOS device users' perceptions of mobile commerce applications except for their perception of advertisements. On the other hand, user perceptions of mobile applications in general does not exhibit significant differences except for the perception of usefulness for both gender and OS.

Keywords: Mobile · M-commerce · Mobile commerce · Operating system

1 Introduction

There is no doubt that the use of the internet and mobile technology has deeply influenced our lives. Mobile commerce (m-commerce) has emerged through the existence of mobile phones and personal devices such as Personal Digital Assistants (PDA) and tablets. M-commerce refers to electronic commerce transactions conducted via mobile phones and it is a relatively new area of research, which has a potential for rapid growth and wide extension. M-commerce has some core characteristics that differentiate it from classic e-commerce [1]. These include ubiquity, personalization, flexibility, dissemination, convenience, instant connectivity and location-specific services. These features, which are specific to mobile platforms, provide important advantages for m-commerce.

Mobile users prefer to use mobile applications rather than browsers to access mobile services. Application markets have grown rapidly as a result of vesting user interest in mobile applications. Our study focuses on measuring and analyzing user perceptions of mobile applications and explores how operating systems being used affect user preferences.

© Springer International Publishing Switzerland 2015
M. Younas et al. (Eds.): MobiWis 2015, LNCS 9228, pp. 63–73, 2015.
DOI: 10.1007/978-3-319-23144-0_6

To measure user preferences, several research models are utilized to depict consumer's behavior and technology acceptance. The theory of reasoned action (TRA) [2] assumes that human behavior is preceded by intentions. TRA claims that performed behavior is determined by behavioral intention. Behavioral intention, on the other hand, is determined by the individual attitude and subjective norm concerning the behavior.

Technology acceptance model (TAM) is the most widely used and most influential research model to explain consumer behavior toward technology. TAM proposes that intention to use technology is determined by the attitude toward using (AT) it. Attitude toward using is determined by its perceived usefulness (PU) and perceived ease of use (PEU) [3]. PU has an immediate effect on adoption intention, whereas PEU has both an immediate effect and an indirect effect on adoption intention via perceived usefulness [4]. Other variables that are used in TAM are adoption intention (AI) and actual system use (AU) [5].

The main contribution of this paper is to explore users' attitudes towards mobile applications. In addition, whether the gender factor and operating system (OS) being used on a user's mobile device has any correlation with that user's perception of the applications is investigated as an issue not explored in previous studies.

The findings in this study may provide a useful insight for service providers, business model developers and actors in m-commerce market. Since the m-commerce market gains importance day by day and provides more potential for new commerce trends, the findings of this study will be valuable for further research.

2   Related Work

Studies on consumer behavior in mobile environments are a rapidly growing field of interest. There are empirical studies on the users' adoption of m-commerce. In the study by Yang [6], the factors that affect the adoption of m-commerce in Singapore are studied. The research results showed that PU, consumer innovativeness, past adoption behavior, technology cluster adoption, age, and gender affect the adoption of m-commerce and the results were consistent with the technology acceptance model employed.

A quantitative study aimed to explore the determinants of m-commerce usage [7]. This study was conducted using a survey, which consisted of 22 items measuring seven variables, namely, perceived risk, cost, compatibility, PU, PEU, actual use and behavioral intention to use. It was found that, except for PEU, all variables were significant in determining m-commerce usage, with the compatibility factor being the most significant among others.

Consumer perception of mobile applications in the m-commerce environment was investigated by Mahatanankoon et al. [8]. Their study intended to address what attributes are important for consumers in their preferences among mobile applications. The authors used a survey that asked the users questions about their perception of the importance of mobile application attributes that ranged from 1 being not important to 5 being very important. It was found that mobile applications should possess maximum effectiveness through context aware, location-centric and customized features. The effect of personalization and context on customers' privacy concerns and intention to adopt commerce applications was investigated by Sheng et al. [9] in an empirical study, which consisted of four scenarios covering different commerce models. The results showed that the adoption intention differs according to the context, namely, it varies among the information, entertainment and payment areas depending on situation and context. The factors that influence users adoption in the m-commerce environment is analyzed in a recent empirical study [10]. The results indicate that perceived value mediates the effect of PU and perceived security on users' intention to use m-commerce.

Kim et al. [11] explained their reservations for well-known TAM. The authors stated that most adopters and users of technology are the employees of firms and organizations. However, for mobile internet, individuals should be considered as both consumers and users of technology. By adopting the theory of consumer choice and decision making from literature, the authors developed the Value-based Adoption Model (VAM). VAM evaluates the consumers' perspective of value maximization for mobile internet. Their study shows that consumers' perception of the value is the principal determinant of adoption intention.

In a study conducted on Turkish consumers [12], mobile phone users' attitudes towards m-commerce tools were explored. It was found that the respondents have positive attitude towards mobile advertising, mobile discount coupons, mobile entertainment services, location-based mobile services, mobile internet and mobile banking whereas they have negative attitudes toward mobile shopping.

Trust is a crucial factor in many of the economic activities and it has been studied in many disciplines ranging from business to psychology. After the landmark study of McKnight and Cervany [13], trust has been studied extensively in e-commerce as a factor in user adoption. Nevertheless, there are relatively few studies in m-commerce context. Siau and Shen [14] developed a framework for trust in m-commerce. They suggested that the two main factors influencing trust in m-commerce are: trust in mobile technology and trust in mobile vendor. The constructs the authors used were; reliability of wireless services, usability of m-commerce website, usability of mobile device, information quality, privacy of customer information, security of mobile transaction, trustworthiness of product vendor and quality of product.

Empirical studies that have been conducted on consumer adoption of Internet devices exhibit similar results. In a study regarding the mass adoption of 3G mobile phones in Taiwan [15], it was shown that consumers' perception of the utility is the key factor that stimulates mass adoption. In their study on explaining consumer acceptance of handheld Internet devices, Bruner and Kumar [16] used Usefulness, Ease of Use (EOU) and Fun to Use (FTU) constructs as scales. Their empirical results showed that while PU contributes to consumer adoption of handheld internet devices, the FTU attribute contributes even more.

Although the above-mentioned studies have focused on technological aspects of m-commerce, only few studies have examined the applications and user profiles in m-commerce. Furthermore, most studies on m-commerce adoptions have focused on the relationships between technology adoption factors and behavioral intentions of users based on demographic variables. Demographic variables are widely used since they are easier to obtain and valuable for identifying potential targets and predicting market trends [17]. Whitley [18] showed that age and gender significantly affect the attitudes towards computer use. Whitley found that men had higher self-efficacy and were more willing to take risks than women. Similarly, Yang [6] reported that men's perception of m-commerce were more positive. Concerning consumer spending on mobile applications, Seneviratne et al. [19] found that male users tend to purchase more apps than female users and they are more likely to spend more money on mobile applications.

Anckar et al. [20] reported contradicting results concerning the attitudes of male and female users towards m-commerce services. Women were found to be more interested in making reservations and purchases via their mobile devices. Men showed more interest in mobile banking and mobile games. In a recent study in 2014 [21] it has been pointed out that although quite a number of studies analyzed the relation between demographic characteristics and mobile internet usage, the impacts of age, gender and extent of mobile internet experience on mobile internet usage are still inconclusive. One of the reasons behind this finding may be due to the increasing maturity of the mobile usage market. Furthermore, since the characteristics of mobile use and features of mobile devices change over time, there is a need to conduct further explorative studies in this domain. To the best of our knowledge, there are no empirical studies, which have investigated m-commerce user perceptions of mobile applications and m-commerce applications with various constructs based on gender. The purpose of the current study is to determine whether gender is a determinant of user perception of mobile applications; in particular m-commerce applications.

Although demographic user profiling is more common due to its wide area of implementation and ease of obtaining, impact of operating system being used is a less studied topic. Since the launch of Apple Store in 2008, there has been a growing competition between Apple Store and Google Play store for iOS and Android operating systems, respectively. In the first quarter of 2015, Android and iOS operating systems covered approximately 96.3% of the global smartphone market: Android dominated the market with a 78.0% share followed by iOS with a market share of 18.3% [22]. Even though smartphones with Android operating systems dominate the market, the revenue of Google Play Store is half that of Apple Store and the average revenue per iOS user is four times that of an Android [23]. Mobile phones are not just a medium of communication but they also imply the status and identity of their users [24]. Plant [24] reported that the color of the handset, the ringtone, and the logos and graphics indicate personal preferences. In this study, in addition to demographics, we explored the effects of the operating system being used on user preferences regarding mobile applications as well as their related attitudes and intention to spend money with mobile applications.

The current study is important for its contribution to a recently developing field. There is a limited number of empirical studies conducted in this field especially for m-commerce applications. This study will provide results that can be used for future research and that may be beneficial for developers and designers in mobile business market.

3   Methodology

3.1   Sample and Data Collection

The empirical data was collected using the questionnaire given in Appendix A, which was e-mailed to undergraduate and graduate university student lists of the Middle East Technical University. Our target population was university students since the young generation heavily relies on their mobile phones. The data used in this study were collected from 287 respondents.

3.2   Questionnaire

In this study, a survey research methodology was employed. The questionnaire was based on a seven point Likert scale, ranging from 1 being "Totally disagree" to 7 being "Totally agree". The survey consisted of four parts. In the first part, the respondents were asked questions on their mobile phone usage. The second part contained items measuring the attributes of mobile application usage. In the third part, questions with regard to the usage of mobile applications for commerce purposes were presented. In the last part, the questions were related to demographic information such as gender and education.

In our study, we focused on user's attitudes towards general-purpose mobile applications and m-commerce applications in particular. To investigate user perceptions of mobile applications, we used the following constructs from Bruner and Kumar [16]; Usefulness, Ease of Use (EOU) and Fun to Use (FTU). Information Quality and Attitude Toward Use (AT) constructs were adopted from Siau and Shen [14]. In this study, user perceptions of m-commerce applications were also investigated using constructs that address specific issues in m-commerce. Usefulness, EOU and FTU constructs were taken from Yang [6], and Security, Advertisement, Actual Use and Intention to Use constructs were adopted from Barutcu [12]. The scales used in the current study are given in Appendix A.

4   Results and Discussion

The data was analyzed using the SPSS software. Of the total 287 participants, 156 used Android, 86 used iOS and 45 used other operating systems corresponding to 54%, 30% and 16% of all the participants, respectively. In terms of the demographic information, 140 participants were female and 114 were male, and the remaining 33 did not state their gender.

4.1   User Perceptions of Mobile Applications

Figure 1 presents the mean scores of user perceptions of mobile applications in terms of two operating systems, namely Android and iOS. The scores of iOS device users concerning mobile applications were found to be higher than Android device users in all constructs. Figure 2 shows the results for user perceptions based on gender distinction. It is observed that the scores of female and male participants were close to each other except for usefulness in which male users scored higher.

To explore whether there is a significant difference, first, normality of data is checked for the user perceptions of mobile applications constructs using Kolmogorov-Smirnov and Shapiro-Wilk Tests. The results revealed that the significance values were lower than 0.05, so the data was not normally distributed. When the data is not normally distributed, based on the rank order of observations, non-parametric tests can be performed by sacrificing some information such as the magnitude of difference.

Since the data was not normally distributed, we used the Mann Whitney U Test as the non-parametric test for the dataset. The results of the Mann Whitney U Tests revealed that there is a significant difference between the scores of iOS and Android device users concerning Mobile Application Usefulness (U=5403, Z=-2.535, p=0.011) whereas there is no significant difference in terms of EOU (U=5925, Z=-1.604, p=0.109), FTU (U=6156, Z=-1.153, p=0.249), AT (U=6121, Z=-1.183, p=0.237) and Information Quality (U=6251, Z=-0.884, p=0.377) constructs. Similarly, the results based on gender distinction show that there is a significant difference between the Usefulness (U=5979, Z=-3.477, p=0.001) scores of females and males while there is no significant difference in EOU (U=7507, Z=-0.862, p=0.389), FTU (U=7763, Z=-0.401, p=0.688), AT (U=7032, Z=-1.704, p=0.088) and Information Quality (U=7709, Z=-0.469, p=0.639).

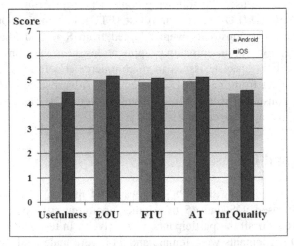

Fig. 1. User Perceptions of Mobile Apps based on OS

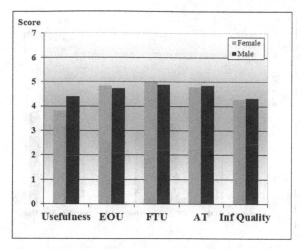

Fig. 2. User Perceptions of Mobile Apps based on Gender

4.2   User Perceptions of Mobile Commerce Applications

The mean scores for user perceptions of m-commerce applications are shown in Figures 3 and 4 based on OS and gender, respectively. Similar to the results obtained from general-purpose mobile application (Figure 1), iOS device users' scores were found to be higher than Android device users in all constructs. When the results were analyzed with regard to gender, it was seen that the perception scores of male users concerning all constructs were higher than those of female users.

For the study on user perceptions of m-commerce applications, normality of data was checked using the Kolmogorov-Smirnov and Shapiro-Wilk Tests. Since the results revealed that the data was not normally distributed, the Mann Whitney U Test was used. The tests on m-commerce application constructs showed that there is a significant difference between the scores of iOS and Android device users concerning Usefulness (U=5169, Z=-2.979, p=0. 003), EOU (U=5687, Z=-1.998, p=0. 046) , FTU (U=5431, Z=-2.503, p=0. 012), Security (U=5374, Z=-2.604, p=0. 009), Actual Use (U=4970, Z=-3.403, p=0. 001) and Intention to Use (U=5320, Z=-2.678, p=0. 007) whereas there is no significant difference in terms of the Advertisement construct (U=6045, Z=-1.291, p=0. 197). The results based on a comparison between the genders showed that there is a significant difference between the scores of female and male users in Security (U=6838, Z=-1.995, p=0. 045) and Intention to Use (U=6460, Z=-2.624, p=0. 0087) whereas other constructs such as Usefulness (U=7463, Z=-2. 895, p=0. 371) , EOU (U=7024, Z=-1. 670, p=0. 095), FTU (U=7190, Z=-1. 384, p=0. 166), Advertisement (U=7954, Z=-0. 44, p=0. 965) and Actual Use (U=7478, Z=-0. 884, p=0. 376) did not significantly differ.

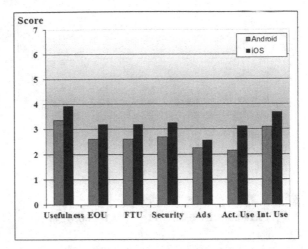

Fig. 3. User Perceptions of Mobile Commerce Apps based on OS

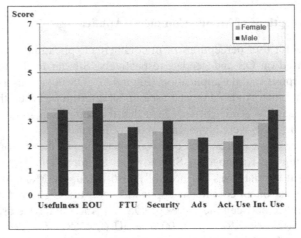

Fig. 4. User Perceptions of Mobile Commerce Apps based on Gender

5   Conclusion

In this study, user perceptions of m-commerce applications were analyzed based on gender and OS being used. To our knowledge, this issue has not been investigated before. The results show that there is a significant difference between Android and iOS users' perceptions of m-commerce applications except their perception of advertisements. iOS device owners showed more positive attitudes towards m-commerce applications and scored significantly higher on the constructs compared to Android users. Therefore, we can assume that iOS device owners are more likely to spend money on mobile applications, which concurs with their actual spending in application markets [23]. The attitude of male users towards security issues and their intention to use m-commerce applications are significantly more positive than female users. This is also in agreement with [22] who reported that the behaviors of male users reflect a desire for independence and separateness, and they are generally more independent in their purchase decisions.

On the other hand, user perceptions of mobile applications did not exhibit significant differences between the two operating systems except the usefulness construct in terms of both gender and the OS being used. Mobile phone users with devices using the iOS operating systems considered mobile applications to be more useful than Android OS users. This may be due to the iOS device owners being more satisfied with their mobile applications and attaching more importance to usefulness. This tendency was similar in male users. Male users obtained higher scores for all the constructs of user perceptions of mobile applications. The only significant construct was found to be the usefulness construct, where the discrepancy between male and female users was most obvious.

We consider that this research has made three main contributions to the academic literature. First, it has shown how iOS device users are more likely to use mobile applications and spend more money with applications, which is a significant contribution given the lack of literature in this area. Second, this study has demonstrated that, when compared to women, men's perceptions of m-commerce applications are more positive and they find security problems to be less threatening. Third, mobile applications are considered more useful by men and iOS device users.

One of the limitations of our study is that the reasons behind our findings could not directly be compared with the findings in the literature. In the future, we intend to conduct qualitative research to explore the different perceptions according to different user profiles. Another limitation of our study was using a convenience sample consisting of graduate and undergraduate university students in Turkey. This sample does not completely represent the general consumer population since they may be more familiar with mobile applications.

Operating system in use and user profiles based on gender are important parameters for mobile business models. The findings on the relationship between these parameters and user attitudes towards m-commerce applications can be useful for different stakeholders such as m-commerce service providers and application developers to explore on m-commerce from the consumers, providers and advertisers side. The results of this study will be useful for those involved in mobile markets in terms of developing personalized strategies in the future.

References

1. Sadeh, N.: Mobile Commerce: Technologies, Services, and Business Models. Wiley Computer Publishing, New York (2002)
2. Ajzen, I., Fishbein, M.: Understanding Attitudes and Predicting Social Behavior. Prentice-Hall, Englewood Cliffs (1980)
3. Davis, F.D.: Perceived Usefulness, Perceived Ease of Use, and User Acceptance of Information Technology. MIS Quarterly 13(3), 318–330 (1989)

4. van der Heijden, H.: Factors Influencing the Usage of Websites: The Case of a Generic Portal in the Netherlands. Information and Management **40**(6), 541–549 (2003)
5. Legris, P., Ingham, J., Collerette, P.: Why Do People Use Information Technology. A Critical Review of the Technology Acceptance Model. Information and Management **40**(3), 191–204 (2003)
6. Yang, K.C.C.: Exploring Factors Affecting the Adoption of Mobile Commerce in Singapore. Telematics and Informatics **22**(3), 257–277 (2005)
7. Wu, J.H., Wang, S.C.: What Drives Mobile Commerce? An Empirical Evaluation of the Revised Technology Acceptance Model. Information and Management **42**(5), 719–729 (2005)
8. Mahatanankoon, P., Wen, H.J., Lim, B.: Consumer-Based M-Commerce: Exploring Consumer Perception of Mobile Applications. Computer Standards and Interfaces **27**(4), 347–357 (2005)
9. Sheng, H., Nah, F.F.H., Siau, K.: An Experimental Study on Ubiquitous Commerce Adoption: Impact of Personalization and Privacy Concerns. Journal of the Association for Information Systems **9**, 344–376 (2008)
10. He, T., Wang, Y., Liu, W.: Empirical Research on Mobile Commerce Use: An Integrated Theory Model. Advances in Information Sciences & Service Sciences **4**(7), 23–32 (2012)
11. Kim, H., Chan, H.C., Gupta, S.: Value-Based Adoption of Mobile Internet: An Empirical Investigation. Decision Support Systems **43**, 111–126 (2007)
12. Barutcu, S.: Attitudes towards Mobile Marketing Tools: A Study of Turkish Consumers. Journal of Targeting, Measurement and Analysis for Marketing **16**, 26–38 (2007). doi:10.1057/palgrave.jt.5750061
13. McKnight, D.H., Cervany, N.L.: What Trust Means in E-Commerce Customer Relationships: An Interdisciplinary Concept Typology. International Journal of Electronic Commerce **6**, 35–59 (2002)
14. Siau, K., Shen, Z.: Building Customer Trust in Mobile Commerce. Communications of the ACM **46**(4), 91–94 (2003)
15. Teng, W., Lu, H., Yu, H.: Exploring the Mass Adoption of Third-Generation (3G) Mobile Phones in Taiwan. Telecommunications Policy **33**, 628–641 (2009)
16. Bruner, G.C., Kumar, A.: Explaining Consumer Acceptance of Handheld Internet Devices. Journal of Business Research **58**(5), 553–558 (2005)
17. Tang, M.L., Kuo, C.W.: Toward an Integrative Model for Consumer Behavior Regarding Mobile Commerce Adoption. In: 2010 International Conference on Cyber-Enabled Distributed Computing and Knowledge Discovery, pp. 142–149 (2010) doi:10.1109/CyberC.2010.34
18. Whitley, B.: Gender Differences in Computer Related Attitudes and Behavior: a Meta-analysis. Human Behavior **13**(1), 1–22 (1997)
19. Seneviratne, S., Seneviratne, A., Mohapatra, P., Mahanti, A.: Your installed apps reveal your gender and more! In: Proceedings of the ACM MobiCom Workshop on Security and Privacy in Mobile Environments, SPME, pp. 1–6 (2014)
20. Anckar, B., D'Incau, D.: Value-added Services in Mobile Commerce: An Analytical Framework and Empirical Finding from A National Consumer Survey. In: Proceedings of the 35th Hawaii International Conference on System Science (2002)
21. Gerpott, T.J., Thomas, S.: Empirical Research on Mobile Internet Usage: A Meta-analysis of the Literature. Telecommunications Policy **38**(3), 291–310 (2014). doi:10.1016/j.telpol.2013.10.003
22. Smartphone OS Market Share, Q1 (2015). http://www.idc.com/prodserv/smartphone-os-market-share.jsp (last visited at June 1, 2015)

23. The problem facing Android: Users don't want to spend money. http://www.zdnet.com/article/the-problem-facing-android-users-dont-want-to-spend-money/ (last visited at June 1, 2015)
24. Plant S.: On the mobile: The effect of mobile telephones on social and individual life. Report commissioned by Motorola (2000)
25. Cross, S.E., Madson, L.: Models of the self: self-construals and gender. Psychological Bulletin **122**(1), 5 (1997)

A   Appendix

Scales Used in the Study

Mobile Applications	Mobile Commerce Applications
Usefulness	Usefulness
1. It helped me be more effective	1. It saves time
2. It helped me be more productive	2. It creates a value
Ease of Use (EOU)	Ease of Use (EOU)
1. It is easy to use	1. It is easy to use
2. I learned to use it quickly	Fun to Use (FTU)
Fun to Use (FTU)	1. I have fun using it
1. I have fun using it	Security
2. I enjoy using it	1. There is no security issue.
Attitude Toward Use (AT)	Advertisement
1. My general opinion is favorable	1. Advertisement placement is acceptable for me
2. It is good for me	Actual Use
Information Quality (IQ)	1. I use mobile shopping applications
1. Applications are easy to find2. I can find more interesting applications	Intention to Use
3. There are many interesting apps to be downloaded	1. I will shop using my mobile phone in the future
	2. I recommend mobile shopping

Toward Knowledge Management Approach to Enhance the Mobile Learning Management Systems

Hatoon S. AlSagri[1,2(✉)] and Nesrine Zemirli[1]

[1] Information System Department, College of Computer and Information Science, King Saud University, Riyadh, Saudi Arabia
h-alsagri@ccis.imamu.edu.sa, nzemirli@ksu.edu.sa
[2] Information System Department, College of Computer and Information Science, Al Imam Mohammad Ibn Saud Islamic University (IMISU), Riyadh, Saudi Arabia

Abstract. In the wave of digital learning, Mobile learning (M-learning) captures more and more attention. Advanced developments in wireless technology and the availability of mobile devices provide the learners the freedom of mobility in using. In this context, the learning process had gained more flexibility, as well as challenges in order to adapt and manage the learning object to this new framework through the use of Mobile Learning Management Systems (M-LMS), a cross domain between LMSs and mobile device . Moreover, as part of the learning process, Knowledge Management (KM) is integrated in the practical teaching activities as one of the methods that enhance the abilities of learners by encouraging them to create, share, apply, and store knowledge. For that, it is necessary to find a way to successfully transform ordinary M-learning to knowledge-based learning. In this study we compare three main M-LMSs that integrated a KM approach in their system: MOODLE, Blackboard and mEKP. We focus our investigation on how these systems apply KM strategy in their system. We compared these tools based on Nonaka and Takeuchi Knowledge Conversion Process Model that represents one of the common KM models helping to extract knowledge from data collection. We found that Moodle has adopted a Mobile Knowledge Management Learning System (MKLMS) that helps capture tacit and explicit knowledge from users through the use of mobile devices; and based on this we propose guidelines that might be followed to enhance integration of KM approach in M-LMSs and ensure gaining valuable results of the integration.

Keywords: Knowledge management · M-Learning · Learning management system · Knowledge management process · Mobile learning management system · Mobile knowledge learning management system

1 Introduction

Over the last decade, coverage of mobile phones development in great speed added the dimension of mobility to learning. M-Learning is an emerging form of distance

© Springer International Publishing Switzerland 2015
M. Younas et al. (Eds.): MobiWis 2015, LNCS 9228, pp. 74–83, 2015.
DOI: 10.1007/978-3-319-23144-0_7

learning that offers both trainers and learners the "opportunity to interact and gain access to educational material using a wireless handheld device, independent of time and space" [1], [2], [3], [4], [5].

M-Learning is the learning accomplished with the use of small, portable computing devices. These computing devices may include smart phones, PDAs and similar handheld devices. Therefore, M-learning intersects mobile computing with e learning; it combines individualized learning with anytime and anywhere teaching [6], [7]. M-learning reduces the complicated and repeated work of the teacher. It allows the teacher to transfer or broadcast readily available materials to the students. Some students may be slower in learning and understanding. Such students can store and revise their lessons any time, any number of times and learn on their own pace [8], [2], [3].

Mobile applications generally allow users to control or filter information flow and interaction through the handheld devices. Portability, interactive, easy to operate, and targeted users are some advantages of M-learning [9]. BenMoussa identified several other benefits for mobile connectivity: First, mobile devices offer personalized or individualized connectivity. Second, mobile connectivity improves collaboration via real-time or instant interactivity that may lead to better decision-making. And third, mobile connectivity enhances users' orientation or direction. These benefits are proved to be equally useful in improving the learning environment [6], [10].

M-LMS is a cross domain between LMSs and mobile device. It is a platform that externalizes the traditional learning system into the mobile environment, manage the learning object and actors, and provides the facility of interaction among learners and instructors in the mobile environment. Some of the existing LMSs have designed "plug-ins" or "extensions" as MLMSs such as MLE-Moodle that has been designed for Moodle [11].

The 21st century technology oriented economy concentrates on creating, managing and sharing information. This indicates that competition will be driven by knowledge revolution in the future. Integrating KM into practical teaching activities is one of the best methods for learners to enhance their abilities in KM and problem solving. KM has been defined as the process of selectively applying knowledge from previous experiences to current and future decision making activities with the explicit purpose of improving effectiveness. Moreover, KM is a strategy to be developed as a way to ensure that knowledge reaches the right learner at the right time. Knowledge can be classified as tacit or explicit [12], [13].

Tacit knowledge is subconsciously understood and applied. It is ineffable and based on personal experience and directly related to personal cognitive skills but may be developed from direct experience and action. Tacit knowledge is usually shared through highly interactive conversation, storytelling, and shared experience [14], [12], [13]. Explicit knowledge can be consciously understood and can be expressed in words, diagrams, or formulas, which can be easily codified, represented, documented, transferred and shared asynchronously [13], [12]. It may have different types; printed minutes of meeting, tutorial sessions on discs and tapes, documentaries, the official correspondence using faxes and e-mails, etc. [15], [16].

Knowledge has become the most critical input factors and the core asset. Therefore, organizations must manage knowledge and adopt a variety of effective means in order to maximize and discover the potential of this resource and assets [17]. KM technology can be used to rapidly capture, organize and deliver large amounts of knowledge to its users. It connects people with the knowledge that they need to take action, when they need it [13].

From m-leaning approach, it is extremely beneficial to learners' growth that KM is highly connected with the use of M-learning systems. It's necessary in order to capture the knowledge spread through the devices, enhance learning effectiveness and to share the knowledge with others. It is also important to provide teachers, educational policy-makers, and researchers with a better representation of educational affordances of M-learning. Due to the previous reasons and because KM is regarded as an important part of developing M-learning and, finding a way to successfully transform ordinary M-learning to knowledge-based learning will be necessary in order to enhance learning effectiveness and to share the knowledge with others [6]. The need for a more applicable framework is emerging nowadays to provide teachers, educational policy-makers, and researchers with a better representation of educational affordances of M-learning [6].

This paper focuses on how KM has been introduced in different kinds of M- LMS. First, KM process in the M-Learning sector will be produced after defining Nonaka and Takeuchi model. Second, a comparative study will be proposed. It concentrates on comparing between different M-LMSs according to how these systems apply KM strategy in their system and to what extent it is effectively used. Later, MKLMS that Moodle adopted will be presented. Finally, we will propose some guidelines be followed to enhance integration of KM approach in M-LMSs and ensure gaining valuable results of the integration.

2   M-Learning KM Process

2.1   KM Model

For the conversion of Tacit to Explicit and Explicit to Tacit knowledge Nonaka and Takeuchi (1995) Knowledge Conversion Process Model has taken great interest of researchers for the creation of new and innovative knowledge. The knowledge conversion process follows specific pattern (figure 1).

Socialization: this is considered as Tacit-Tacit knowledge conversion, the individuals share their experiences and knowledge in a form of team in an organization or network.

Externalization: also referred as Tacit- Explicit knowledge. The externalization is storing the tacit knowledge, which is strongly the context-based fact into explicit knowledge with context-free knowledge condition in knowledge repository.

Internalization: this is also considered as Explicit- Tacit knowledge. The knowledge in the explicit form is taken out from the repository, which is required by the person according to his need and relevance.

Combination: also considered as Explicit-Explicit knowledge. The categorization, sorting, addition and deletion of explicit knowledge in repository are performed in this stage [15], [18].

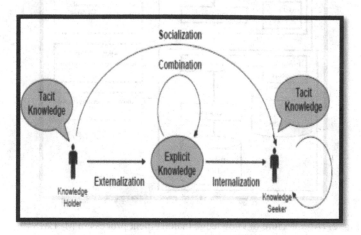

Fig. 1. (Nonaka and Takeuchi Model [15])

2.2 Knowledge Management Process in M-Learning

KM process is converted into practical teaching methods. Without being limited by a classroom, learners can browse materials and share the experience with others. They can also personalize knowledge organization and save it through the wireless network. Learners can carry out self-learning which enhances problem solving skills [19]. The need for a more applicable framework is emerging nowadays, a MKLMS framework that inspires learners to acquire, store, share, apply and create knowledge [19]. A KM process in m-learning proposed by Liaw et al is presented and used in this study to compare KM processes used in different M-LMSs.

Liaw et al. proposed a five-stage approach to lead learners to master new knowledge: knowledge retrieval, knowledge gathering, knowledge analysis, knowledge construction, and knowledge management [6].

Knowledge retrieval stage helps individuals to ensure that attention is concentrated on relevant knowledge that can then be retrieved. Knowledge gathering is the stage in which relevant knowledge can be found. Both knowledge retrieval and knowledge gathering can be performed by users using a mobile device (PDA). It means users can search, retrieve, and collect Internet resources via handheld tools. Knowledge analysis stage is based on individual experience and helps an individual to understand what the demanded knowledge is [20]. The stage of knowledge construction is attained through learning and previous task performances. Finally, knowledge management stage in which individuals manage knowledge and share knowledge with others [9]. After the first two steps, users process knowledge analysis, knowledge construction, and knowledge management by using laptop computers. Figure 2 shows the architecture of the knowledge management process m-learning system [6].

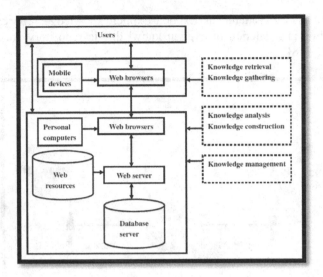

Fig. 2. (Architecture of knowledge management process in M- LMS [9])

3   Comparative Study

Just when the M-learning revolution came along and LMS companies reached a limit of saturation, LMS companies started to present new M-LMSs to market their products. Some have done cosmetic changes, redesigning their interface to fit on a small screen. A few have designed M-LMSs that actually work on smart phones and tablets. Some have even developed stand-alone LMSs that do not need to be connected to a non M-LMS [11].

A few of the LMSs have been designed with mobile computing in mind. For example, the Moodle interface consists of a three-column layout that is very mobile friendly [11]. M-LMS (Moodle) has been integrated with a KM system to enhance the effectiveness of learning outcomes. Learners and instructor can interact and discuss specific topic with the relevant material available in the system. Knowledge analysis and construction is being applied through giving the user the authority to modify and extend the knowledge according to his needs, considering that access is given to registered users only [21]. Discussion forums are used to share knowledge between users which ensures consideration of knowledge management [15]. Moodle's course management system has the facilities of knowledge retrieval and gathering.

Another approach is to design "plug-ins" or "extensions" for existing LMSs. Blackboard has an extension for their Learn 9.1 platform called Blackboard Mobile that lets users receive notification of updates to their Blackboard courses, including new assignments, course content, study group updates, community discussions, and their grades/assessment results [11]. Blackboard applies knowledge gathering and retrieving through allowing the automatic coupling of existing student databases with Blackboard, making course visible to the worldwide Blackboard community. Courses published by instructors from other institutions can be searched from the course cartridge library and accessed after getting the permission from the course owner [22]. It also includes an asynchronous discussion board as a tool through which learners might socially interact in one-way or another assuring the use of knowledge management. Blackboard can collect and archive the online discussions that take place in its discussion board and later copy it into a word-processing document for further knowledge analysis [23], [24].

There are signs of innovative new solutions that will transform the world of M-LMSs, and not simply reuse the concepts of desktop LMSs. One example is the mEKP (Mobile Enterprise Knowledge Platform) M-learning management system from Net Dimensions that delivers a full-featured LMS on a USB stick. This allows students to go off-line, do their work, and have it tracked without a connection to the Internet. They simply take their USB stick with them and plug it into an Internet-connected computer at the first opportunity [11]. It is multi-user (20, 30 or more users can use it concurrently or separately) – making it a powerful option for remote locations [25]. All training documents are distributed through mEKP system making the latest version available for knowledge gathering. Students can participate in virtual classroom training or take courses online. Knowledge construction is applied through allowing all content creators and experts to contribute content, store content centrally and deliver content so that it is readable on a variety of devices. It supports different collaboration tools some take the form of questions and answers between members or feedback and suggestions about the products or courses, their acceptance in the field and ideas for the future which assures covering knowledge management. Reports are generated and provided on demand giving feedback on the state of various learning activities [26].

According to the previous analysis of current situation of the M-LMSs depending on their appliance of KM process that has been introduced by Liaw et al, we were able to propose comparison between the different M-LMSs presented in table 1. The comparison shows what stages in Liaw et al KM process has been applied in each M-LMS.

Table 1. (Knowledge Management Process in different M- LMSs)

KMP in M learning / M- LMSs	knowledge retrieval	knowledge gathering	knowledge analysis	knowledge construction	knowledge management
MOODLE	✓	✓	✓	✓	✓
Blackboard	✓	✓	✓		✓
mEKP		✓		✓	✓

4   Guidelines for MKLMS

4.1   Moodle KM Model

Most of the discussed LMSs consider the need for KM to enhance educational process, although lacking some of the important KM processes such knowledge construction in the blackboard system. Both blackboard and mEKP didn't rely on a certain KM process to ensure the coverage of all steps of KM.

On the other hand, MOODLE integrated a KM process to insure efficient capturing of knowledge and its delivery for quality learning. It has adopted Nonaka and Takeuchi model for transferring knowledge. Nonaka focuses on the vitality of knowledge formation by considering the implicit and explicit elements of knowledge creation[15]. Figure 3 shows the integration of KM and E Learning that Moodle adopted [15].

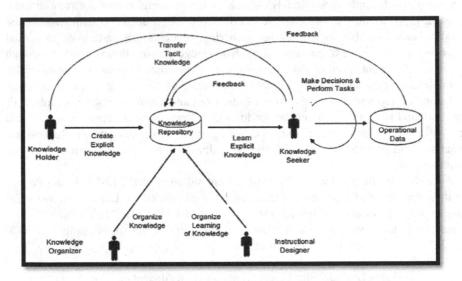

Fig. 3. (Integration of KM and E Learning adopted my MOODLE (MKLMS) [15])

- The instructor (knowledge holder) can store his experience and knowledge (Tacit knowledge) in both the knowledge repository through externalization and can also transfer that to the learner (Knowledge seeker) via socialization.
- The knowledge organizer will help in the placement of relevant information in it proper place for the purpose of refining and indexing the knowledge.
- The instructional designer works on the new learning aids creation, assignment posting and creating new modules.
- The learner is able to receive more knowledge from the knowledge repository through internalization and also from the instructor through socialization. The working and performance of the leaner is operationalize and then again returned to the knowledge repository as a feedback. In discussion forums of MOODLE students and instructor perform socialization and then internalization and externalization for

creating the explicit knowledge; however the CMS perform the task of combination for the new and quality knowledge creation [15].

4.2 Guidelines

After investigating the current situation of the three M- LMSs and to what extent did they cover KM processes, and based on Moodle's implementation of MKLMS, we came to some guidelines that would help other M- LMSs to integrate KM processes in its' systems:

1. Adopt a knowledge management process and integrating it into the M- LMSs to ensure capturing, transforming, storing and sharing different types of knowledge through the use of M-learning.
2. Use of KM process or model that is suitable for education to ensure that both tacit and explicit knowledge is being considered for the benefit of instructors and learners.
3. Focus on capturing tacit knowledge of instructors and learners and add functions to make it clear and easy.
4. Analyze documents stored and categorize them to help reach them much faster and easier.

5   Conclusion and Future Work

This paper shows the importance of applying KM approach in M- LMSs. It presents how this will increase the effectiveness of learning and sharing knowledge. The integration of KM in the M- LMSs will be useful for the efficient capturing of knowledge and its delivery for quality learning. It also sheds light on current M- LMSs' achievements toward KM in the M-learning environment and ways to improve it through proposing some guidelines and hints.

As future work, we plan to further apply the MKMLS for other M-LMSs and test its' usefulness and effectiveness in the M-Learning sector. Adding some functions to optimize KM and learning activities for current M-LMSs will also enhance benefits of M-Learning.

References

1. Dye, A., Solstad, B.-E., Joe, A.K.: Mobile Education - A Glance at the Future: 1 Introduction (2003). http://www.dye.no/articles/a_glance_at_the_future/introduction.html. (accessed: December 8, 2013)
2. Abfalter, D., Mirski, P.J., Hitz, M.: Mobile learning: knowledge enhancement and vocational training on the move. In: 5th OKLC (2004)
3. Brown, T.H.: The role of m-learning in the future of e-learning in Africa. In: 21st ICDE World Conference, vol. 110 (2003).(retrieved from) http://wwwtml.tkk.fi/OpinnotT

4. Liu, Q., Zuo, M., Zhang, X.: The Personal Knowledge Management in Mobile Learning In: IEEE International Symposium on Knowledge Acquisition and Modeling Workshop, KAM Workshop 2008, pp. 1129–1132 (2008)
5. Wang, J., Li, X., Haung, T., Wu, B.: Personalized Knowledge Service Framework for Mobile Learning. Presented at the Second International Conference on Semantics, Knowledge, and Grid (SKG 2006), p. 102 (2006)
6. Liaw, S.-S., Hatala, M., Huang, H.-M.: Investigating acceptance toward mobile learning to assist individual knowledge management: Based on activity theory approach. Comput. Educ. **54**(2), 446–454 (2010)
7. Sharma, S.K., Kitchens, F.L.: Web services architecture for m-learning. Electron. J. E-Learn. **2**(1), 203–216 (2004)
8. Hemabala, J., Suresh, E.S.M.: The Frame Work Design of Mobile Learning Management System. Int. J. Comput. Inf. Technol. IJCIT **1**(2), 179–184 (2012)
9. Zhuang, S., Hu, L., Xu, H., Tian, Y.: M-Learning Design Based on Personal Knowledge Management. In: 2011 International Conference on Information Management, Innovation Management and Industrial Engineering (ICIII), vol. 2, pp. 135–138 (2011)
10. BenMoussa, C.: Workers on the move: New opportunities through mobile commerce. Stockh. Mobil. Roundtable, 22–23 (2003)
11. Mobile Learning Management Systems: a spectrum of choices Float Mobile Learning http://floatlearning.com/2011/09/mobile-learning-management-systems-a-spectrum-of-choices/. (accessed: Octobder 30, 2013)
12. Li, L., Zheng, Y., Zheng, F., Zhong, S.: Knowledge Management in Computer-supported Learning. In: 2010 International Conference on Management and Service Science (MASS), pp. 1–4 (2010)
13. Ahmad, M., Husain, A., Zulkifli, A.N., Mohamed, N.F.F., Wahab, S.Z.A., Saman, A.M., Yaakub, A.R.: An investigation of knowledge creation process in the LearningZone Learning Management System amongst postgraduate students. In: 2011 7th International Conference on Advanced Information Management and Service (ICIPM), pp. 54–58 (2011)
14. Nonaka, I., Konno, N.: The Concept of 'Ba': Building a Foundation for Knowledge Creation. Calif. Manage. Rev. 40(3), 40–54 (1998)
15. Waheed, M.: Integration of Knowledge Conversion Process and Electronic Learning Environment: Use of Course Management System. In: Knowledge Globalization Conference, Boston, Massacusetts October 16–17, p. 69 (2011)
16. Gunnlaugsdottir, J.: Seek and you will find, share and you will benefit: organizing knowledge using groupware systems. Int. J. Inf. Manag. **23**(5), 363–380 (2003)
17. Ni, G., Wang, W., Wang, J., Zong, Z., Xie, M.: Research on the Knowledge Management System of the Vicarious Management Corporation, pp. 62–67 (2010)
18. Dalkir, K.: Knowledge management in theory and practice. Elsevier/Butterworth Heinemann, Amsterdam (2005)
19. Chen, H.-R., Huang, H.-L.: User Acceptance of Mobile Knowledge Management Learning System: Design and Analysis. Educ. Technol. Soc. **13**(3), 70–77 (2010)
20. Uden, L., Brandt, D.S.: Knowledge Analysis of Tasks for Instructional Design. Educ. Technol. Publ. **41**, 59–63 (2001)
21. Sammour, G., Schreurs, J., Al-Zoubi, A.Y., Vanhoof, K.: The role of knowledge management and e-learning in professional development Jeanne Schreurs - Academia.edu. Int. J. Knowl. Learn. 4(5) (2008)
22. Sallis, E., Jones, G.: Knowledge management in education: enhancing learning & education. Kogan Page; Stylus Pub., London; Sterling, VA (2002)

23. Johnson, H.: European Journal of Open, Distance and E-Learning. Dialogue and the Construction of Knowledge in E-Learning: Exploring Students' Perceptions of Their Learning While Using Blackboard's Asynchronous Discussion Board http://www.eurodl.org/index.php?tag=120&article=151&article=251 (accessed: November 24, 2013)
24. Marshall, B., Zhang, Y., Chen, H., Lally, A., Shen, R., Fox, E., Cassel, L.N.: Convergence of knowledge management and E-learning: the GetSmart experience. In: Proceedings of the 2003 Joint Conference on Digital Libraries, pp. 135–146 (2003)
25. mEKP: New Possibilities in Mobile Learning. NetDimensions
26. Nantel, R., Werner, T.: The Extended Enterprise: Six Steps to Gaining a Competitive Advantage. NetDimensions (2011)

Visualization Approaches in Augmented Reality Applications

Markus Aleksy[1]([⊠]) and Elina Vartiainen[2]

[1] ABB Corporate Research, Wallstadter Str. 59, 68526 Ladenburg, Germany
markus.aleksy@de.abb.com
[2] ABB Corporate Research, Forskargränd 7, 72178 Västerås, Sweden
elina.vartiainen@se.abb.com

Abstract. Augmented reality applications are gaining increased popularity due to the advances in mobile and wearable technologies and devices. In this paper, we categorize augmented reality applications with regard to the used visualization elements and techniques. Moreover, we present corresponding application areas and used metaphors to emphasize their usefulness.

1 Introduction

Augmented Reality (AR) enhances real-world view with additional virtual information. According to [3], an AR system has the following properties:

- Blends real and virtual objects in a real environment,
- Runs interactively and in real time, and
- Registers real and virtual objects with each other.

The variety of AR applications is extensive and includes localization / navigation assistance, training, technical support, safety improvement, and many more. These applications apply AR for multiple different scenarios. They can, for example, present guidance to the user based on his/her location or environment, reveal hidden information, and extend the physical objects. As a result, AR has become a powerful visualization tool that can benefit several applications used for different purposes. In this paper, we summarize and categorize the visualization techniques already used in existing AR applications to map and give inspiration for the use of AR in future developments. Moreover, we provide the underlying metaphors that were utilized as a basis for the presented visualization approaches. Figure 1 provides an overview of different visualization categories in AR applications.

The presented visualization categories include:

- Object information
  This category includes information about the object itself and related information. Moreover, it is not limited to visible objects but can be also utilized to depict information about hidden and non-existing objects.

M. Younas et al. (Eds.): MobiWis 2015, LNCS 9228, pp. 84–90, 2015.
DOI: 10.1007/978-3-319-23144-0_8

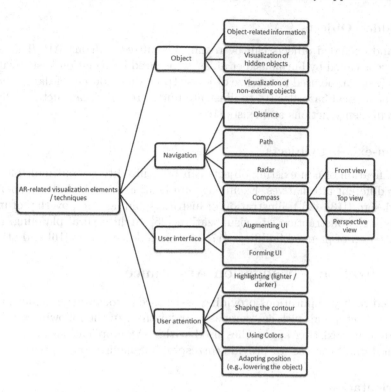

Fig. 1. AR-related visualization elements and techniques.

- Navigation
  Navigation support is one of the well known application areas that benefit from AR. Here information with regard to the route and ambient objects can be visualized.
- User interface
  AR applications can make use of virtual user interface elements together with advanced techniques, such as gesture recognition and tactile feedback to facilitate user interaction.
- User attention
  This category summarizes techniques that can be used to attract user's attention.

2   Objects

The visualization of an object is application specific to a large extent. Generally, it should be ensured that the display is not cluttered with too much information [14]. Moreover, virtual objects and labels should be positioned and scaled without obscuring important real objects and avoiding overlapping [7].

2.1   Hidden Objects

Hidden and occluded objects can be readily visualized utilizing AR. This specialized use is called by Furmanski et al. as "Obscured Information Visualization (OIV)" [6]. It can be used to localize objects [1], to show sources of danger, such as hidden chemical hazards [21], to illustrate underground infrastructure [18], or to depict hidden junctions and exists [16].

2.2   Non-existing Objects

The visualization of non-existing objects can be utilized to try out multiple scenarios or different alternatives. Exemplary application areas include augmented interior design ([13], [20]), illustration of historic buildings [10], overlay of medical scans [12], construction site visualization [25], architectural planning, such as visualization of planned buildings [17], virtual follow-me cars [16] and others.

3   Localization / Navigation Assistance

Augmented reality applications providing assistance to localization / navigation fall back on metaphors such as "compass" or "paths". In the following sections, we will describe existing approaches used within AR applications to visualize the orientation of the user or provide corresponding navigation support.

3.1   Orientation

"Compass" is a metaphor that is usually used to display the orientation of the user. This information can be obtained using the magnetometer sensor often provided by a variety of mobile devices. Although, the accuracy of the magnetometer sensor may vary due to several reasons, such as environmental settings [5], many AR applications rely on orientation information.

The visualization of a virtual compass can be achieved in various ways. Generally, it can be realized using a front view, a top view or a perspective view visualization approach. A front view based visualization shows the values of the compass in a bordered row. The center of the row represents the heading. This approach can be found in [23]. It can be enhanced by highlighting the visible angle of view. The top view based solution presents the compass as a circle representing the 360 degree view and highlighting the visible segment in form of a pie slice. The center of the segment represents the point of the compass. This approach can be found in the open source augmented reality engine Mixare [15]. The perspective compass view ([21], [11]) implements an attractive visualization alternative but doesn't provide additional value.

All approaches can be enhanced by the visualization of detailed information related to compass degrees. Additionally, the top view approach can be extended to a "radar". In this approach, all existing points of interest (POIs) or all POIs within a particular range are represented in the radar view, e.g., as dots. This approach is used in Mixare again. Figure 2 depicts the aforementioned approaches.

Fig. 2. Approaches to compass visualization.

3.2 Routes

The visual presentation of routes can be done in various ways. It can range form approaches, such as "virtual trails" introduced in [10] that represent the route by traverse lines to path visualization utilizing aligned triangles to depict the route used in [21]. In most of the approaches, additional information, such as distance, time to arrival, speed etc. can be also included.

Table 1 provides an overview of visualization related metaphors used in AR-based applications. Interaction metaphors related to AR applications can be found in [4].

Table 1. Metaphors used in AR-based visualization

Visualization	Metaphors
navigation	compass, radar, path / trail
hidden objects	x-ray, lens

4 User Interface

Generally, it can be differentiated between two styles of user interface (UI) elements used in AR applications:

- Virtual UI elements as part of the UI and
- Virtual UI elements as stand-in for real UI elements.

The next sections will describe the two UI styles in more detail.

4.1 Augmenting UI

The first category incorporates virtual UI elements as part of the UI of the application. In this category, well known user interface elements, such as buttons, windows, sliders etc. are used to facilitate user interactions. These approaches can be extended by including gesture recognition and tactile feedback. Heidemann et al. [9] enhance menu control by finger tipping. The user interacts with buttons by executing a "pressing" gesture on it. The personal interaction panel [19] combines tactile feedback with overlaid graphics and enables the integration of conventional user interface elements, such as buttons and sliders. The Mobile Augmented Reality Interface Sign Interpretation Language System (MARISIL) introduced by [2] describes a scenario, which deals with placing a call using a virtual keyboard displayed on the user's hand enabling him dialling a number.

4.2   Forming UI

The second category is related to the usage of virtual UI elements that represent physical UI elements of a device (see Figure 3). That way, real devices that are connected to portable devices can be controlled.

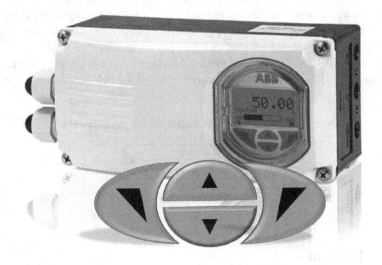

Fig. 3. Virtual UI elements as a stand-in for physical UI elements.

5   User Attention

Attracting user attention can be done utilizing different techniques. Güven and Feiner describe techniques for locating and viewing occluded objects, such as tilting, lifting, and shifting [8]. Uratani et al. [24] suggest using colored frames to indicate absolute paths, semi-transparent frames for annotations that are out of interest, and dotted frames to indicate occlusions. Tönnis et al. [22] discuss different presentation schemes for navigation arrows and their impact on user's perception.

Emphasizing some of the objects can also be used to increase safety. E.g., Narzt et al. [16] suggest highlighting of current traffic and driving situations to recognize hazards.

6   Conclusions

In this paper, we have provided a survey on different AR-related visualization approaches. First, we introduced a categorization of the presented elements and techniques. Thereafter, we discussed them including exemplary application scenarios and utilized metaphors. The presented application areas cover a multitude of domains and can help practitioners to apply appropriate visualization techniques. Therefore, they should be considered in new projects related to AR application development to ensure proper visualization of virtual objects and related information.

Acknowledgments. This research was supported by the German Federal Ministry of Education and Research (BMBF) under grant number 16KIS0244. The responsibility for this publication lies with the authors.

References

1. Aleksy, M., Vartiainen, E., Domova, V., Naedele, M.: Augmented reality for improved service delivery. In: 28th IEEE International Conference on Advanced Information Networking and Applications (AINA 2014), Victoria, BC, Canada, May 13–16, 2014, pp. 382–389. IEEE
2. Antoniac, P.: Augmented Reality Based User Interface for Mobile Applications and Services. Dissertation. University of Oulu (2005)
3. Azuma, R.T., Baillot, Y., Behringer, R., Feiner, S.K., Julier, S., MacIntyre, B.: Recent Advances in Augmented Reality. IEEE Computer Graphics and Applications **21**(6), 34–47 (2001)
4. Billinghurst, M., Grasset, R., Looser, J.: Designing augmented reality interfaces. In: ACM SIGGRAPH Computer Graphics - Learning through computer-generated visualization, vol. 39, Issue 1, pp. 17–22. ACM, February 2005
5. Blum, J.R., Greencorn, D.G., Cooperstock, J.R.: Smartphone sensor reliability for augmented reality applications. In: Zheng, K., Li, M., Jiang, H. (eds.) MobiQuitous 2012. LNICST, vol. 120, pp. 127–138. Springer, Heidelberg (2013)
6. Furmanski, C., Azuma, R., Daily, M.: Augmented-reality visualizations guided by cognition: perceptual heuristics for combining visible and obscured information. In: Proceedings of the 1st International Symposium on Mixed and Augmented Reality (ISMAR 2002), Darmstadt, Germany, September 30, October, 1, p. 215. IEEE (2002)
7. Gervautz, M., Schmalstieg, D.: Anywhere Interfaces Using Handheld Augmented Reality. IEEE Computer **45**(7), 26–31 (2012)
8. Güven, S., Feiner, S.: Visualizing and navigating complex situated hypermedia in augmented and virtual reality. In: Proceedings of the 5th IEEE/ACM International Symposium on Mixed and Augmented Reality (ISMAR 2006), Santa Barbara, California, USA, October 22–25, 2006, pp. 155–158. IEEE
9. Heidemann, G., Bax, I., Bekel, H.: Multimodal interaction in an augmented reality scenario. In: Proceedings of the 6th International Conference on Multimodal Interfaces (ICMI 2004), State College, PA, USA, October 13–15, 2004, pp. 53–60. ACM
10. Höllerer, T.H.: User Interfaces for Mobile Augmented Reality Systems. Dissertation. Columbia University (2004)

11. Kluge, M.: Fußgängernavigation: Reality view der einsatz von computerspielnavigation in der realen welt. In: Strobl, J., Blaschke, T., Griesebner, G. (eds.) Angewandte Geoinformatik 2009: Beiträge 21. AGIT-Symposium Salzburg. Universität Salzburg, Austria, July 8-10, 2009

12. van Krevelen, D.W.F., Poelman, R.: A Survey of Augmented Reality Technologies, Applications and Limitations. The International Journal of Virtual Reality 9(2), 1-20 (2010)

13. Kymäläinen, T., Siltanen, S.: Co-designing novel interior design service that utilizes augmented reality, a case study. In: Second International Symposium on Communicability, Computer Graphics and Innovative Design for Interactive Systems, CCGIDIS 2012, Italy, July 5-6, 2012

14. Julier, S., Lanzagorta, M., Baillot, Y., Rosenblum, L.J., Feiner, S., Höllerer, T., Sestito, S.: Information filtering for mobile augmented reality. In: Proceedings of the IEEE and ACM International Symposium on Augmented Reality (ISAR 2000), October 5-6, 2000, Munich, Germany, pp. 3-11. IEEE (2000)

15. mixare - Open Source Augmented Reality Engine. http://www.mixare.org/

16. Narzt, W., Pomberger, G., Ferscha, A., Kolb, D., Müller, R., Wieghardt, J., Hörtner, H., Lindinger, C.: Augmented Reality Navigation Systems. Universal Access in the Information Society 4(3), 177-187 (2006)

17. Olsson, T., Savisalo, A., Hakkarainen, M., Woodward, C.: User evaluation of mobile augmented reality in architectural planning. In: Gudnason G., Scherer R. (eds.) eWork and eBusiness in Architecture, Engineering and Construction, ECPPM 2012, Reykjavik, Island, July 25-27, 2012, pp. 733-740

18. Schall, G., Mendez, E., Kruijff, E., Veas, E., Junghanns, S., Reitinger, B., Schmalstieg, D.: Handheld Augmented Reality for underground infrastructure visualization. Personal and Ubiquitous Computing 13(4), 281-291 (2009)

19. Schmalstieg, D., Fuhrmann, A., Hesina, G.: Bridging multiple user interface dimensions with augmented reality. In: Proceedings of the International Symposium on Augmented Reality (ISAR 2000), Munich, Germany, October 5-6, 2000, pp. 20-29. IEEE

20. Siltanen, S., Oksman, V., Ainasoja, M.: User-Centered Design of Augmented Reality Interior Design Service. International Journal of Arts & Sciences 06(01), 547-563 (2013)

21. Swan II, J.E., Gabbard, J.L.: Survey of User-Based Experimentation in Augmented Reality. In: Proceedings 1st International Conference on Virtual Reality, Las Vegas, Nevada, USA, July 22-27, 2005

22. Tönnis, M., Klein, L., Klinker, G.: Perception thresholds for augmented reality navigation schemes in large distances. In: 7th IEEE and ACM International Symposium on Mixed and Augmented Reality (ISMAR 2008), Cambridge, UK, September 15-18, 2008, pp. 189-190. IEEE

23. Tokusho, Y., Feiner, S.: Prototyping an outdoor mobile augmented reality street view application. In: Let's Go Out: Workshop on Outdoor Mixed and Augmented Reality, ISMAR 2009, Orlando, FL, USA, October 19, 2009. IEEE

24. Uratani, K., Machida, T., Kiyokawa, K., Takemura, H.: A study of depth visualization techniques for virtual annotations in augmented reality. In: Proceedings of the 2005 IEEE Conference 2005 on Virtual Reality (VR 2005), Bonn, Germany, March 12-16, 2005, pp. 295-296. IEEE (2005)

25. Woodward C., Hakkarainen M., Korkalo O., Kantonen T. Aittala M., Rainio K., Kähkönen, K.: Mixed Reality for mobile construction site visualization and communication. In: Proc. 10th International Conference on Construction Applications of Virtual Reality (CONVR 2010), Sendai, Japan, November 4-5, 2010, pp. 35-44

Mobile Networks and Applications

Atomic Species and Applications

A Bandwidth Allocation Method Based on Psychological Factors Considering QoE of Users

Huong Pham-Thi[✉] and Takumi Miyoshi[✉]

Graduate School of Engineering and Science, Shibaura Institute of Technology,
307 Fukasaku, Minuma-ku, Saitama-shi, Japan
{nb13510,miyoshi}@shibaura-it.ac.jp

Abstract. The explosion of the internet and its service are changing our daily lives and making our lives more convenient by becoming easily accessible from anywhere. However, the popularity of the internet also poses a challenge for network managers and internet service providers (ISPs): how is it possible meet the needs of users and optimize network resources? To solve this problem, it is necessary to find a feasible solution that allocates limited network resources to users reasonably. One allocation method, which has been investigated in previous studies, is based on the viewpoint of fairness in the quality of service (QoS). However, user satisfaction may vary depending on a users characteristics and individual psychological factors, even with the same network resources. To overcome this limitation, an allocation method based on the viewpoint of fairness in the quality of experience (QoE) is developed. From the viewpoint of the QoE, this paper proposes a bandwidth allocation method for mobile services that is based on the users psychological factors using the Newton-Raphson method. The proposed method can meet the requirements of both users and ISPs: it guarantees a fair QoE for users and increases the efficient management of network resources by ISPs.

Keywords: QoE · Bandwidth allocation · Utility function · Fairness

1 Introduction

Currently, the internet and internet services play important roles in peoples lives. As the internet spreads and personal digital assistants (PDAs) and mobile devices mature, they enable people to easily access multimedia applications for entertainment at almost any place and anytime. The convenience of users, however, poses a challenge for ISPs in terms of network planning and design. Currently, the demand of users for significant information exchange and a high quality of service is continuously increasing, while network resources are limited. Therefore, a question arises: how should network resources be effectively allocated or distributed to satisfy users while maintaining good network performance?

© Springer International Publishing Switzerland 2015
M. Younas et al. (Eds.): MobiWis 2015, LNCS 9228, pp. 93–101, 2015.
DOI: 10.1007/978-3-319-23144-0_9

A simple bandwidth allocation method, which is currently used in real systems and is commonly known as the conventional method, allocates bandwidth from the viewpoint of fairness in quality of service (QoS). This means that the same amount of bandwidth is allocated to all users; this amount is calculated by dividing the total bandwidth by the number of users. From the QoS viewpoint, all of the users experience the same communication quality when they have the same amount of bandwidth. However, user satisfaction or quality of experience (QoE) is the overall metric for applications or services, and it is affected by all of the end-to-end factors [1]. Therefore, QoS parameters and other technical metrics affect the QoE. In addition, the QoE is also affected by psychological factors such as a users situation, demands, or degree of relaxation [2]-[6]. For this reason, users QoE can be different, even in the same network environment.

To overcome the limitations of the conventional method, it is necessary to consider both objective and subjective factors that influence users perceptions of the network resource allocation. An approach that many researchers are interested in is to allocate network resources to users based on the QoE. From the QoE viewpoint, users can experience the same level of satisfaction in different network environments because of the way psychology affects the human perception of time. Based on this consideration, this paper proposes a bandwidth allocation method that is based on users psychological factors to guarantee that all users experience the same perceived QoE.

To achieve this aim, the proposed method first categorizes users into groups according to their perceived degrees of relaxation. Each group of users is assigned a specific utility function to map the relationship between the allocated bandwidth and users QoE. The method then allocates bandwidth to users based on their groups. As a result, the same amount of network resources will be allocated to all of the users in each group. The numerical results, which are obtained for various cases, show that the proposed method can improve the QoE of dissatisfied users.

The rest of this paper is organized as follows. The next section details the proposed method of allocating network resources and explains how the Newton-Raphson method is used in this paper. To illustrate our proposed method, section 3 presents the obtained results in some cases. Finally, the last section presents the conclusion and suggestions for future research.

2   Proposed Bandwidth Allocation Method

As mentioned above and as shown in previous studies [2]-[6], user satisfaction can depend on various subjective factors such as an individuals demands, level of experience, degree of concentration, and degree of relaxation. In particular, a users degree of relaxation is a typical psychological factor that significantly influences the subjective results of the evaluation [3]-[5]. For this reason, the classification of users in this paper is based on their degree of relaxation.

From the same perspective, a previous study [3] categorizes users into four classes: not relaxed, neutral, relaxed, and very relaxed. Users, however, may be confused about whether to describe themselves as very relaxed or relaxed in a real system. Therefore, we do not distinguish between very relaxed and relaxed and, instead, use a single category, relaxed, that combines the results of the very relaxed and relaxed users in [3]. As a result, users are classified into three groups: not relaxed (B), neutral (N), and relaxed (R) in this paper. When accessing a file containing S Mbits of data, the relationships between the QoE and the allocated bandwidth for the three user types are as follows:

$$U_B(B_B) = -1.29 \ln(\frac{S}{B_B}) + 5.12, \tag{1}$$

$$U_N(B_N) = -1.31 \ln(\frac{S}{B_N}) + 5.32, \tag{2}$$

$$U_R(B_R) = -1.46 \ln(\frac{S}{B_R}) + 5.778, \tag{3}$$

where S is the file size [Mbits], B_B, B_N, and B_R are the amounts of bandwidth allocated [Mbps], and U_B, U_N, and U_R are the utility values for not relaxed, neutral, and relaxed users, respectively. Eqs. (1)-(3 can be rewritten as follows:

$$U_B(B_B) = \ln(C_B B_B^{r_{1B}}), \tag{4}$$
$$U_N(B_N) = \ln(C_N B_N^{r_{1N}}), \tag{5}$$
$$U_R(B_R) = \ln(C_R B_R^{r_{1R}}), \tag{6}$$

where r_{1B}=1.29, r_{1N}= 1.31, $r_{1R} = 1.46$, $C_B = e^{5.12}/S^{1.29}$, $C_N = e^{5.32}/S^{1.31}$, and $C_R = e^{5.778}/S^{1.46}$. The bandwidth allocation is realized using the QoE relationships between the groups of users,

$$k_1 U_B = k_2 U_N = k_3 U_R, \tag{7}$$

where k_1, k_2, and k_3 are the controlling parameters. When $k_1 = k_2 = k_3$, all of the users experience the same satisfaction level. However, the proposed method can allocate bandwidth to provide different QoEs for users or give priority to certain users depending on the management policy. From Eqs. (4)-(7), the following equations are derived:

$$k_1 \ln(C_B B_B^{r_{1B}}) = k_2 \ln(C_N B_N^{r_{1N}}), \tag{8}$$
$$k_1 \ln(C_B B_B^{r_{1B}}) = k_3 \ln(C_R B_R^{r_{1R}}). \tag{9}$$

Eq. (8) can be expressed as follows:

$$(C_B B_B^{r_{1B}})^{k_1} = (C_N B_N^{r_{1N}})^{k_2}. \tag{10}$$

From Eq. (10), the relationship between the amounts of bandwidth allocated to users who are not relaxed and neutral can be expressed as follows:

$$B_N = C_1 B_B^{\alpha_1}, \tag{11}$$

where

$$C_1 = \left(\frac{C_B^{\frac{k_1}{k_2}}}{C_N}\right)^{\frac{1}{r_{1N}}}, \tag{12}$$

$$\alpha_1 = \frac{k_1 r_{1B}}{k_2 r_{1N}}. \tag{13}$$

In the same way, the relationship between the bandwidth allocated to users who are not relaxed and those who are relaxed is as follows:

$$B_R = C_2 B_B^{\alpha_2}, \tag{14}$$

where

$$C_2 = \left(\frac{C_B^{\frac{k_1}{k_3}}}{C_R}\right)^{\frac{1}{r_{1R}}}, \tag{15}$$

$$\alpha_2 = \frac{k_1 r_{1B}}{k_3 r_{1R}}. \tag{16}$$

In addition, the total bandwidth (B_{ALL}) is distributed to users according to the following condition,

$$N_B B_B + N_N B_N + N_R B_R = B_{ALL}, \tag{17}$$

where N_B, N_N, and N_R are the numbers of users in the not relaxed, neutral, and relaxed groups, respectively. From Eqs. (11), (14), and (17), the amount of bandwidth allocated to users who are not relaxed is as follows:

$$N_B B_B + N_N C_1 B_B^{\alpha_1} + N_R C_2 B_B^{\alpha_2} - B_{ALL} = 0. \tag{18}$$

The amount of bandwidth allocated to users who are not relaxed is determined by solving Eq. (18), and the amounts allocated to neutral and relaxed users are determined by solving by Eqs. (11) and (14). Eq. (18) can be rewritten as the following general equation,

$$ax^\alpha + bx^\beta + cx^\gamma + d = 0 \quad (a, b, c, d, \alpha, \beta, \gamma \in R+), \tag{19}$$

where

$$a = N_B, \tag{20}$$

$$b = N_N C_1 = N_N \left(\frac{C_B^{\frac{k_1}{k_2}}}{C_N}\right)^{\frac{1}{r_{1N}}}, \tag{21}$$

$$c = N_R C_2 = N_R \left(\frac{C_B^{\frac{k_1}{k_3}}}{C_R} \right)^{\frac{1}{r_{1R}}}, \tag{22}$$

$$d = -B_{ALL}, \tag{23}$$

$$\alpha = 1, \tag{24}$$

$$\beta = \alpha_1 = \frac{k_1 r_{1B}}{k_2 r_{1N}}, \tag{25}$$

$$\gamma = \alpha_2 = \frac{k_1 r_{1B}}{k_3 r_{1R}}. \tag{26}$$

In previous studies [5], [7], the equations for the amount of bandwidth allocated to users have the form of general quadratic or cubic equations [8], [9]. In these studies, the quadratic and cubic equations can be solved using the discriminant and a geometric interpretation, respectively [8], [9]. In this paper, the function expressing the amount of bandwidth allocated to users, which is expressed by Eq. (19), is an algebraically complicated function. This type of function is difficult to solve using the methods of previous studies. To find the roots of this type of function, we use the Newton-Raphson method [10]. This method uses an iterative process to estimate the roots of a function.

It is assumed that the initial value x_0 is a good estimate of the actual solution to Eq. (19). This value is randomly selected based on the conditions of a specific function. The next estimate, x_1, is given by

$$x_1 = x_0 - \frac{f(x_0)}{f'(x_0)}. \tag{27}$$

The following estimate is obtained in the same way. The general form of an estimate for a root is

$$x_{n+1} = x_n - \frac{f(x_n)}{f'(x_n)}, \tag{28}$$

where

$$f(x) = ax^\alpha + bx^\beta + cx^\gamma + d, \tag{29}$$

and x_n and x_{n+1} are the current and next estimates of the root. In this study, the iteration continues until $x = x_k$ and $f(x_k)$ is less than 10^{-5}. Therefore, x_k is the closest estimate of the root of Eq. (19). This means that the computational error of the proposed method is less than 10^{-5}.

3   Numerical Results

For evaluating the QoE, the mean opinion score (MOS) method is widely used as a subjective measurement [11]. A five-grade MOS scale is popular and rates the QoE from 1 (bad) to 5 (excellent). When the MOS is more than 3, the perceived quality is acceptable because 3 is the center of the evaluation range. In the paper, the utility value is used with a corresponding MOS value between 0 and 100. When the utility value is not less than 60, users accept the service quality. In this case, an acceptable QoS means that users find the length of time they must wait for a website to load tolerable.

In this paper, it is assumed that all of the users share a total bandwidth of 100Mbps and access the same service, Yahoo news [12]. The average amount of data per web site, measured on an Android smart phone (Sony Xperia model C5303), is 4.29Mbits. In addition, the control parameters are set to the same value so that $k_1 = k_2 = k_3$. This means that all of the users experience the same level of satisfaction or the same perceived QoE. Two case studies are introduced in this paper to demonstrate proposed method.

(1) Case study 1: The total number of users is 130, and the number of neutral users changes.

Fig. 1 shows the bandwidth allocation and users QoE based on both the conventional and proposed methods. In this case study, 10% of the users are not relaxed. Fig. 1(a) shows the results of the conventional method, and Fig. 1(b)-(d) show the results of the proposed method when 10%, 20%, and 40%, respectively,

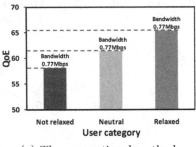

(a) The conventional method.

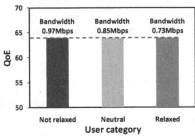

(b) The proposed method with 10% of the users in the neutral group.

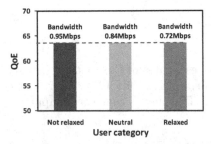

(c) The proposed method with 20% of the users in the neutral group.

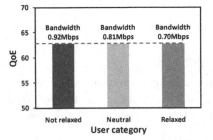

(d) The proposed method with 40% of the users in the neutral group.

Fig. 1. Bandwidth allocation and users QoE using the conventional and proposed methods; (a) the conventional method, (b)-(d) the proposal method with 10%, 20%, and 40%, respectively, of the users in the neutral group.

of the users are in the neutral group. As shown in Fig. 1(a), the relaxed and neutral users are satisfied with the service quality, but the users who are not relaxed experience a lower QoE. However, the proposed method can improve the QoE for the users who are not relaxed while the relaxed and neutral users still experience a good QoE, as shown in Fig. 1(b)-(d).

According to Fig. 1, when the number of neutral users increases from 10% to 40%, the bandwidth allocated to users in all of the groups decreases slightly. Therefore, the relaxed users share their bandwidth with the users who are neutral or not relaxed. When the number of neutral users increases and the number of users who are not relaxed remains constant, relaxed users become neutral. In addition, neutral users require more bandwidth than relaxed users to be satisfied with the service quality. The total bandwidth, however, remains at 100Mbps. For this reason, the bandwidth allocated to users decreases when the number of neutral users increases.

(2) Case study 2: The number of neutral users is 10%, and the total number of users is 100, 120, 130, or 150.

Fig. 2 shows the QoE of each group of users according to the conventional and proposed methods when the number of neutral users is constant and the number of users who are not relaxed changes from 0 to 90%. The bandwidth allocated to each user decreases when the number of users who are not relaxed

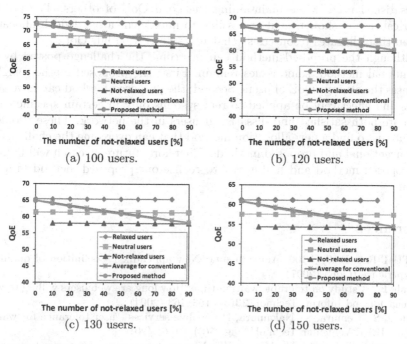

(a) 100 users.

(b) 120 users.

(c) 130 users.

(d) 150 users.

Fig. 2. The QoE of the conventional and proposed methods when 10% of the users are neutral, and the number of total users changes: (a) 100 users, (b) 120 users, (c) 130 users, and (d) 150 users.

increases. Although the average QoE of the users is slightly higher with the conventional method is slightly better than it is with the proposed method, the proposed method always improves the QoE of users who are not relaxed.

As shown in Fig. 2(a) and (b), all of the users experience a high utility value, which is greater than 60. This means that all of the users are satisfied with the service quality. Furthermore, when the number of users who are not relaxed is not more than 50%, the proposed method improves the QoE for them and for neutral users.

In Fig. 2(c) and (d), when the number of users who are not relaxed is not more than 40%, the proposed method improves the QoE for them and for neutral users. In contrast, the QoE improves only for users who are not relaxed when those users comprise over 40% of all users.

4 Conclusion

This paper proposed a bandwidth allocation method that is based on not only the network resources but also users perceptions of their experiences. The proposed method reallocates bandwidth from the users who do not require high-speed communication to others based on psychological factors. The method guarantees a fair QoE for each user by applying the Newton-Raphson method. Compared with the conventional method, the proposed method successfully improves QoE of dissatisfied users while maintaining the good QoE of others. The positive numerical results show that it is possible to implement a bandwidth allocation method that allocates resources so that users perceive a fair QoE.

Although the proposed method can overcome the challenge posted by the conventional method, some issues remain. First, the proposed method slightly decreases the average QoE of users. Second, the proposed method can have good results and effectively be applied to real systems only in certain specific cases. There are both satisfied and dissatisfied users in the network. These problems motivate us to find a new allocation method that can overcome the challenges of the conventional and proposed methods. Therefore, future research will improve the proposed method and find a way to realize our proposed method in a real system.

References

1. ITU-T Rec. P.10/G.100, Amendment1: New appendix I - definition of quality of experience (QoE) (2007)
2. Nah, F.: A study on tolerable waiting time: How long are web users willing to wait. Behavior and Inform. Technol. **23**(3), 153–163 (2004)
3. Niida, S., Uemura, S., Nakamura, H.: Mobile services - user tolerance for waiting time. IEEE Vehicular Technol. Mag. **5**(3), 61–67 (2010)
4. Yamazaki, T., Eguchi, M., Miyoshi, T., Yamori, K.: Quality of experience modeling with psychological effect for interactive web services. In: IEEE Workshop QoE Centric Management (QCMan) (2014)

5. Yamazaki, T., Miyoshi, T.: Resource allocation method based on QoE for multiple user types. In: 7th Int. Conf. Commun. Theory, Reliability, and Quality of Service (CTRQ) (2014)

6. Egger, S., Hossfeld, T., Schatz, R., Fiedler, M.: Waiting times in quality of experience for web based services. In: 4th Int. Workshop Quality of Multimedia Experience (QoMEX), pp. 86–96 (2012)

7. Pham-Thi, H., Hoang-Van, H., Miyoshi, T., Yamazaki, T.: QoE-driven bandwidth allocation method based on user characteristics. In: 16th Asia-Pacific Network Operations and Management Symposium (APNOMS), Taiwan (2014)

8. Quadratic equation. http://mathworld.wolfram.com/QuadraticEquation.html

9. Cubic function. http://mathworld.wolfram.com/CubicFormula.html

10. Newton-Raphson method. http://www.shodor.org/unchem/math/newton/

11. ITU-T Rec. P800: Methods for subjective determination of transmission quality (1996)

12. Yahoo news. http://news.yahoo.co.jp/

Piecewise Linear Formulations for Downlink Wireless OFDMA Networks

Pablo Adasme[1]([⊠]) and Abdel Lisser[2]

[1] Departamento de Ingeniería Eléctrica, Universidad de Santiago de Chile,
Avenida Ecuador, 3519 Santiago, Chile
pablo.adasme@usach.cl
[2] Laboratoire de Recherche En Informatique, Université Paris-Sud XI,
Bâtiment 650, 91190 Orsay Cedex, France
abdel.lisser@lri.fr

Abstract. In this paper, we propose piecewise mixed integer linear programming (PWMIP) models for joint subcarrier and power allocation in downlink wireless orthogonal frequency division multiple access (OFDMA) networks. In particular, we consider the problem of maximizing the total capacity of an OFDMA system subject to user power, subcarrier and quality of service constraints. For this purpose, we model the problem as a (0-1) mixed integer nonlinear programming problem. Then, we obtain two PWMIP models by means of a convex combination approach [17] and with the approach proposed in [21]. The latter consists of reducing the cardinality of a subset of binary variables to a logarithmic number of binary variables. Finally, we propose a variable neighborhood search (VNS) procedure [10,11]. Our preliminary numerical results indicate that the first model is more effective and that the VNS approach allows to obtain feasible solutions in less computational cost.

Keywords: Wireless OFDMA networks · Downlink resource allocation · Mixed integer nonlinear programming · Piecewise mixed integer linear programming

1 Introduction

Wireless orthogonal frequency division multiple access (OFDMA) networks use a wireless multi-carrier transmission scheme currently embedded into modern technologies such as IEEE 802.11a/g WLAN and IEEE 802.16a. It has also been implemented in mobile WiMax deployments ensuring high quality of service [18,23]. In a wireless OFDMA network, multiple access is achieved by assigning different subsets of subcarriers (or subchannels) to different users using orthogonal frequencies. In theory, this means that interference is completely minimized between subcarriers which allows simultaneous data rate transmissions from/to several users to/from the base station (BS). We can have an OFDMA system consisting of one or more BSs surrounded by several mobile users within a given radial transmission area. The former is known as a single-cell OFDMA network

© Springer International Publishing Switzerland 2015
M. Younas et al. (Eds.): MobiWis 2015, LNCS 9228, pp. 102–114, 2015.
DOI: 10.1007/978-3-319-23144-0_10

while the latter forms a multi-cell OFDMA network. In a downlink OFDMA network, the transmission of signals is performed from the BS to users. In this paper, we formulate two equivalent piecewise mixed integer linear programming (PWMIP) models for joint subcarrier and power allocation in downlink wireless OFDMA networks. In particular, we consider the problem of maximizing the total capacity of an OFDMA system subject to user power, subcarrier and proportional quality of service assignment constraints. For this purpose, we model the problem as a (0-1) mixed integer nonlinear programming (MINLP) problem from which we derive the equivalent PWMIP models. The first model is obtained by using a convex combination approach due to [17] whereas the second one uses both approaches proposed in [17,21]. In particular, the latter approach consists of reducing the cardinality of a subset of binary variables in the optimization problem to a logarithmic number of binary variables. Finally, we propose a simple variable neighborhood search procedure that uses the piecewise linear models to compute feasible solutions for the problem [10,11]. From a theoretical point of view, the proposed models allow to obtain optimal solutions for the OFDMA problem as long as the number of line segments used in the piecewise models grows to infinity. In practice, it would suffice to increase the number of line segments until no further improvement can be obtained with the piecewise models. Therefore, the proposed models can be used as reference when comparing the efficiency of new algorithmic approaches in terms of optimality for this hard combinatorial optimization problem. The equivalent PWMIP models use locally ideal formulations with proven desirable theoretical properties and enhanced computational performance [17,21]. As defined in [15,17], a locally ideal mixed integer linear programming (MILP) formulation is one where the vertices of its corresponding linear programming (LP) relaxation satisfy all required integrality conditions. In [6,13], the authors extend this definition and define a locally ideal SOS-2 MILP formulation as one whose LP relaxation has extreme points that all satisfy the SOS-2 property. This property means that at most two variables of an special ordered set (SOS) of non-negative variables in the optimization problem should be positive and consecutive in the SOS. These types of variables are commonly used as an additional way to specify integrality conditions in an optimization model and allow branch and bound algorithms to speed up the search procedure. In particular, they are often used to model nonlinear functions in piecewise linear approximations methods [20].

Maximizing capacity in an OFDMA network is relevant as it allows to select the best subcarriers for the different users while simultaneously exploiting multi-user diversity. The multi-user diversity phenomena occurs since subcarriers perceive large variations in channel gains which are different for each user and then each subcarrier can vary its own transmission rate depending on the quality of the channel. The better the quality of the channel, the higher the number of bits that can be transmitted. Several mathematical programming formulations for resource allocation in OFDMA networks have been proposed in the literature so far [1,12,19,24]. As far as we know, none of them attempts to solve the problem to optimality. Piecewise linear formulations allow to transform nonlinear programming problems into pure MILP problems which can be efficiently handled by specialized solvers [4]. We refer the reader to [7,8,13,14,21] for a deeper comprehension on this subject.

The paper is organized as follows. Section 2 briefly introduces the system description and presents the mathematical formulation of the downlink resource allocation problem. In Section 3, we present the equivalent PWMIP models. Then, in Section 4 we present the VNS approach while in Section 5, we conduct preliminary numerical tests in order to compare the proposed models and the VNS approach as well. Finally, in section 6 we give the main conclusions of the paper and provide some insights for future research.

2   System Description and Problem Formulation

In this section, we give a brief system description of a downlink wireless OFDMA network and formulate a MINLP model for this problem.

2.1   System Description

A general downlink wireless OFDMA network consists of a base station (BS) which is placed at the centre of a given radial transmission area and surrounded by several mobile users. The BS transmits its signals to each user using different subcarriers which have orthogonal frequencies. Each subcarrier must be assigned to a particular user in the system and the bandwidth channel capacity should be maximized subject to user power, subcarrier and proportional quality of service assignment constraints. The latter constraints are relevant in an OFDMA network as they ensure that each user is assigned a specific capacity requirement. These requirements depend on the application each user performs, e.g., video on demand, voice, multimedia, or any real and non-real time data transmission application.

These types of networks may arise in many difficult situations. In emergency, war battlefield or natural disaster scenarios where no strict planning of the network is possible due to short time constraints. The BS must perform the allocation process over time in order to exploit the so-called multi-user diversity and hence increasing the capacity of the system [5]. Different modulation types can be used in each subcarrier. The modulation types depend on the number of bits to be transmitted in each subcarrier. Commonly, M-PSK (M-Phase Shift Keying) or M-QAM (M-Quadrature Amplitude Modulation) modulations are used in OFDMA networks [22].

2.2   Mathematical Formulation

We consider a downlink wireless OFDMA network composed by a set of $\mathcal{N} = \{1, .., N\}$ subcarriers in the BS and a set of $\mathcal{K} = \{1, .., K\}$ users. The BS has to assign different subsets of subcarriers to each user within a given frame[1]. The downlink resource allocation model we consider can be written as follows

$$P_0: \quad \max_{\{x,p\}} \sum_{k=1}^{K} \sum_{n=1}^{N} x_{k,n} \log_2 \left(1 + \frac{p_{k,n} h_{k,n}}{\sigma_{k,n}} \right) \tag{1}$$

$$\text{st:} \quad \sum_{k=1}^{K} \sum_{n=1}^{N} p_{k,n} x_{k,n} \leq P_{Tot} \tag{2}$$

$$\sum_{k=1}^{K} x_{k,n} = 1, \quad \forall n \in \mathcal{N} \tag{3}$$

$$\sum_{n=1}^{N} x_{k,n} \log_2 \left(1 + \frac{p_{k,n} h_{k,n}}{\sigma_{k,n}} \right) =$$

$$\phi_k \sum_{l=1}^{K} \sum_{n=1}^{N} x_{l,n} \log_2 \left(1 + \frac{p_{l,n} H_{l,n}}{\sigma_{l,n}} \right), \forall k \tag{4}$$

$$x_{k,n} \in \{0,1\}, p_{k,n} \geq 0, \forall k, n \tag{5}$$

where $x_{k,n}$ and $p_{k,n}$ are the decision variables. In particular $x_{k,n} = 1$ if user k is assigned subcarrier n and $x_{k,n} = 0$ otherwise. Variable $p_{k,n}$ denotes the amount of power used by the BS to transmit signals to user k when using subcarrier n. In P_0, the objective function maximizes the total capacity of the OFDMA system. The capacity formula follows from the well known Shannon-Hartley Theorem [1,16,22,23,25]. Constraint (2) represents a maximum power constraint for the BS which cannot exceed P_{Tot}. Constraint (3) is a subcarrier assignment constraint and imposes the condition that each subcarrier should be assigned to only one user. Constraint (4) represents a quality of service assignment constraint and ensures that each user should be assigned a proportional amount $\phi_k, \forall k \in \mathcal{K}$ of the total maximum capacity achieved by the system where $\sum_{k \in \mathcal{K}} \phi_k = 1$. Constraints (5) are the domain constraints for the decision variables. Finally, the matrix $(h_{k,n})$ denotes the channel gain associated with user k when using subcarrier n while the matrix $(\sigma_{k,n})$ represents the Additive White Gaussian Noise (AWGN) experimented by user k in subcarrier n, respectively [22,25].

Notice that P_0 is formulated as a (0-1) MINLP problem and thus it is hard to solve directly. Furthermore, notice that by relaxing the integrality condition on variables $x_{k,n}, \forall k, n$ yet leads to a nonconvex problem which cannot be directly solved with traditional exact branch and bound methods. The nonconvexity of P_0 can be easily checked from the nonlinear equality constraint (4). Finally, observe that if $x_{k,n} = 0$, then $p_{k,n}$ should be equal to zero since no power will be available for that particular subcarrier. On the opposite, when $x_{k,n} = 1$ variable $p_{k,n}$ may be upper bounded by P_{Tot}. This observation allows writing an equivalent formulation for P_0 as follows

---

[1] A frame is a packet in which the data to be transmitted is placed. Each frame is composed by T time slots and N subcarriers.

$$P_1: \quad \max_{\{x,p\}} \sum_{k=1}^{K}\sum_{n=1}^{N} \log_2\left(1 + \frac{p_{k,n}h_{k,n}}{\sigma_{k,n}}\right) \tag{6}$$

$$\text{st:} \quad \sum_{k=1}^{K}\sum_{n=1}^{N} p_{k,n} \leq P_{Tot} \tag{7}$$

$$\sum_{k=1}^{K} x_{k,n} = 1, \quad \forall n \in \mathcal{N}$$

$$\sum_{n=1}^{N} \log_2\left(1 + \frac{p_{k,n}h_{k,n}}{\sigma_{k,n}}\right) =$$

$$\phi_k \sum_{l=1}^{K}\sum_{n=1}^{N} \log_2\left(1 + \frac{p_{l,n}H_{l,n}}{\sigma_{l,n}}\right), \forall k \tag{8}$$

$$p_{k,n} \leq x_{k,n}P_{Tot}, \quad \forall k, n \tag{9}$$

$$x_{k,n} \in \{0,1\}, p_{k,n} \geq 0, \forall k, n$$

Notice that neither the objective function (6) nor the constraints (7) and (8) include the variable $x_{k,n}$ anymore. Instead, we add the constraints (9) to control the value of $p_{k,n}$ by means of $x_{k,n}$ using the maximum available power P_{Tot} that the BS can use. In order to derive equivalent PWMIP formulations for P_1, we exploit the on-off logical condition in constraints (9). As demonstrated in [17], this logical condition allows to obtain improved formulations with proven desirable theoretical properties and better computational performances.

3   Piecewise Linear Formulations

In this section, we present two equivalent PWMIP models for P_1 which allow to obtain optimal solutions for the downlink OFDMA problem. Notice that the piecewise linear formulations can only guaranty the optimal solution of the problem if the line segments considered in the optimization problem is large enough.

3.1   Convex Combination Model

In order to write a PWMIP model for P_1, so far we consider the convex combination based approach proposed in [17]. For this purpose, consider the tabular data $\left(\bar{p}_{k,n}^{i}, \log_2\left(1 + \frac{\bar{p}_{k,n}^{i}h_{k,n}}{\sigma_{k,n}}\right)\right) \forall i \in \mathcal{I} = \{0, 1, \ldots, m\}$ for each logarithmic term in P_1. Notice that two consecutive indices in the set $\mathcal{I}$ allow to form an interval, i.e., a piecewise linear segment. We give more details on how we generate these intervals in the numerical results section. By introducing continuous nonnegative variables $\lambda_{k,n}^{i} \forall k, n, i \in \mathcal{I}$, accordingly we can write the following equivalent optimization problem for P_1 as

$$PW_1: \quad \max_{\{x,p,z,\lambda,b\}} \sum_{k=1}^{K} \sum_{n=1}^{N} z_{k,n} \tag{10}$$

$$\text{st: } p_{k,n} = \sum_{i=0}^{m} \lambda_{k,n}^i \bar{p}_{k,n}^i, \quad \forall k,n \tag{11}$$

$$z_{k,n} = \sum_{i=0}^{m} \lambda_{k,n}^i \log_2 \left(1 + \frac{\bar{p}_{k,n}^i h_{k,n}}{\sigma_{k,n}} \right), \quad \forall k,n \tag{12}$$

$$\sum_{i=0}^{m} \lambda_{k,n}^i = x_{k,n}, \quad \forall k,n \tag{13}$$

$$\sum_{i=1}^{m} b_{k,n}^i = x_{k,n}, \quad \forall k,n \tag{14}$$

$$\sum_{k=1}^{K} \sum_{n=1}^{N} p_{k,n} \leq P_{Tot}$$

$$\sum_{k=1}^{K} x_{k,n} = 1, \quad \forall n \in \mathcal{N}$$

$$\sum_{n=1}^{N} z_{k,n} = \phi_k \sum_{l=1}^{K} \sum_{n=1}^{N} z_{l,n}, \quad \forall k \tag{15}$$

$$\lambda_{k,n}^0 \leq b_{k,n}^1, \quad \forall k,n \tag{16}$$

$$\lambda_{k,n}^m \leq b_{k,n}^m, \quad \forall k,n \tag{17}$$

$$\lambda_{k,n}^i \leq b_{k,n}^i + b_{k,n}^{i+1}, \quad \forall k,n,i \in \{1,\ldots,m-1\} \tag{18}$$

$$b_{k,n}^i \in \{0,1\}, \quad \forall k,n,i \in \{1,\ldots,m\} \tag{19}$$

$$\lambda_{k,n}^i \geq 0, \quad \forall k,n,i \in \{0,\ldots,m\} \tag{20}$$

$$x_{k,n} \in \{0,1\}, z_{k,n} \geq 0, p_{k,n} \geq 0, \forall k,n$$

where the constraints (11) and (12) are the domain and function evaluation constraints for the tabular data. Constraints (13) are convexity constraints that together with constraints (14), (16)-(20) enforce the SOS-2 type condition on variables $\lambda_{k,n}^i, \forall k, n, i$. This means that only two consecutive variables $\lambda_{k,n}^i$ and $\lambda_{k,n}^{i+1}, \forall k, n, i$ are allowed to be nonnegative. This is controlled by the binary variables $b_{k,n}^i, \forall k, n, i$. Notice that constraints (13)-(14) and (16)-(18) are only active when $x_{k,n} = 1, \forall k, n$. As shown in [17], these constraints allow to obtain significantly improvements in terms of CPU time and in terms of number of branching nodes when solving the optimization problem to optimality with branch and bound based MIP solvers [3]. Finally, we use the nonnegative variable $z_{k,n}, \forall k, n$ to replace the logarithmic terms in the objective function (6) and in the quality of service constraints (8).

In the next subsection, we propose a second piecewise linear formulation for P_1 that uses a logarithmic number of binary variables in order to represent the SOS-2 type condition.

3.2   Convex Combination Model with Logarithmic Number of Binary Variables for the SOS-2 Condition

As it can be observed in PW_1, for a particular user $\bar{k}$ and subcarrier $\bar{n}$, the number of binary variables $b^i_{\bar{k},\bar{n}}, \forall i$ grows linearly with the number of line segments considered in the optimization problem which allows encoding 2^m possible solution vectors $b^\bullet_{\bar{k},\bar{n}}$. This is a huge amount of solution vectors. However, it has been shown in [21] that one can formulate conditions like the SOS-2 condition with dramatically fewer number of binary variables. More precisely, with $\lceil \log_2(m) \rceil$ number of binary variables. The idea is to use a Gray code [9] in order to encode the definition intervals of the piecewise linear functions. In turn, this allows using an injective function $\varphi = \{1, \dots, m\} \to \{0,1\}^{\lceil \log_2(m) \rceil}$ with the additional property that for any number j, the vectors $\varphi(j)$ and $\varphi(j+1)$ only differ in one component. This allows replacing constraints (16)-(19) with the equivalent constraints (21)-(22). Finally, dropping constraints (14) from PW_1 allows to write the following equivalent problem

$$PW_2: \quad \max_{\{x,p,z,\lambda,b\}} \quad \sum_{k=1}^{K} \sum_{n=1}^{N} z_{k,n}$$

$$\text{st: } p_{k,n} = \sum_{i=0}^{m} \lambda^i_{k,n} \bar{p}^i_{k,n}, \quad \forall k,n$$

$$z_{k,n} = \sum_{i=0}^{m} \lambda^i_{k,n} \log_2 \left(1 + \frac{\bar{p}^i_{k,n} h_{k,n}}{\sigma_{k,n}} \right), \quad \forall k,n$$

$$\sum_{i=0}^{m} \lambda^i_{k,n} = x_{k,n}, \quad \forall k,n$$

$$\sum_{k=1}^{K} \sum_{n=1}^{N} p_{k,n} \leq P_{Tot}$$

$$\sum_{k=1}^{K} x_{k,n} = 1, \quad \forall n \in \mathcal{N}$$

$$\sum_{n=1}^{N} z_{k,n} = \phi_k \sum_{l=1}^{K} \sum_{n=1}^{N} z_{l,n}, \quad \forall k$$

$$\sum_{i=0}^{j-2} \lambda^i_{k,n} + \sum_{i=j+1}^{m} \lambda^i_{k,n} \leq$$

$$\sum_{\{l \mid (\varphi(j))_l = 1\}} (1 - b^l_{k,n}) + \sum_{\{l \mid (\varphi(j))_l = 0\}} b^l_{k,n}, \forall j = \{1, \dots, m\}, k, n \quad (21)$$

$$b^i_{k,n} \in \{0,1\}, \quad \forall k,n,i \in \{1,\ldots,\lceil \log_2(m) \rceil\} \tag{22}$$

$$\lambda^i_{k,n} \geq 0, \quad \forall k,n,i \in \{0,\ldots,m\}$$

$$x_{k,n} \in \{0,1\}, z_{k,n} \geq 0, p_{k,n} \geq 0, \forall k,n$$

Notice that modeling SOS-2 type conditions with fewer binary variables and constraints might seem advantageous, however a smaller formulation does not necessarily provide a better formulation of the problem [21] since more constraints and variables usually provide tighter LP relaxations [2]. Therefore, our aim in formulating PW_2 is mainly focussed in collecting empirical evidence in order to find out whether this model can provide better feasible solutions in less computational cost.

4   Variable Neighborhood Search Procedure

VNS is a metaheuristic approach [10,11] that uses the idea of neighborhood change during the descent toward local optima and to avoid valleys that contain them. Recall that metaheuristic procedures do not guaranty to find globally optimal solutions. In general, suboptimal and possibly near optimal solutions can be found with significantly less computational effort than exact branch and bound methods [10,11]. We define only one neighborhood structure as $Ngh(x)$ for PW_1 and PW_2 as the set of neighbor solutions x' in PW_1 and PW_2 at a distance "h" from x where the distance "h" corresponds to the number of 0-1 values which are different in x' and x, respectively. We propose a variable neighborhood search procedure in order to compute feasible solutions for PW_1 (Resp. for PW_2) as depicted in algorithm 4.1. The algorithm receives an instance of problem PW_1 (Resp. of PW_2) and provides a feasible solution for it. We denote by $(xOpt^*, p^*, z^*, \lambda^*, b^*, g^*)$ the final solution obtained with the algorithm where g^* represents the objective function value and $(xOpt^*, p^*, z^*, \lambda^*, b^*)$ the solution found. The algorithm is simple and works as follows. First, it computes randomly an initial feasible solution for $RPW_1(x)$ (Resp. for $RPW_2(x)$) that we keep. We denote by $RPW_1(\bar{x})$ (Resp. by $RPW_2(\bar{x})$) the resulting linear programming problem obtained while simultaneously fixing the variable $x = \bar{x}$ and relaxing the binary variable $0 \leq b \leq 1$ in PW_1 (Resp. in PW_2). Next, the algorithm performs a variable neighborhood search process by randomly assigning $\mathcal{H} \leq \theta$ different subcarriers to different users. Initially, $\mathcal{H} \leftarrow 1$ and it is increased in one unit when there is no improvement after new "η" solutions have been evaluated. On the other hand, if a new current solution is better than the best found so far, we set $\mathcal{H} \leftarrow 1$, the new solution is recorded and the process goes on. Notice that the value of $\mathcal{H}$ is increased until $\mathcal{H} = \theta$, otherwise $\mathcal{H} \leftarrow 1$ again after new "η" solutions have been evaluated. This gives the possibility of exploring in a loop manner from local to wider zones of the feasible space. The whole process is repeated while the cpu time variable "$Time$" is less than or equal to the maximum available "$maxTime$". Finally, for the best $\bar{x} = xOpt$ found, we solve $PW_1(\bar{x})$ (Resp. $PW_2(\bar{x})$) which corresponds to the resulting MIP problem obtained while simultaneously fixing variable $x = xOpt$ and using the binary variable b in PW_1 (Resp. in PW_2).

Algorithm 4.1. VNS approach

Data: A problem instance of PW_1 (Resp. of PW_2)
Result: A feasible solution for PW_1 (Resp. for PW_2)
$Time \leftarrow 0$; $\mathcal{H} \leftarrow 1$; $count \leftarrow 0$; $x_{k,n} \leftarrow 0, \forall k, n$;
Step 1: **foreach** $n \in \mathcal{N}$ **do**
   | Choose randomly $k' \in \mathcal{K}$;
   | $\bar{x}_{k',n} \leftarrow 1$;

$xOpt^* = \bar{x}$;
For the fixed $\bar{x}$, let $(\tilde{p}, \tilde{z}, \tilde{\lambda}, \tilde{b})$ be the output solution of $RPW_1(\bar{x})$ (Resp. of $RPW_2(\bar{x})$) with objective function value $\tilde{f}$;
if $((\tilde{p}, \tilde{z}, \tilde{\lambda}, \tilde{b})$ *is infeasible)* **then**
   | $x_{k,n} \leftarrow 0, \forall k, n$;
   | Return to Step 1 ;

else
   | Go to Step 2 ;

Step 2: **while** *(Time $\leq$ maxTime)* **do**
   for $i = 1$ *to* $\mathcal{H}$ **do**
     | Choose randomly $k' \in \mathcal{K}$ and $n' \in \mathcal{N}$;
     | $\bar{x}_{k,n'} \leftarrow 0, \quad \forall k \in \mathcal{K}$;
     | $\bar{x}_{k',n'} \leftarrow 1$;

   For the new fixed $\bar{x}$, let $(p^*, z^*, \lambda^*, b^*)$ be the new solution found for $RPW_1(\bar{x})$ (Resp. for $RPW_2(\bar{x})$) with objective function value g^*;
   if $(g^* > \tilde{f}$ *and* $(p^*, z^*, \lambda^*, b^*)$ *is feasible)* **then**
     | $\mathcal{H} \leftarrow 1$; $(\tilde{p}, \tilde{z}, \tilde{\lambda}, \tilde{b}) \leftarrow (p^*, z^*, \lambda^*, b^*)$; $\tilde{f} \leftarrow g^*$; $Time \leftarrow 0$; $count \leftarrow 0$;
     | $xOpt^* = \bar{x}$;

   else
     | $\bar{x} = xOpt^*$; $count \leftarrow count + 1$;

   if *(count $> \eta$)* **then**
     | $count \leftarrow 0$;
     if *($\mathcal{H} \leq \theta$)* **then**
       | $\mathcal{H} \leftarrow \mathcal{H} + 1$;
     else
       | $\mathcal{H} \leftarrow 1$;

For the fixed $xOpt^*$, let $(p^*, z^*, \lambda^*, b^*)$ be the solution obtained with $PW_1(xOpt^*)$ (Resp. with $PW_2(xOpt^*)$) with objective function value g^*;
Return $(xOpt^*, p^*, z^*, \lambda^*, b^*, g^*)$;

---

5   Preliminary Numerical Results

We present preliminary numerical results for PW_1 and PW_2 using CPLEX 12.6 and for the proposed VNS algorithm. CPLEX is used with default options. We generate randomly the input data as follows. We set the maximum available power in the BS to $P_{Tot} = 1000$ miliWatts (mW) and generate the wireless channel matrix $(h_{k,n})$, $\forall k, n$ using a wireless channel from [25]. Further details regarding how mobile users are placed and what the dimensions are in an OFDMA cell can be found in IEEE 802.11a/g WLAN and IEEE 802.16a standards. We consider instances with up to $N = 128$ subcarriers and $K = 12$ users. Commonly, in an OFDMA cell, these instances dimensions are, in average, not larger than $N = 64$ subcarriers and $K = 12$ users [22,25]. Notice, that there are K^N feasible assignments for the subcarriers in the OFDMA network. Each entry in matrix $(\sigma_{k,n})$, $\forall k, n$ is uniformly distributed in the interval $[0, 2]$. For the PWMIP formulations we generate line segments first by dividing the interval $[0, P_{Tot}]$ into two subintervals $\{[0, 500], [500, P_{Tot}]\}$. Then, the interval $[0, 500]$ is further divided into equally spaced line segments of length 5 whereas the interval $[500, 1000]$ is divided into subintervals equally spaced of length 20. Finally, we calibrated the values of $\eta = 10$ and $\theta = 5$ in Algorithm 4.1, respectively. The numerical experiments have been carried out on an AMD Athlon 64X2 Dual-Core 1.90 Ghz with 1.75 GoBytes of RAM under windows 7. In Table 1, column 1 gives the instance number and columns 2-3 give the instances dimensions. In columns 4-7 we present the optimal objective function value of PW_1, its CPU time in seconds, the number of nodes used by CPLEX, and the objective function value of P_0 obtained with the optimal solution of PW_1, respectively. In columns 8-11 we present the same information for PW_2. In Table 2, columns 1-3 present the same information as in Table 1. Columns 4-6 present the optimal objective function value of PW_1, its CPU time in seconds, and the objective function value of P_0 obtained with the optimal solution of PW_1, respectively. Then, in columns 7-10 we present the objective function value obtained with the VNS approach, its CPU time in seconds, and the objective function value of P_0 obtained with the feasible solution of VNS_1, respectively. By VNS_1, we refer to Algorithm 4.1 when using $RPW_1(\bar{x})$ and $PW_1(xOpt^*)$ as defined in Section 4. Finally, in columns 11-14 we present the same information for VNS_2. Analogously, by VNS_2 we refer to Algorithm 4.1 when using $RPW_2(\bar{x})$ and

Table 1. Numerical results obtained with the piecewise linear models.

#	N	K	PW_1	CPU(s)	B&Bn	$P_0(x_1, p_1)$	PW_2	CPU(s)	B&Bn	$P_0(x_2, p_2)$
1	32	4	365.9281	357.05	6286	344.8729	365.9281	306.85	5409	344.8729
2	32	6	368.2689	909.20	15781	342.4525	368.2689	1057.30	12389	342.4525
3	32	8	368.6386	3600	36887	333.7932	-	2323.05	15135	-
4	32	10	365.2246	3600	27851	327.7168	366.7200	2550.71	12566	334.2562
5	32	12	347.7560	3600	8027	326.4608	348.7228	3600	12688	326.3653
6	64	4	637.1779	104.94	970	601.9434	637.1779	189.51	1187	601.9434
7	64	6	664.8312	3600	32095	603.0704	664.8312	3600	11817	603.0704
8	64	8	669.9684	2963.13	40298	608.3116	669.9655	3600	11863	608.7298
9	64	10	-	2736.55	6145	-	683.9805	3600	10686	610.3342
10	64	12	677.3243	3600	3404	600.7871	-	576.50	0	-
11	128	4	1124.8288	1572.28	8740	1075.0267	1124.8288	724.96	4958	1075.0267
12	128	6	1204.2892	3600	28872	1087.5581	-	648.37	0	-
13	128	8	1223.6594	3600	9060	1090.0766	-	186.59	0	-
14	128	10	-	2228.05	2912	-	-	71.45	0	-
15	128	12	-	2575.65	1938	-	-	101.13	0	-
Min.			347.7560	104.94	970	326.4608	348.7228	71.45	0	326.3653
Max.			1223.6594	3600	40298	1090.0766	1124.8288	3600	15135	1075.0267
Ave.			-	2576.45	15284.4	-	-	1542.42	6579.8	-

"-": No solution found with CPLEX in at most one hour.

Table 2. Numerical results obtained with PW_1 and with the VNS approach.

#	N	K	PW_1	CPU(s)	$P_0(x_1,p_1)$	VNS_1	CPU(s)	#Iter	$P_0(VNS_1)$	VNS_2	CPU(s)	#Iter	$P_0(VNS_2)$
1	32	4	363.2280	1108.81	332.8280	346.3483	319.10	319	335.1820	331.2224	265.37	77	340.7584
2	32	6	358.1708	3600	329.6743	307.5490	193.66	163	312.6892	282.4700	528.23	92	295.5082
3	32	8	348.7124	3600	339.5729	282.5991	320.19	182	325.3545	266.2212	233.97	37	288.4816
4	32	10	364.7378	3600	330.3201	305.2848	282.36	132	300.8118	80.2625	46.97	13	109.7926
5	32	12	-	2729.71	-	289.6406	212.72	92	295.5502	209.2945	474.99	43	284.9162
6	64	4	658.9609	26.94	622.4422	601.3463	504.75	268	601.0131	559.1510	498.30	64	607.9442
7	64	6	663.8848	2213.53	609.9619	592.2736	805.44	274	592.7362	498.5069	856.58	70	540.9147
8	64	8	677.2995	3600	612.1996	580.1416	504.74	135	612.8284	218.2924	40.08	7	237.9056
9	64	10	673.5958	3600	606.0439	531.3900	400.95	88	596.4567	396.1174	159.57	11	450.3003
10	64	12	678.4744	3600	605.2070	519.7449	492.12	87	537.2961	413.9242	32.92	4	448.8457
11	128	4	1197.2692	33.96	1087.2750	1149.9367	2869.08	680	1085.3320	1017.8216	801.16	48	1117.5813
12	128	6	1219.9842	532.66	1102.9785	1022.8716	1250.29	200	1084.5559	769.1204	172.38	9	796.2384
13	128	8	1233.0722	594.13	1096.4564	739.0429	1517.74	164	764.1754	418.3734	77.56	2	420.8889
14	128	10	1243.3079	3600	1099.3401	703.2871	361.16	39	716.7762	438.2657	180.96	2	459.9043
15	128	12	1252.2929	3600	1091.7133	572.4907	238.03	22	587.9126	673.5254	140.87	1	734.6070
Min.			348.7124	26.94	329.6743	282.5991	193.66	22	295.5502	80.2625	32.92	1	109.7926
Max.			1252.2929	3600	1102.9785	1149.9367	2869.08	680	1085.3320	1017.8216	856.58	92	1117.5813
Ave.			-	2402.64	-	569.5964	684.82	189.6	583.2446	438.1712	300.66	32	475.6391

"-": No solution found with CPLEX in at most one hour.

$PW_2(xOpt^*)$. Finally, we arbitrarily set the maximum cpu time available for CPLEX to be at most 1 hour. While for the VNS algorithm, we set in all our tests the maximum available time to $maxTime = 100$ seconds.

From the numerical results presented in Table 1, we mainly observe that PW_1 can find feasible solutions for most of the instances which is not possible to achieve using PW_2. In general, we see that CPLEX cannot get feasible solutions for some of the instances in less than 1 hour due to shortage of memory using both models. Finally, we observe that the feasible solutions obtained with both models lead to very close objective function values in P_0. In summary, we observe that PW_1 outperforms PW_2 despite the fact that CPLEX requires more nodes to get these solutions. From Table 2, we confirm the effectiveness of PW_1. In this case, we observe that the VNS approach needs more iterations when using PW_1. This shows that the LP relaxation $RPW_1(\bar{x})$ can be solved significantly faster than $RPW_2(\bar{x})$. As a consequence, higher objective function values are obtained for P_0 when using the feasible solutions obtained with VNS_1. Although the CPU times required by VNS_1 are higher than those required by VNS_2. In particular, we observe that the VNS approach cannot solve the instances 11-15 effectively as one would expect. This can be explained by the fact that solving $RPW_1(\bar{x})$ becomes rapidly prohibitive when the instances dimensions increase. This is reflected in the number of iterations required by VNS_1 which decreases as well. On the opposite, for the instances 1-10, the VNS approach outperforms PW_1 in terms of CPU time, although the feasible solutions found are slightly inferior when evaluated in the objective function of P_0.

6   Conclusions

In this paper, we formulate two equivalent piecewise mixed integer linear programming models for joint subcarrier and power allocation in downlink wireless orthogonal frequency division multiple access (OFDMA) networks. In particular, we consider the problem of maximizing the total capacity of an OFDMA system subject to user power, subcarrier and proportional quality of service assignment constraints. For this purpose, we model the problem as a (0-1) mixed integer nonlinear programming problem from which we derive the equivalent piecewise linear models. Additionally, we propose a simple variable neighborhood search (VNS) procedure that uses the piecewise models to compute feasible solutions for the problem. Our preliminary numerical results indicated that the first model is more effective and that the VNS approach allows to obtain feasible solutions in less computational cost. Finally, we mention that the best piecewise linear model can be used for comparison purposes when designing new algorithmic approaches as it allows to compute optimal solutions for this hard combinatorial optimization problem.

As future research, we plan to develop new piecewise linear models and low complexity algorithmic approaches for this challenging optimization problem.

References

1. Amzallag, D., Armarnik, T., Livschitz, M., Raz, D.: Multi-cell slots allocation in OFDMA systems. In: 16th Mobile and Wireless Communications Summit (IST), pp. 1–5 (2007)
2. Balas, E.: Projection, lifting and extended formulation in integer and combinatorial optimization. Ann. Oper. Res. **140**, 125–161 (2005)
3. Beale, E., Tomlin, J.: Special facilities in a general mathematical programming system for non-convex problems using ordered sets of variables. In: Lawrence, J. (ed.) Proceedings of the Fifth International Conference on Operational Research, pp. 447–454. Tavistock Publications, London (1970)
4. Bixby, R.: Solving Real-World Linear Programs: A Decade and More of Progress. Oper. Res. **50**(1), 1–13 (2002)
5. Cao, Z., Tureli, U., Liu, P.: Optimum subcarrier assignment for OFDMA uplink. In: IEEE International Conference on Communications, pp. 11–15 (2003)
6. Croxton, K., Gendron, B., Magnanti, T.: Comparison of mixed-integer programming models for nonconvex piecewise linear cost minimization problems. Manage. Sci. **49**, 1268–1273 (2003)
7. Dantzig, G.: Linear programming and extensions. Princeton University Press (1963)
8. Geiler, B., Martin, A., Morsi, A., Schewe, L.: Mixed Integer Nonlinear Programming. The IMA Volumes in Mathematics and its Applications, vol. 154, pp. 287–314 (2012)
9. Gray, F.: Pulse code communication, March 17, 1953 (filed November 1947). U.S. Patent 2,632,058
10. Hansen, P., Mladenovic, N.: Variable neighborhood search: Principles and applications. Eur. J. Oper. Res. **130**, 449–467 (2001)
11. Hansen, P., Mladenovic, N., Perez Brito, D.: Variable Neighborhood Decomposition Search. J. Heuristics. **7**, 335–350 (2001)
12. Hernández, A., Guio, I., Valdovinos, A.: Interference management through resource allocation in multi-cell OFDMA networks. In: IEEE 69th Vehicular Technology Conference VTC, pp. 1–5 (2009)

13. Keha, A., de Farias, I., Nemhauser, G.: Models for representing piecewise linear cost functions. Oper. Res. Lett. **32**(1), 44–48 (2004)
14. Markowitz, H., Manne, A.: On the solution of discrete programming-problems. Ecometrica **25**, 84–110 (1957)
15. Padberg M., Rijal, M.: Location, Scheduling, Design and Integer Programming. International Series in Operations Research & Management Science, vol. 3. Springer, Boston (1996)
16. Shannon, C.E.: A Mathematical Theory of Communication. AT&T Tech. J. **27**, 379–423 (1948)
17. Srikrishna, S., Linderoth, J., Luedtke, J.: Locally ideal formulations for piecewise linear functions with indicator variables. Oper. Res. Lett. **41**(6), 627–632 (2013)
18. Sternad, M., Svensson, T., Ottosson, T., Ahlen, A., Svensson, A., Brunstrom, A.: Towards Systems Beyond 3G Based on Adaptive OFDMA Transmission. Proceedings of the IEEE **95**, 2432–2455 (2007)
19. Venturino, L., Risi, C., Buzzi, S., Zappone, A.: Energy-efficient coordinated user scheduling and power control in downlink multi-cell OFDMA networks. In: IEEE 24th International Symposium on Personal Indoor and Mobile Radio Communications (PIMRC), pp. 1655–1659 (2013)
20. Vielma, J., Ahmed, S., Nemhauser, G.: Mixed-integer models for nonseparable piecewise-linear optimization: unifying framework and extensions. Oper. Res. **58**, 303–315 (2009)
21. Vielma, J., Nemhauser, G.: Modeling disjunctive constraints with a logarithmic number of binary variables and constraints. Math Program **128**, 49–72 (2009)
22. Wong, I., Zukang, C., Evans, B., Andrews, J.: A low complexity algorithm for proportional resource allocation in OFDMA systems. In: IEEE Workshop on Signal Processing Systems, pp. 1–6 (2004)
23. Yaghoobi, H.: Scalable OFDMA physical layer in IEEE 802.16 WirelessMAN. Intel Technology Journal **8**, 201–212 (2004)
24. Zhaorong, Z., Jianyao, Z., Jingjing, L., Weijiang, L., Yunjie, R.: Resource allocation based on immune algorithm in multi-cell cognitive radio networks with OFDMA. In: Fifth International Conference on Computational and Information Sciences (ICCIS), pp. 1644–1647 (2013)
25. Zukang, S., Jeffrey, G., Evans, B.: Short range wireless channel prediction using local information, signals, systems and computers. In: Conference Record of the Thirty-Seventh Asilomar Conference, vol. 1, pp. 1147–1151 (2003)

Reconfigurable Packet FEC Architecture
for Mobile Networks

Wael M. El-Medany[✉]

Computer Engineering Department, College of Information Technology,
University of Bahrain, 32038, Zallaq, Bahrain
welmedany@uob.edu.bh

Abstract. This paper presents a reconfigurable hardware architecture of Forward Error Correction (FEC) coding algorithm for mobile networks, with high throughput on Field Programmable Gate Array (FPGA). The design can be reconfigured for different message length and different generator number, the encoder and decoder has been described using VHDL (VHSIC Hardware Description Language). The decoder has the ability to detect and correct different types and different numbers of errors based on the message length and the length of redundant data. The design has been simulated and tested using ModelSim PE student edition 10.4. Spartan 3 FPGA starter kit from Xilinx has been used for implementing and testing the design in a hardware level.

Keywords: FPGA · FEC · VHDL · Mobile networks

1 Introduction

Error Correcting Code (ECC) is a technique used to increase link reliability and to lower the required transmitted power. It enables reconstruction of the original data at the receiving end of the communication channel [1-7]. Forward Error Correction (FEC) plays the main role for correcting errors in mobile networks, particularly when poor Signal to Noise Ratio (SNR) environments are encountered [8]. In FEC the encoder adds redundant information that allows the receiver to detect and possibly estimate the error location, and hence correct the detected error, for that reason FEC is a suitable ECC technique when single source is broadcasting data to many destinations, as it does not require handshaking between sender and receiver.

GPRS (General packet radio service) is a packet oriented mobile data service on mobile network; it allows transmitting IP packets to external networks such as the Internet. GPRS has been developed from the GSM (Global System for Mobile) communications, which is the standard mobile network developed by ETSI (European Telecommunications Standards Institute) to describe protocols for the second and third generation (2G&3G) of mobile networks, GSM uses 1800 MHz and 1900 MHz frequency bands that are defined as Digital Cellular System (DCS) [9-12].

In the Transmission Control Protocol (TCP) and the Internet Protocol (IP) architecture, the data transmission in the IP layer, in case of errors occurs in the data packet,

© Springer International Publishing Switzerland 2015
M. Younas et al. (Eds.): MobiWis 2015, LNCS 9228, pp. 115–121, 2015.
DOI: 10.1007/978-3-319-23144-0_11

which will lead to IP network packet loss problem. A forward error correction technique is more feasible approach to solve the IP network packet loss problem. In GPRS networks, the design of a real-time erasure ability and have good erasure coding is necessary [13].

In this paper we are introducing a reconfigurable FEC decoding algorithm based on a well known cyclic linear block coding technique that has the ability of detecting and correcting channel errors in an efficient and reliable manner, it is a modified version of a well known error trapping technique that use cyclic shifting in order to trap and correct the error in the fly, the algorithm has the ability of correcting single bit, double bit, and multiple bit errors, based on the predefined minimum Hamming distance. The design can easily be reconfigured for different message and code lengths, with different generator numbers. The implemented technique is based on the syndrome decoding technique [14, 15].

The materials in this article are organized as follows: in Section 2, a discussion of syndrome decoding is given; Section 3 gives a brief discussion about reconfigurable architecture; a brief description of the register transfer logic design given in section 4; the simulation results and discussion is given in Section 5; at the end, a conclusions will be given in Section 6.

2   Syndrome Decoding

Syndrome decoding is an efficient linear block code that allows decoding of the received codeword over a noisy channel; it is a minimum distance decoding. Assume that a code $\mathbf{C} \subset \mathbf{F}_2^n$ is a linear block code with ($\mathbf{n}$) code length and minimum distance ($\mathbf{d_{min}}$), the number of detected errors is given by:

$$\mathbf{X} = \lfloor \mathbf{d_{min}} - \mathbf{1} \rfloor$$

Where $\mathbf{X}$ is the number of errors that can be detected, the capability of correcting errors is clearly given by:

$$\mathbf{t} = \left\lfloor \frac{\mathbf{d_{min}} - \mathbf{1}}{\mathbf{2}} \right\rfloor$$

Where $\mathbf{t}$ is number of errors that can be corrected.

The implemented coding architecture is based on syndrom decoding that can trap the error, and then correct the error in the fly based on the redundant information provided by the parity-check equations.

3   Reconfigurable Architecture

Reconfigurable architecture is the ability of rapidly changing to achieve different functionalities of their components and the interconnection between them to a customized design. There most commercially available reconfigurable platform is the Field Programmable Gate Arrays (FPGAs). The main difference with the hardwired ASICs (Application Specific Integrated Circuits) is the possibility of loading a modified circuit of the design on the reconfigurable chip; on the other hand reconfigurable architecture has an advantage of rapid prototyping compared to ASICs that takes more time for long fabrication processing steps. The advantage of FPGA implementation compared to ASIC for the packet FEC architecture is that the design has a reconfigurable minimum distance according to the codelenghth and gerator polynomial with different message length as well.

4   Register Transfer Logic Design

The RTL (Register Transfer Logic) system design abstraction is used to create the high level representations of the encoding/decoding circuits. The RTL schematic of the encoding circuit is given in figure 1, it is mainly composed of Mod-2 additions (XOR functions). Figure 2 Shows the technology schematic created from Xilinx tools. It is simply 4-bit buffer for the message, and Mod-2 arithmetic for calculating the parity-check bits (3-bits) in the given example. The RTL schematic given in figure 1, and technology schematic given in figure 2 are the first level of the top-down design, each components in figures 1 & 2 has one or more levels up to the logic gate level.

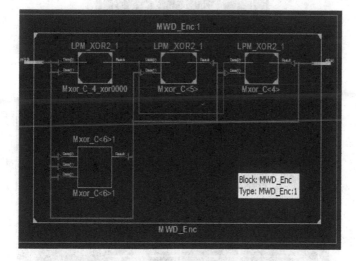

Fig. 1. RTL Schematic for the Encoder Circuit

The RTL schematic of the decoding circuit is given in figure 3, it has 6 components, most of them are Mod-2 additions (XOR functions), in addition to decoding circuit for the syndrome and error pattern detection. Figure 4. Shows the technology schematic of the decoder circuit created using Xilinx tools. It has 7 components that are also based on Mod-2 arithmetic for calculating the syndrome bits (3-bits) in the given example.

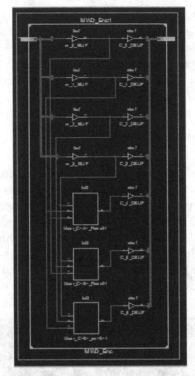

Fig. 2. Xilinx Technology Schematic for the Encoder Circuit

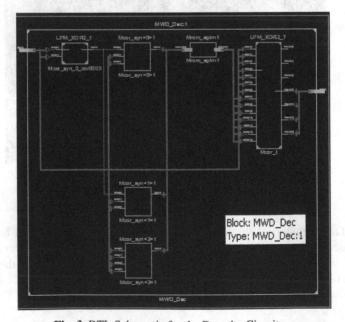

Fig. 3. RTL Schematic for the Decoder Circuit

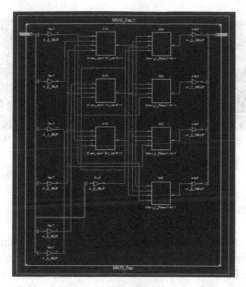

Fig. 4. Xilinx Technology Schematic for the Decoder Circuit

5   Simulation Results and Discussion

The simulation results for the decoding and encoding processes are given in figures 5 & 6 respectively. There are five rows of binary values in figure 5, the first one is the received word (7-bits), second one is estimated transmitted message (4-bits), the third and fourth rows are the estimated codeword (7-bits) and error pattern (7-bits) respectively, and the last row is the syndrome (3-bits), the LSB on the left and MSB on the right. In figure 6, the first row of binary data is the message, and the second one is the encoded codeword.

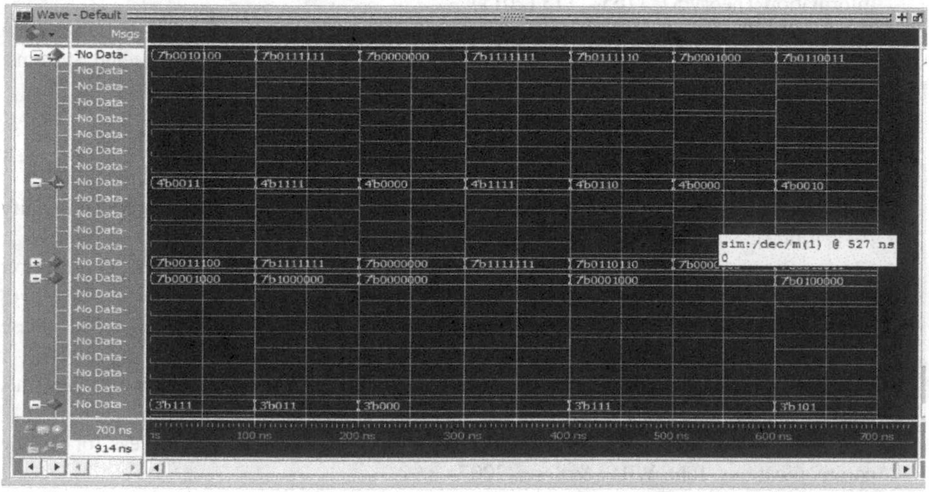

Fig. 5. Simulation Results for Decoder Circuit

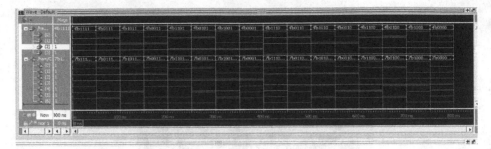

Fig. 6. Simulation Results for Encoder Circuit

6   Conclusions

Reconfigurable packet FEC design for mobile network has been simulated and implemented with different code length and different generator number using ModelSim and Xilinx tools. The hardware design has been described using VHDL language, the design has been tested in the hardware environment level using Spartan-3A/3AN FPGA Starter Kit Board. The VHDL source code has been edited and synthesized using Xilinx ISE 14.5, and then simulated and tested using ModelSim (VHDL/Verilog). The final design is targeting Xilinx XC3S700AN FPGA.

References

1. Islam, M.R.: Error correction codes in wireless sensor network: An energy aware approach. International Journal of Computer and Information Engineering **4**, 59–64 (2010)
2. Etzion, T., Vardy, A.: Error-correcting codes in projective space. IEEE Transactions on Information Theory **57**, 1165–1173 (2011)
3. Naseer, R., Draper, J.: DEC ECC design to improve memory reliability in sub-100nm technologies. In: 15th IEEE International Conference on Electronics, Circuits and Systems, ICECS 2008, pp. 586–589 (2008)
4. Frigo, M., Stewart, L.C.: Error-correcting code. Google Patents (2014)
5. Egner, S.: Error correcting code. Google Patents (2011)
6. Morelos-Zaragoza, R.H.: The art of error correcting coding. John Wiley & Sons (2006)
7. Huffman, W.C., Pless, V.: Fundamentals of error-correcting codes. Cambridge University Press (2003)
8. Chang, F., Onohara, K., Mizuochi, T.: Forward error correction for 100 G transport networks. Communications Magazine, IEEE **48**, S48–S55 (2010)
9. Brasche, G., Walke, B.: Concepts, services, and protocols of the new GSM phase 2+ general packet radio service. Communications Magazine, IEEE **35**, 94–104 (1997)
10. Cai, J., Goodman, D.: General packet radio service in GSM. Communications Magazine, IEEE **35**, 122–131 (1997)
11. Holma, H., Toskala, A.: HSDPA/HSUPA for UMTS: high speed radio access for mobile communications. John Wiley & Sons (2007)

12. Bettstetter, C., Vogel, H.-J., Eberspacher, J.: GSM phase 2+ general packet radio service GPRS: Architecture, protocols, and air interface. Communications Surveys & Tutorials, IEEE **2**, 2–14 (1999)
13. Xiao-kai, W., Yong-jin, S., Da-jin, C., Bing-he, M., Qi-li, Z.: Transfer Error and Correction Approach in Mobile Network. Physics Procedia **25**, 1270–1276 (2012)
14. Zhang, Y., Song, H., Burd, G.: QC-LDPC decoder with list-syndrome decoding. Google Patents (2012)
15. Schmidt, G., Sidorenko, V.R., Bossert, M.: Syndrome decoding of Reed-Solomon codes beyond half the minimum distance based on shift-register synthesis. IEEE Transactions on Information Theory **56**, 5245–5252 (2010)

Strategies and Techniques for Relay Node Placement in Multi-hop Wireless Networks

Abeer AlSanad[1,2(✉)], Lulwah AlSuwaidan[1,2(✉)], and Mohammed Alnuem[1(✉)]

[1] College of Computer and Information Sciences, Department of Information Systems, King Saud University, P.O. Box. 51178, Riyadh 11534, Saudi Arabia
{Abeer.AlSanad,lalsuwaidan}@ccis.imamu.edu.sa,
malnuem@ksu.edu.sa
[2] College of Computer and Information Sciences, Al-Imam Muhammad Ibn Saud Islamic University, Riyadh, Saudi Arabia

Abstract. The concept of relaying was raised recently in networking world. This technology has a great impact on multi-hop wireless networks. There had been many research studies on the role of Relay Node placement in Multi-hop Wireless Networks. Therefore, in this paper a comprehensive review on the strategies and techniques of Relay Node placement in MWNs, categorized based on either ad hoc or infrastructure-based, is presented. Ad hoc category contains WSNs strategies and techniques which classified into quality of service, fault tolerance, Federating disjoint segments and connectivity restoration. While Infrastructure-based includes WiMAX, Wireless Mesh Networks and LTE-Advanced networks. This work proposes open research ideas in this filed. As a result, several findings and recommendations are emerged that greatly direct the researchers to new and important research areas.

Keywords: Multi-hop wireless network · Wireless network · Relay node placement

1   Introduction

Multi-hop Wireless Networks (MWNs) are captivating significant attention because of their suitability for enormous range of applications that requires ease of deployment compared with wired networks. MWNs allow transmission of data from source to destination through intermediate nodes (i.e., multiple hops) instead of direct communication. MWNs include ad hoc and sensor networks, Worldwide Interoperability for Microwave Access (WiMax) networks, as defined by the IEEE 802.16j standard. Also, it include Wireless Mesh Networks (WMNs) [1], and Long-Term Evolution (LTE)-Advanced networks as defined by 3GPP [2].These networks have received much attention in the last decade and will continue to be a prominent research topic in the future.

The concept of relay node was introduced in ad hoc networks because the lacks of centralized control require nodes to organize themselves. It becomes popular in sensor

© Springer International Publishing Switzerland 2015
M. Younas et al. (Eds.): MobiWis 2015, LNCS 9228, pp. 122–133, 2015.
DOI: 10.1007/978-3-319-23144-0_12

networks due to several reasons, such as their influence by the surrounding environments [3, 4]. Therefore, finding a solution to enhance connectivity and availability is being important [5]. It has been shown in literature that using RNs in infrastructure-based networks is getting growing interest because of many reasons such as their fast deployment, low cost backhaul, …etc. [6, 7, 8, 9, 10, 11].

Relay node placements covered different kind of problems in Multi-hop wireless networks (MWNs) [12]. In addition, WSN has considered the relay node placement problem (RNP) under different requirements and objectives such as connectivity [13, 14], extend the network lifetime [15, 16], energy-efficient or balanced data gathering [17, 18, 19], and survivability and fault tolerance [12].

In this paper, we investigate the strategies and techniques for relay node placement in MWNs. This review broadly categorizes and discusses the relay node placement schemes in ad hoc and infrastructure based networks. Many open research issues and recommendations are proposed. Since there is no difference between RN and RS we will use them interchangeably in this work.

The following section, section 2, covers strategies of RN placement in MWNs based on previous categorizations. Section 3 discusses open research issues. Finally, a conclusion of this work is presented in section 4.

2   Relay Node Placement Strategies in Multi-hop Wireless Networks

In this section, we investigate the strategies and techniques for relay node placement. This section divides the relay node placement schemes into ad hoc and infrastructure based networks. The focus in this review is particularly in WSNs. WSN is classified based on the objective of placing the RN either to quality of service, connectivity restoration, federating disjoint segments or fault-tolerance.

2.1   Ad hoc Networks

Ad hoc networks are self-organizing and do not have preinstalled infrastructure. WSN considered as ad hoc network due to the dynamic link it uses [20].

Wireless Sensor Networks
Wireless sensor networks are a collection of a huge number of sensor nodes that deployed in a way that helps in collecting information. Sensor networks have some limitations such as battery power, node densities and huge data volume [21]. Their role is to ensure connectivity and coverage. One of the methods used to guarantee this target is using of relay nodes. It is more capable than sensor network and it provides strong computation power, long communication range, and energy reserve [12]. This section focus on methods used to get, firstly, the optimal quality of service through ensuring coverage [22, 23, 24, 25, 26]. Secondly, fault-tolerance to tolerating the fault and make the network keep functioning [38], [27]. Thirdly, federating disjoint segments because failure of node(s) may partition the network into disjoint segments

[28, 29, 30, 31, 32]. Fourthly, connectivity restorations since sensors in WSN are susceptible to physical damage and component malfunction [46], [33], [34].

WSN architecture is shown in Figure 1. The blue nodes represent the relay node connected with base station with wireless links. The relay node form a connected path between the base station and sensor nodes which represented by gray nodes [35].

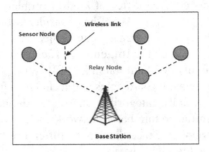

Fig. 1. Architecture of Relay Node in WSNs.

Quality of Service

Mostly, WSN is affected by environment. There are two works done under minimum Steiner tree structure. First, [22] by proposing a new algorithm called "Optimized Relay node placement algorithm using a minimum Steiner tree on the Convex hull (OCR)". Second, [23] by OCR greedy heuristics. Authors in [24] worked on WSN powered by Ambient Energy Harvesting to find the optimal routing algorithm and relay node placement scheme. Another idea was proposed in [25] which used a strategy to place RNs in WSN to monitoring underground tunnel infrastructure in UK London. In addition, [36] was claimed to achieve a high level of connectivity in a heterogeneous WSN. In [26] stated that many relaying protocols for WSN presented in the literature to show how relay node process the packet received. Sookyoung and Meejeong [37] proposed heuristics which is QoS-aware Relay node placement using Minimum Steiner tree on Convex hull (QRMSC) which guaranteed the QoS and connectivity.

Fault Tolerance

Fault-tolerance means that failure of any node will make the BS able to recover the faulty nodes and backup the original data [38]. However, the factors that affected WSN vary. Sensor coverage, sensor battery power, and dependability are some of them. Gupta and Younis [39] proposed a mechanism to detect and recover faulty gateway. In the work of [40] Bari et al. formulated their problem as integrated Integer Linear Program (ILP). The same approach was used by [27]. Recently, Gao et al. [41] have dealt with fault tolerance in relay node by model it in 2tWSN as a graphic problem, called DBY-HCG.

Federating Disjoint Segments

Generally, federation means connect or interact which leads to fabricate a connected entities. Federation in term of WSN formulates a relay node placement that maximizes the connectivity of WSN nodes. However, many reasons make federating between sectors as a complex task. These reasons are the huge distances between sectors, and the harsh operational conditions [28]. Therefore, there are many solutions worked on solving WSN disjunction, and we will summarize them in this section

In term of federating disjoint WSN, there were strategies proposed by [29] in order to optimize relay node placement. Most of federation problems showed in infinite large search space [29, 30, 31, 32] and they solved by applied 3-D grid model which limits the search space. In addition, Shiow-Fen et al. [42] proposed a relay node placement scheme in WSNs. It aimed at federating disjoint segments to form a 2-connected topology with fewer relay nodes. It also found the best possible place of relay node to connect two topologies.

Connectivity Restoration

WSNs experienced large scale damage because it usually found in harsh environment. This damage may cause the network to be partitioned. Therefore, restoring the network connectivity is very critical and important to avoid side effects on the application [43].

Table 1. Advantages and problems in adapting relay nodes in WSN.

Ref#	Objective	Advantages	Problems	Comments
[22], [23], [24], [25], [36], [26], [50]	Performance	— Minimize used no. of RN — Balance terrific load — Average coverage of data — Increase connectivity — Guarantee scalability and efficiency.	— Noisy environment — Time consuming — Inefficiency	— Guaranteed in different kinds of WSN
[39], [40], [27], [41]	Fault Tolerance	— Detecting and recovering faulty gateway — Connectivity	— Limited stability	— No comments
[28], [29], [30], [31], [32], [42]	Federating Disjoint Segments	— Enhancing the connectivity. — Limiting cost	— Not applicable in large scale WSN	— No comments
[33], [34], [43], [44], [45]	Connectivity Restoration	— Ensuring connectivity and survivability — Reducing no. of needed RNs, RNs movement cost, total tour length — Fault tolerance	— Time consuming	— No comments

In terms of connectivity restoration WSN, there are many works take this objective in consideration. One of these works is by [43] who addressed the establishment of inter-segment connectivity of RN placement strategy. Other work by [44] dealt with the con the RNs movements cost.

At the same year, [33] worked on restoring the connectivity of inter segment when the network gets partitioned into multiple disjoint segments. They use Mobile Data Collectors (MDCs), as mobile RNs, to help in establishing the communication links between segments, instead of using stationary RNs. Moreover, [34] worked on ensuring the connectivity and survivability of sensor nodes and base stations. Lee et. al. [45] proposed a Connectivity Restoration with Assured Fault Tolerance (CRAFT) algorithm.

Table.1 summarized advantages and problems related to the approaches used in WSNs along with their objectives behind using them. It also gives comments related to each objective.

2.2   Infrastructure-Based

In this section, we investigate the strategies and techniques for relay node placement in infrastructure-based networks. Infrastructure-based means that the networks require pre-installed infrastructure in order to offer services to the users [20]. This section covers the three newer MWN types (WiMAX, Mesh network, and LTE-Advanced).

WiMAX

IEEE 802.16 is a chain of wireless broadband standards. It is dedicated for issues regarding Multi-hop Relay Networks (MRN). According to IEEE 802.16j task group, two types of architecture are available for WiMAX. The first type, shown in Figure 2, is MP-tree (point to multipoint tree) where PMP connections are set between each subscriber station (SS) and RN or BS. In addition, PMP connections are set between each RN and BS or other RS. The second type, shown in Figure 3 is Hybrid-PMP-mesh (HPM) architecture where RNs are connected among themselves in mesh. RN will be connected through PMP to BS. Also, SS will be connected through mesh connection to RN. Moreover, RNs can create mesh among them to give reliable connectivity to SSs [46].

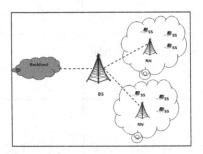 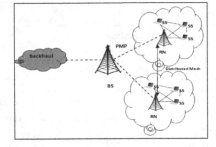

Fig. 2. Architecture of Relay Node in WiMAX, PMP-Tree.   **Fig. 3.** Architecture of Relay Node in WiMAX, HPM.

Lin et. al. in [47] pretend that they published the first study which use a cooperative relay technology to handle the RS placement and relay time allocation problem in Mobile Multi-hop Relay (MMR) Networks. After this work, the same group of scientists published in [48] a new research that focuses on solving the minimum cost RS placement problem. The main goal was founding the optimal location for nodes. In [7] the same group developed an optimization framework to solve a problem of Capacity Maximization RS Placement (CMRP). This framework was aimed to maximize the network capacity and satisfy the minimum traffic for SS.

In the newly defined IEEE 802.16j standard, two types of RSs are defined Transparent Relay Stations (TRSs) and Non Transparent Relay Stations (NTRS). In [50] developed a planning model for Multi-hop Relay Networks. Its models work on determining the optimal locations for RSs and BSs with a lowest cost. The problem was formulated as Integer Programming problem. In [51] a clustering approach was proposed for network planning. The challenge of this approach is to solve a large problem in less time with limited equipment of hardware and software. A work of [8] develops a model that work on determining the optimal locations for RSs with a lowest cost. A mixed integer linear program was used to find the solution of the problem. In [52] Chang and Li present a deployment algorithm for WiMAX multi-hop relay networks. This algorithm works based on the traffic history of internet usage and work on deploying as few as possible RSs at specific locations.

Wireless Mesh Networks

Wireless Mesh Networks (WMNs) composed of mesh routers and clients. WMNs used to overcome network limitation problem and enhance wireless metropolitan area networks (WMANs) performance [53]. They are organized and configured by themselves. They have many advantages such as easy to maintain, robustness, etc. [54].

WMN has its architecture in term of relay placement. Figure 4 shows the WMN structure in using relay nodes. It uses the two main components base station and relay nodes with its subscribed station (SS). All connections are in wireless manner, and formed by support of relay nodes [1].

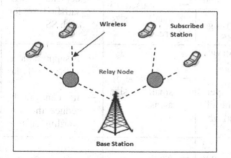
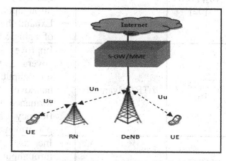

Fig. 4. Architecture of Relay Node in WMNs   **Fig. 5.** Architecture of Relay Node in LTE-Advanced.

The authors in [54] aimed in their work to find the optimal place for relaying nodes which increase the throughput per node In addition, placing the relay node at the center between the transmitter and the receiver maximize the throughput [54]. In [55] authors recommended a relay node placement schema in a WMN, which aimed to improve the throughput and link connectivity. In [56] Huan et. al. dealt with the rechargeable router placement problem in a green WMN.

LTE-Advanced Networks

LTE-Advanced is an enhanced version of Long Term Evolution (LTE) which is one of the 3rd Generation Partnership Project (3GPP) standards. LTE-Advanced adds new features which are Carrier Aggregation (CA), advanced use of multi-antenna techniques. In LTE, user devices are called User Equipments (UEs) and base stations are called Evolved Node B (eNBs) [57], [58], [59], [2].

LTE-Advanced architecture, as shown in Figure 5, contains RN, Donor eNB (DeNB), radio interface Un, E-UTRAN air interface Uu and UE [60]. Yang et. al. in [38] focused on LTE-Advanced networks. Many schemes are used and the result shows that the selective (DCF) can give better performance achievement. They resulted that the centralized schemes can achieve higher performance than distributed schemes but it requires a signaling overhead [27]. In [57] authors proposed a forwarding mechanism to enhance handover performance. In [61] Venkataraman et. al. presented a new architecture called multi-hop multi-band intelligent relay architecture (MMI).

Table.2 summarized advantages and problems related to the approaches used in Infrastructure-based approaches.

Table 2. Advantages and problems in adapting relay nodes in Infrastructure-based approaches.

Ref#	Application Area	Advantages	Problems	Comments
[47], [48], [50], [51], [7], [49], [8], [10], [52]	WiMAX	— Solve the minimum cost RS placement problem. — Enhance time, quality, and throughput. — Expand the range of a single BS.	— Network capacity — Required bandwidth in not satisfied. — It is used in small size areas.	— The overall system capacity was maximize and the traffic demands was satisfied for each SS.
[27], [57], [61]	LTE-Advanced	— Improve service coverage, throughput, handover performance, the efficiency and the performance.	— It is used in small size areas.	— It supports hops with small latency. — It can fairly reduce the forwarding cost.
[54], [55], [56]	Mesh	— Increase the throughput per node. — Increase link connectivity.	— Network capacity.	— No comments.

3   Open Research Issues

Based on the extensive survey presented in previous section, we identify several open research issues and challenges. Table.3 shows each type of network examined against multiple aspects. From the table, we can conclude that there are no researches about the security using RNs in MWNs. Also, only the WSNs and LTE-Advanced networks covered quality of service (QoS) with RNs while the others are not. Moreover, fault tolerance which is an important aspect only covered in WSNs.

Table 3. Network Type- Aspect Schedual

Network Type	Aspect	Connectivity	Coverage	Throughput	Security	QoS	Failure tolerating
Ad hoc	WSN	✓	✗	✗	✗	✓	✓
Infrastruc- ture based	WiMAX	✓	✓	✓	✗	✗	✗
	WMN	✓	✗	✓	✗	✗	✗
	LTE-Advanced	✗	✓	✓	✗	✓	✗

The concept of RN placement is popular in WSN. Since the other MWNs allowing placement of RNs to extend capacity and range, there is a feasibility of adopting some approaches from WSN to other MWNs. Table.4 summarizes all WSN approaches mentioned in this paper with their references and shows whether each approach adopted in any of the infrastructure-based networks or not.

Table 4. WSN Approaches in WiMAX, WMN or LTE-Advanced (A: adopted, N: Not adopted)

Network Type / WSN Approaches	WiMAX		WMN		LTE-Advanced	
	A/N	Ref #	A/N	Ref #	A/N	Ref #
Greedy heuristics [23] [43]	A	[10]	N	-	N	-
Cluster-based [25]	A	[51]	N	-	N	-
Decode-Forward [26]	A	[7], [47], [48]	N	-	A	[57]
Divide-and-Conquer [25]	N	-	N	-	N	-
Steiner tree and Steiner Point [22] [36] [28] [62] [63]	A	[64]	N	-	N	-
Multiplicative Increase Li- near Decrease (MILD) [39]	N	-	N	-	N	-
RLNOD, and RLNODwFC [32]	N	-	N	-	N	-
Grid-based and Non Grid- based [29]	N	-	N	-	N	-
FADI [30], [31]	N	-	N	-	N	-
Polynomial Time Approxi- mation Algorithms [34]	N	-	N	-	N	-
Distributed Positioning Ap- proach [44]	N	-	N	-	N	-
Polynomial Time Heuristic [33]	N	-	N	-	N	-

From the table, we can see that Greedy heuristics is adopted in WiMAX in [10] but not in WMN and LTE-Advanced whereas the last seven approaches are not adopted on any of WiMAX, WMN or LTE-Advanced networks. As a consequence, a recommendation is made for testing the possibility of making an adoption for those approaches which are not adopted on the other MWNs.

4   Conclusion and Recommendation

A comprehensive review on the strategies of RN placement in MWNs categorized based on ad hoc or infrastructure-based was produced. Ad hoc contains WSNs while infrastructure-based includes WiMAX, WMNs and LTE-Advanced networks. Several important and valuable open research topics that would greatly help interested researchers in this field were found.

References

1. Bešťák, R., Mach, P.: Wireless Mesh and Relay Networks. http://fireworks.intranet.gr/Publications/Fireworks_6CTUPB011a.pdf (accessed November 2, 2012)
2. LTE System Overview, September 1, 2011. http://www.3gpp.org (accessed October 31, 2012)
3. Al-Kofahi, M.O., Kamal, E.A.: Survivability strategies in multihop wireless networks. IEEE Wireless Communications 17(5), 71–80 (2010)
4. Chattopadhyay, A., Sinha, A., Coupechoux, M., Kumar, A.: Optimal Capacity Relay Node Placement in Multi-hop Network on a Line, April 19, 2012. arxiv.org/abs/1204.4323 (accessed November 30, 2012)
5. Bari, A.: Relay Nodes in Wireless Sensor Networks: A Survey (2005)
6. Kumar, D.S., Nagarajan, N.: Simulation of Relay modes in IEEE 802.16j Mobile Multi-hop Relay (MMR) WIMAX Networks. Innovative Systems Design and Engineering, 75–85 (2011)
7. Lin, B., Mehrjoo, M., Ho, P.-H., Xie, L.-L., Shen, X.: Capacity enhancement with relay station placement in wireless cooperative networks. In: Wireless Communication and Networking Conference (2009)
8. Abichar, Z., Kamal, A.E., Chang, J.M.: Planning of Relay Station Locations in IEEE 802.16 (WiMAX) Networks, pp. 1–6. IEEE (2010)
9. Braun, T., Kassler, A., Kihl, M., Siris, V., Heijenk, G.: Multihop wireless networks. In: Traffic and QoS Management in Wireless Multimedia Networks. Springer Science and Business Media, LLC, pp. 201–265 (2009)
10. Lu, H.-C., Liao, W., Lin, F.Y.-S.: Relay Station Placement Strategy in IEEE 802.16j WiMAX Networks. IEEE Transactions on Communications, 1–8, January 2011
11. Zhu, G., Lin, X., Hu, J.: Optimal Relay Node Placement for Multi-Commodity Concurrent Flow Maximization, USA
12. Di Caro, G., Flushing, E.: Optimal relay node placement for throughput enhancement in wireless sensor networks. In: Dalle Molle Inst. for Artificial Intell., Lugano, Switzerland (2011)
13. Lin, G.: Steiner tree problem with minimum number of steiner points and bounded edge-length. Information Processing Letters 69(2), 53–57 (1999)

14. J. Tang, B. Hao and A. Sen: Relay node placement in large scale wireless sensor networks. Computer Communications **29**(4) 2005
15. Hou, Y., Shi, Y., Sherali, H., Midkiff, S.: Prolonging sensor network lifetime with energy provisioning and relay node placement. In: Proc. of IEEE SECON 2005 (2005)
16. Wang, G., Huang, L., Xu, H., Li, J.: Relay node placement for maximizing network lifetime in wireless sensor networks. In: Proc. Of WiCOM 2008. IEEE (2008)
17. Patel, M., Chandrasekaran, R., Venkatesan, S.: Energy efficient sensor, relay and base station placements for coverage, connectivity and routing. In: 24th IEEE International Performance Computing and Communications Conference (IPCCC) (2005)
18. Falck, E., Floreen, P., Kaski, P., Kohonen, J., Orponen, P.: Balanced ´data gathering in energy-constrained sensor networks. Algorithmic Aspects of Wireless Sensor Networks **3121**, 59–70 (2004)
19. Varaiya, S., Ergen, P.: Optimal placement of relay nodes for energy efficiency in sensor networks. In: Proc. of ICC 2006 (2006)
20. Jangra, A., Swati, Richa, Priyanka: Wireless Sensor Network (WSN): Architectural Design issues and Challenges. International Journal on Computer Science and Engineering **02**(09), 3089–3094 (2010)
21. Cheng, P., Chuah, C.-N., Liu, X.: Energy-aware node placement in wireless sensor networks. In: Global Telecommunications Conference (2004)
22. Lee, S., Younis, M.: Optimized Relay Node Placement for Connecting Disjoint Wireless Sensor Networks **56**(12) 2788–2804 (2012)
23. Lloyd, E.L., Xue, G.: Brife Contributions Relay Node Placement in Wireless Sensor Networks. IEEE Transactions on Computers **56**(1), 134–138 (2007)
24. Ang, E., Hwee-Pink, T., Seah, W.: Routing and Relay Node Placement in Wireless Sensor Networks Powered by Ambient Energy Harvesting. In: Wireless Communications and Networking Conference (2009)
25. Liu, R., Wassell, I., Soga, K.: Relay Node Palcement for Wireless Sensor Networks Deployed in Tunnels (2010)
26. Zhang, G.-C., Peng, X.-H., Gu, X.-Y.: Performance analysis of an experimental wireless relay sensor network. Concurrency and Computation: Practice and Experience **22**(4), 462–480 (2010)
27. Yang, Y., Hu, H., Xu, J., Mao, G.: Relay technologies for WiMax and LTE-advanced mobile systems. IEEE Communications Magazine **47**(10), 100–105 (2009)
28. Al-Turjman, F., Alsalih, W., Hassanein, H.: Towards augmented connectivity in federated wireless sensor networks. In: Wireless Communications and Networking Conference (WCNC) (2012)
29. Al-Turjman, F., Hassanein, H., Alsalih, W., Ibnkahla, M.: Optimized relay placement for wireless sensor networks federation in environmental applications. Wireless Communications and Mobile Computing, 1677–1688 (2011)
30. Al-Turjman, F.M., Hassanein, H.S., Oteafy, S.A.: Towards augmented federated wireless sensor networks. In: International Conference on Ambient Systems, Networks and Technologies (2012)
31. Al-Turjman, F., Hassanein, H., Oteafy, S., AlSalih, W.: Towards augmented federation wireless sensor networks in forestry application. Journal of Personal and Ubiquitous Computing (2012)
32. Al-Turjman, F., Al-Fagih, A., Hassanein, H., Ibnkahla, M.: Deploying fault-tolerant grid-based wireless sensor networks for environmental applications. In: IEEE 35th Conference on Local Computer Networks (LCN) (2010)

33. Younis, F., Senel, M.: Optimized Interconnection of disjoint wireless sensor network segments using K mobile data collectors. In: IEEE International Conference on Communications, Ottawa, Canada (2012)
34. Misra, S., Hong, S.D., Xue, G., Tang, J.: Constrained relay node placement in wireless sensor networks to meet connectivity and survivability requirements. In: The 27th Conference on Computer Communications. IEEE, Phoenix (2008)
35. Mena, J.: Dynamic Relay Node Placement in Wireless Networks (2007). http://citeseerx.ist.psu.edu/viewdoc/summary?doi=10.1.1.127.2408 (accessed November 3, 2012)
36. Deepak, P.D., Dandekar, R.: Relay node placement for multi-path connectivity in heterogeneous wireless sensor networks. In: 2nd International Conference on Computer, Communication, Control and Information Technology (2012)
37. Sookyoung, L., Meejeong, L.: QRMSC: efficient QoS-aware relay node placement in wireless sensor networks using minimum steiner tree on the convex hull. In: 2013 International Conference on Information Networking (ICOIN) (2013)
38. Yang, D., Misra, S., Xue, G.: Joint base station placement and fault-tolerant routing in wireless sensor networks. In: IEEE Global Telecommunication Conference, Honolulu (2009)
39. Gupta, G., Younis, M.: Fault-tolerant clustering of wireless sensor networks, New Orleans (2003)
40. Bari, A., Xu, Y., Jaekel, A.: Integrated Placement and Routing of Relay Nodes for Fault-Tolerant Hierarchical Sensor Networks, US Virgin Islands (2008)
41. Gao, Z., Chen, K., Cheng, W., Hao, Y., Li, X.: K-extended constrain independent relay node placement with base stations in two-tiered wireless sensor network. In: Tenth International Conference on Intelligent Information Hiding and Multimedia Signal Processing (IIH-MSpP) (2014)
42. Shiow-Fen, H., Wen-Lin, C., Chen-Liang, W., Chyi-Ren, D.: 2-Connected relay node placement scheme in disjoint wireless sensor networks. In: 2014 5th IEEE International Conference on Software Engineering and Service Science (ICSESS), Beijing (2014)
43. Senel, F., Younis, M.: Optimized connectivity restoration in a partitioned wireless sensor network. In: 2011 IEEE Global Telecommunications Conference (GLOBECOM 2011) (2011)
44. Senturk, I.F., Akkaya, K., Yilmaz, S.: Distributed Relay Node Positioning for Connectivity Restoration in Partitioned Wireless Sensor Networks, p. 6. IEEE (2012)
45. Lee, S., Younis, M., Lee, M.: Connectivity restoration in a partitioned wireless sensor network with assured fault tolerance. Ad Hoc Networks 24, Part A, 1–19 (2015)
46. Sagar, V., Das, D.: Modified EDF algorithm and WiMAX architecture to ensure end-to-end delay in multi-hop networks. In: TENCON 2008 - 2008 IEEE Region 10 Conference, Hyderabad (2008)
47. Lin, B., Xie, L.-L., Shen, X., Ho, P.-H.: Optimal Relay Station Placement in IEEE 802.16j Networks, Honolulu, Hawaii, USA (2007)
48. Lin, B., Xie, L.-L., Shen, X., Ho, P.-H.: Relay Station Placement in IEEE 802.16j Dual-Relay MMR Networks, pp. 1–5. IEEE (2008)
49. Chang, C.-Y., Chang, C.-T., Chang, C.-H.: A novel relay placement mechanism for capacity enhancement in IEEE 802.16j WiMAX networks. In: IEEE International Conference on Communication (2009)
50. Yu, Y., Murphy, L., Murphy, S.: Planning Base Station and Relay Station Locations in IEEE 802.16j Multi-hop Relay Networks, pp. 1–5. IEEE (2008)

51. Yu, Y., Murphy, S., Murphy, L.: Clustering approach to planning base station and relay station locations in IEEE 802.16j multi-hop relay networks. In: International Conference on Communication (2008)
52. Chang, C.-Y., Li, M.-H.: A placement mechanism for relay stations in 802.16j WiMAX networks. Wireless Networks 20(2), 227–243 (2014)
53. Akyildiz, I., Wang, X., Wang, W.: Wireless Mesh Networks: A Survey. Computer Networks 47(4) (2005)
54. Wang, X.G., Guan, L., Xuefen, C., Xin, G.: Investigation of Relaying Node Placement in Wireless Mesh Networks (2010)
55. Prasad, S.P., Agrawal, P.: Opportunistic Relay Placement in Mobile Multihop Opportunistic Relay Placement in Mobile Multihop, Texas (2010)
56. Huan, X., Wang, B., Mo, Y., Yang, L.T.: Rechargeable router placement based on efficiency and fairness in green wireless mesh networks. Computer Networks, December 8, 2014
57. Chen, J.-Y., Mai, Y.-T., Yang, C.-C.: Handover Enhancement in LTE-Advanced Relay Networks (2012)
58. Ruby, R., Mohamed, A., Leung, V.: Utility-Based Uplink Scheduling Algorithm for Enhancing Throughput and Fairness in Relayed LTE Networks, Denver (2010)
59. Bou Saleh, A., Redana, S., Hämäläinen, J., Raaf, B.: On the Coverage Extension and Capacity Enhancement of Inband Relay Deployments in LTE-Advanced Networks (2010)
60. Wannstrom, J.: LTE-Advanced, May 2012. http://www.3gpp.org/LTE-Advanced (accessed November 3, 2012)
61. Venkataraman, H., Gandhi, D., Tomar, V.: Multi-hop Multi-band Intelligent Relay-Based Architecture for LTE-Advanced Multi-hop Wireless Cellular Networks. Wireless Personal Communications: An International Journal 75(1), 131–153 (2014)
62. Wang, D., Liu, J.: Traffic-aware relay node deployment for data collection in wireless sensor networks. In: 6th Annual IEEE Communications Society Conference, SECON 2009, Rome (2011)
63. Wang, F., Wang, D., Liu, J.: Traffic-aware relay node deployment: maximizing lifetime for data collection wireless sensor networks: In: IEEE Transactions on Parallel and Distributed Systems, vol. 8, pp. 1415–1423
64. Zhang, W., Bai, S., Xue, G., Tang, J., Wang, C.: DARP: distance-aware relay placement in WiMAX mesh networks. In: IEEE INFOCOM (2011)

Mobile and Data Services

A Framework for Transactional Service Selection Based on Crowdsourcing

Rafael Angarita[1]([⊠]), Maude Manouvrier[1], and Marta Rukoz[1,2]

[1] LAMSADE UMR 7243, CNRS, PSL Université Paris-Dauphine,
75775 Paris Cedex 16, France
{rafael.angarita,manouvrier,marta.rukoz}@lamsade.dauphine.fr
[2] Université Paris Ouest Nanterre, Nanterre, France

Abstract. The growing number of services in the Web providing the same functionality but different QoS (e.g., price, execution time, and availability) and transactional properties (e.g., compensable or not) has lead to the emergence of several approaches for service selection and recommendation. Some of these approaches use collaborative filtering, QoS prediction, service reputation, among others. Existing works lack from a way to integrate all those methods and benefit from their multiple perspectives to decide how to select a service. The problem tackled in this work is the selection of the most suitable service from a set of functionally equivalent services according to the opinions of multiple contributors. We propose a framework to easily rely on crowdsourcing for service selection, where crowdsourcing contributors can be independently developed services or human experts. Our framework emphasizes on the definition of a collaborative system to allow contributors to join and participate in the selection of services.

Keywords: Web service · Service selection · Crowdsourcing · QoS · Transactional properties · Voting systems

1 Introduction

Nowadays, SOA is increasingly used as a platform for business applications frameworks for accessing data and services in distributed environments [6]. The latest SOA techniques, such as Web services and the Web 3.0, support the constantly increasing number of such applications deployed over the Internet, and it is a consequence of the need for business integration and collaboration. Moreover, the growing number of services providing the same functionality but different QoS (e.g., price, execution time, and availability) and transactional properties (e.g., compensable or not) has lead to the emergence of several approaches for service selection and recommendation [15].

Different approaches for QoS based service selection have been proposed; for example, using collaborative filtering [19], service reputation [17], multi-devices approaches [12], and user context [10]. In [14], authors propose a consensus-based

© Springer International Publishing Switzerland 2015
M. Younas et al. (Eds.): MobiWis 2015, LNCS 9228, pp. 137–148, 2015.
DOI: 10.1007/978-3-319-23144-0_13

service selection approach in which different agents evaluate a service QoS; then, their evaluations are aggregated into one accepted QoS assessment.

Each one of the existing approaches has its advantages; nonetheless, existing literature lacks from mechanisms to coordinate all those methods and benefit from their multiple perspectives to perform service selection.

The problem tackled in this work is the selection of the most suitable transactional service from a set of functionally equivalent services according to the opinions of multiple independent contributors. We propose a framework to easily rely on crowdsourcing for service selection; crowdsourcing contributors can be independently developed services or human experts. Our framework emphasizes on the definition of a collaborative system to allow contributors to join and participate in the selection of services. Contributors have neither to know each other nor to form social networks to reach consensus about QoS of candidate services. Furthermore, there are no restrictions about how contributors must rank services: they can use any technique for QoS assessment, or they can consider different QoS criteria. The only requisite for contributors is to rank a list of candidate services. Contributors can be evaluated according to their reputation and the quality of their choices.

We structure the rest of this paper as follows. Section 2 presents basic definitions used in this work; Section 3 introduces our framework, and the modeling and details of its components; in Section 4, we explain our experimental study; Section 5 discusses the related work and highlights our contribution; finally, Section 6 outlines the conclusions and future research.

2   Definitions

2.1   Transactional Service

Web services are distributed software components that communicates over the Web. We define a service, denoted as s_c, as follows:

$$s_c(I, O, QoS, TP) \tag{1}$$

where I is a set of inputs the service needs to be invoked, O is a set of outputs the service produces after its execution, QoS its advertised QoS, and TP its transactional property. Inputs and outputs attributes are associated to an ontology. Some examples of QoS are: price, execution time, and availability.

Services that provide transactional support are useful to guarantee reliable execution even in the presence of failures. The most used transactional properties for services are **pivot**, **compensable**, and **retriable** [2]. A service is **pivot** (p), if once it successfully completes, its effects remain forever and cannot be undone; if it fails, it has no effect at all. A service is **compensable** (c), if it exists another service which can undo its execution. A service is **retriable** (r), if it guarantees a successful termination after a finite number of invocations; the **retriable** property can be combined with properties p and c defining **pivot retriable** (pr) and **compensable retriable** (cr) Web services.

2.2 Service Selection

We define a query for service selection as:

$$Q = (I_Q, O_Q, QoS_Q, TP_Q) \tag{2}$$

where I_Q is a set of given inputs, O_Q is a set of required outputs, QoS_Q the required QoS, and TP_Q is the required transactional property. A selected service s_c to answer Q verifies:

$$s_c(I_C, O_C, QoS_C, TP_C) \tag{3}$$

where $I_C \subseteq I_Q$ and $O_C \supseteq O_Q$, $QoS_C \geq QoS_Q$, and

$$
\begin{aligned}
&\text{if } TP_Q = p, \ TP_c \in \{p, pr, c, cr\} \\
&\text{if } TP_Q = pr, \ TP_c \in \{pr, cr\} \\
&\text{if } TP_Q = c, \ TP_c \in \{c, cr\} \\
&\text{if } TP_Q = cr, \ TP_c \in \{cr\}
\end{aligned}
\tag{4}
$$

Equation 4 means that the selected service must provide at least the transactional support required by Q; for example; if we require the **pivot** transactional property, then we can select any transactional service, since they all satisfy the all-or-nothing property of a **pivot** service; however, if we need **pivot retriable** support, we can only select services with the **retriable** property [3].

Given a set of services whose functionality, transactionality, and advertised QoS satisfy Q: should we choose one of them randomly? Should we chose on an existing QoS based selection approach? To answer this questions, we propose a framework called Service Election System that coordinates different QoS based selection methods to benefit from their multiple perspectives, and to assist the service selection process.

3 Service Election System

The general architecture of our approach is presented in Figure 1. The Service Election System is composed by a Candidate Selection Module, an Election module, and a set of voting services $\mathcal{V}$. The Candidate Selection Module takes a query as input and finds the set of candidate services that can answer the query. The Election Module submits the candidate services to voting services, waits for their answers, and selects the winning service. Voting services can use a local execution log containing historical information of considered services. The Web service execution log goal is to provide as much information as possible over candidate services; for example, historical QoS, who or what invoked the service, and the satisfaction of the service invoker after the service execution. The Voting Services Manager is in charge of applying management policies for voting services: the criteria to accept joining voting services; the trust levels for voting service choices; and the exclusion of useless or harmful voting services.

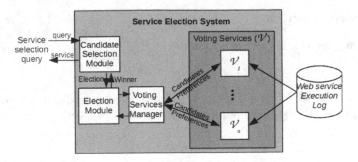

Fig. 1. Framework architecture of our Election System

3.1   Candidate Selection Module

Given a query Q, the candidate selection module obtains a set of candidate services with their corresponding matching degree to Q. This matching degree is a measure to know how much a candidate service satisfies Q in terms of functionality, and it can be calculated using a service matcher such as OWLS-MX [9]. All candidate services are regrouped in classes by matching degrees, as follows:

$$C_Q = \langle \mathcal{C}_1 \succ \mathcal{C}_2 \succ ... \succ \mathcal{C}_{k-1} \succ \mathcal{C}_k \rangle \tag{5}$$

where each class $\mathcal{C}_i$ groups services with the same matching degree, $|\mathcal{C}_i| \geq 1$, and k is the number of different classes, $\mathcal{C}_i$, generated. In other words, $\mathcal{C}_1$ contains the best services regarding their matching degree.

3.2   Voting Services

Voting services are services that can join our system to participate in the process of service selection. A voting service s_v is registered in the set $\mathcal{V}$ and must comply the following functional specification:

$$s_v = (I = \{\mathcal{C}_1, \mathcal{L}\}, O = \{\mathcal{P}_{s_v}\}), \text{ or } s_v = (I = \{\mathcal{C}_1\}, O = \{\mathcal{P}_{s_v}\})$$

where I and O are its inputs and outputs, respectively, and $\mathcal{C}_1$ is the set of candidate services, $\mathcal{L}$ is the execution log (it is an optional input), and $\mathcal{P}_{s_v}$ is the set of candidate services ranked according to s_v:

$$\mathcal{P}_{s_v} = \langle s_{c_1} \succ ... \succ s_{c_{|\mathcal{C}_1|}} \rangle \tag{6}$$

where $|\mathcal{C}_1|$ is the number of candidate services.

3.3   Election Module

At this point, we have an election comprised by a set of voting services $\mathcal{V} = \{s_{v_1}, ..., s_{v_n}\}$ and a set of m candidates in $\mathcal{C}_1$, with $\mathcal{C}_1 \in C_Q$ for a query Q. Each voting service in $\mathcal{V}$ will give its preferences over the candidates in $\mathcal{C}_1$.

Each voting service s_{v_i} has a relation of preference $\succ_i$ (strict total order); therefore, an election will have a *preferences profile* $\mathcal{P}$, which is a tuple of preferences structures, one for each voting service:

$$\mathcal{P} = \langle \mathcal{P}_{s_{v1}}, ..., \mathcal{P}_{s_{vn}} \rangle \tag{7}$$

where $\mathcal{P}_{s_{v_i}}$ are the preferences expressed by the voting service s_{v_i}. The *election module* selects the candidate s_c which maximizes the following equation:

$$z(s_c) = \sum_{i=1}^{n} votingScore_{s_{v_i}}(s_c) * w_{s_{v_i}} \tag{8}$$

where $votingScore_{s_{v_i}}(s_c)$ is the score given to s_c by the voting service s_{v_i} according to the implemented voting system. Different voting systems can be used; for example, Plurality, Borda, k-Approval, and Repeated Alternative Vote [11]. $w_{s_{v_i}}$ is the weight given to the choice of s_{v_i} with $\sum_{i=1}^{n} w_{s_{v_i}} = 1$.

We can have the case where none of the candidates can be elected using only the preferences profile $\mathcal{P}$; for example, if we have two voting services, then we have $\mathcal{P} = \langle \mathcal{P}_{s_{v1}}, \mathcal{P}_{s_{v2}} \rangle$. If the preferred service in $\mathcal{P}_{s_{v1}}$ is different than the preferred $\mathcal{P}_{s_{v2}}$, then we have a tied election, since there are more than one winner service. If it is the case, we select any service in $\mathcal{C}_1$.

Table 1. Notation

Symbol	Description
Q	Service selection query
TP	Transactional property
$\mathcal{L}$	Execution log
$\mathcal{S}$	Service registry
$\mathcal{C}_Q$	Preference relation classes for a query Q
$\mathcal{C}_i$	A class in $\mathcal{C}_Q$, where $\mathcal{C}_1$ is the best ranked class
m	Number of candidate services in $\mathcal{C}_1$
s_c	Candidate service in $\mathcal{S}$
$\mathcal{V}$	Set of voting services
n	Number of voting services in $\mathcal{V}$
s_v	Voting service
$\mathcal{P}_{s_v}$	Candidate services ranked according to a voting service s_v
$\mathcal{P}$	Preferences profile containing rankings of all voting services
$votingScore_{s_{v_i}}(s_c)$	Score given by a voting service s_{v_i} to s_c
$z(s_c)$	Total voting score for s_c

3.4 Algorithms

In this section, we briefly describe the algorithms of the Service Election System. Algorithm 1 is the main algorithm of the system. It receives Q as input and

returns the selected service. It begins by filtering candidate services by transactional property and advertised QoS; then, it calls a service matcher to get
the score of each candidate service s_c. We can parametrize the system with a
threshold for matching degrees (θ) (line 1). If the score of s_c is greater or equal
than θ, it is associated to a class in $\mathcal{C}_Q$ (line 2, see Section 3.1). Algorithm 2 is in
charge of collecting the set of preferences $\mathcal{P}$, which is composed by the individual
answers of voting services in $\mathcal{V}$ (lines 1 and 2). We can use the system parameter
$TIMEOUT$ to set a maximum waiting time for voting services. Once it collects
all the answers, it performs the service election (line 3).

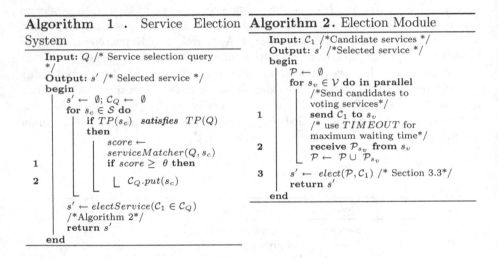

Algorithm 1. Service Election System

Input: Q /* Service selection query */
Output: s' /* Selected service */
begin
  $s' \leftarrow \emptyset; C_Q \leftarrow \emptyset$
  for $s_c \in S$ do
    if $TP(s_c)$ *satisfies* $TP(Q)$ then
      $score \leftarrow serviceMatcher(Q, s_c)$
  1 if $score \geq \theta$ then
  2    $\lfloor\ C_Q.put(s_c)$

  $s' \leftarrow electService(C_1 \in C_Q)$ /*Algorithm 2*/
  return s'
end

Algorithm 2. Election Module

Input: C_1 /*Candidate services */
Output: s' /*Selected service */
begin
  $\mathcal{P} \leftarrow \emptyset$
  for $s_v \in \mathcal{V}$ do in parallel
    /*Send candidates to voting services*/
  1 send C_1 to s_v
    /* use $TIMEOUT$ for maximum waiting time*/
  2 receive $\mathcal{P}_{s_v}$ from s_v
    $\mathcal{P} \leftarrow \mathcal{P} \cup \mathcal{P}_{s_v}$
  3 $s' \leftarrow elect(\mathcal{P}, C_1)$ /* Section 3.3*/
  return s'
end

4 Experimental Evaluation

In this section, we present the experimental evaluation of our approach. We start
by giving details about the implementation and used datasets; we continue with
the analysis of our system in terms of implementation performance and results.

4.1 Implementation and General Setup

All components where written in Java using the Oracle JDK 7. The MPJ Express
[1] 0.38 library was used for parallel processing. The Election Module manages each
voting service in parallel.

We use Web service descriptions from OWLS-TC 2 dataset[2] along with
OWLS-MX. For QoS forecasting, we use Time Series Analysis and Forecasting module of Weka [7]. We have chosen the dataset WS-DREAM [18]. This
dataset contains the monitoring of 100 real services using 150 distributed nodes,
recording more than 1.5 millions service invocations. Each service invocation

---

[1] http://mpj-express.org/
[2] http://projects.semwebcentral.org/projects/owls-tc/

result is described with the IP address of the client using for the invocation and monitoring, service ID, response time in milliseconds, data size, HTTP code, and HTTP message. All components were deployed in a cluster of PCs with the same configuration: Intel Pentium 3.4GHz CPU, 2GB RAM, Debian GNU/Linux 6.0 connected through 100Mbps Ethernet. Finally, all time measurements evaluations were done using `System.nanoTime()` of Java.

We present three default voting services implemented in our framework. They can be removed, or other voting services can be added. For these experiments, we consider that the weights for the choices of voting services are equal.

Basic Voting Service
This basic voting services ranks services according to their normalized advertised QoS parameters. The higher the normalized service QoS is, the better the evaluated service is.

Historical Voting Service
This voting service performs log evaluation, in pursuance of finding the QoS of the candidate service based on their past behavior. We analyze the execution log for a service s_c by considering the following dimensions: *QoS average* $(Qos_{avg}(s_c))$, *availability* $(availability(s_c))$, and *frequency* $(f(s_c))$. The execution log is bounded by a parameter $\mathcal{T}$, indicating until how old services executions will be considered.

The *QoS average* $(Qos_{avg}(s_c))$ based on historical data is calculated by adding up the weighted average of the QoS of the historical executions of s_c. Each execution of s_c is weighted according to how old it is. The *oldness* of a record $r_i^{s_c}$ for a service s_c in the execution log is calculated by:

$$oldness(r_i^{s_c}) = \frac{\mathcal{T} - ts(r_i^{s_c})}{\mathcal{T}} \tag{9}$$

where $ts(r_i^{s_c})$ returns *how much time* has passed since the execution of $r_i^{s_c}$; therefore, the closer the value returned by $oldness(r_i^{s_c})$ to 1, the more recent the execution of $r_i^{s_c}$ is. Then, the QoS weighted average is calculated as following:

$$QoS_{avg}(s_c) = \frac{\sum_{i=1}^{rn} QoS_r(r_i^{s_c}) \times oldness(r_i^{s_c})}{\sum_{i=1}^{n} oldness(r_i^{s_c})} \tag{10}$$

where rn is the number of records of s_c in the execution log. $QoS_r(r_i^{s_c})$ is the sum of the continuous QoS values (e.g., execution time) of the i-th record of a service s_c. Only records of successful executions are taking into account.

The availability of a service s_c is the ratio of the number of successful executions to total executions:

$$availability(s_c) = \frac{|\{r_i^{s_c}, r_i^{s_c} \text{ is a successful execution}\}|}{|\{r_i^{s_c}\}|} \tag{11}$$

and finally, the *frequency* is the the number of executions recorded for a service s_c. The more s_c has been executed, the more impact s_c will have at the moment of choosing the service with the best historical data. We have that *incidence*(s_c) returns the number of executions of s_c recorded in the log, so we can compute the *frequency* as follows:

$$f(s_c) = \frac{incidence(s_c)}{currentDate - \mathcal{T}} \tag{12}$$

We now define the QoS for a service s_c based on historical data:

$$QoS_{Log}(s_c) = [QoS_{avg}(s_c) \times availability(s_c)] + f(s_c) \tag{13}$$

Forecaster Voting Service

At the moment of being consulted about a service, the forecaster voting service will look at the past QoS values of that service, and predict the QoS values using a prediction technique. We have chosen *linear regression* [13] as forecasting model for this service. The QoS forecasting for a given date φ is define as:

$$QoS_\varphi = \alpha + \beta X_\varphi + \varepsilon_\varphi \tag{14}$$

where QoS_φ is the dependent variable, and it is a linear function of X_φ, which represents the date φ and it is the independent variable. α and β will be computed using the principle of least squares and they characterize the population regression line. ε_φ is the randomly error term. In our model, φ will always be the current date.

4.2   Efficiency Evaluation

Figure 2 shows the average execution time taken by the *candidate selection module*. It shows the time of analyzing all candidate services (Candidates in C); the time of analyzing only services that satisfy the required transactional property (Filtered by TP); and the time of analyzing only the services in C_1 (Candidates in C_1).

QoS prediction was performed using 6 instances of the log, with 365, 730, 1095, 1460, 1825, and 2190 log records. Figure 3 shows the execution time for 30

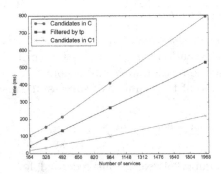 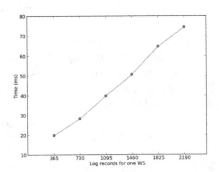

Fig. 2. Candidate selection execution time **Fig. 3.** Forecaster service execution time

days QoS for a given service. Figure 4 shows the average execution time of the *historical voting service* in milliseconds for the 100 services of the dataset using the same 6 log instances.

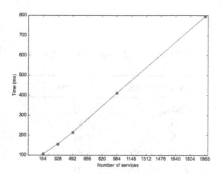
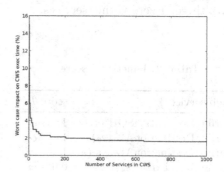

Fig. 4. Historical service execution time   **Fig. 5.** Worst impact over composite Web service execution

Figure 5 shows the worst case additional execution time using our approach for service replacement during composite service executions. We consider 164 equivalent services per service. Depending on the location of the service to replace in the composite service, the replacement may have no impact at all in the execution time. It is represented as a percentage of the composite service execution time. For composite services composed between 1 and 5 services the impact varies from 15% and 5%, while for bigger composite Web services it remains around 2%.

4.3   Effectiveness Evaluation

We submit the query $Q = (\{surfing\}, \{destination\}, c)$. The *candidate selection module* finds 23 candidate services for Q; however, we set $\theta = 0.6$ (see line 1 Algorithm 1), so only 6 are considered, as showed in Table 2. There are 3 exact equivalent candidate services for Q with 1, and other 3 services with score 0.6.

Services are grouped in the following classes: $C_1 = \{s_1, s_2, s_3\}$ and $C_2 = \{s_4, s_5, s_6\}$, where C_1 contains services with score 1, and C_2 services with score 0.6, producing the following preference relation:

$$C_Q = \langle C_1 \succ C_2 \rangle = \langle \{s_1, s_2, s_3\} \succ \{s_4, s_5, s_6\} \rangle \qquad (15)$$

meaning that any service in C_1 is preferred over any other in C_2; therefore, we send only C_1 to the voting services. The voting services return the following preferences:

$$\mathcal{P}_h = \langle s_1 \succ s_3 \succ s_2 \rangle; \; \mathcal{P}_\varphi = \langle s_3 \succ s_1 \succ s_2 \rangle; \; \mathcal{P}_b = \langle s_1 \succ s_3 \succ s_2 \rangle$$

where $\mathcal{P}_h$ are the preferences of the historical voting service, $\mathcal{P}_\varphi$ are the preferences of the forecaster voting service, and $\mathcal{P}_b$ are the preferences of the basic voting service.

Finally, we can have a different elected service depending on the voting services involved; for example, Table 3 shows different possible winners using one, two, three or zero voting services.

Table 2. Functional score

Web service	score	TP
SurfingDestinationSOH (s_1)	1	cr
SurfingDestinationAU (s_2)	1	c
SurfingDestinationAlways (s_3)	1	cr
SurfingRuralArea (s_4)	0.6	cr
SportsDestination (s_5)	0.6	cr
SurfingBeach (s_6)	0.6	cr

Table 3. Elected Web service

Participants	winner
QoS_{log}	s_1
QoS_φ	s_3
QoS_b	s_1
QoS_{log}, QoS_φ	$s_1 \vee s_3$
QoS_{log}, QoS_b	s_1
QoS_φ, QoS_b	$s_1 \vee s_3$
$QoS_{log}, QoS_\varphi, QoS_b$	$s_1 \vee s_3$
$\emptyset$	$s_1 \vee s_2 \vee s_3$

5   Related Work

QoS driven service selection is a well known problem in the service computing area [14]. Some approaches use recommender systems [4,19]; for example, Zheng et al. [19] propose a collaborative filtering approach for predicting service QoS values and making service recommendation based on past user experience. The authors use a user-collaborative mechanism for collecting historical service QoS data; and a QoS prediction approach by combining user-based and item-based collaborative filtering.

Other works use other techniques [1,5,8,10,12,16] for service selection. In [5], the authors propose a recommendation approach inspired in Google Instant Search to provide suggestions during an incremental Web service composition process. A composite Web service execution log is used to identify reliable Web services, while an A* algorithm is used to find composite Web service in real-time, recommending a list of candidate composite Web services according to the partially composite Web service and execution logs. Noteworthy, this work only considers sequential composite Web services, which makes it very limited. The context of intended Web service usage is analyzed in [10] to provide recommendations. Each Web service is semantically annotated with context values, indicating for which context it is suitable, and the context is also modeled in an ontology, so context similarity is calculated by evaluating common description, recommending the most suitable Web service for that context. In [1], different Web service representations are compared considering discovery and recommendation. These representations include the ones extracted from Web service descriptions, Web service textual descriptions, and contextual information (Web service neighbors). Finally, the Web service discovery is proposed based on those different Web service descriptions. In [12], an agent-based system is proposed to recommend multimedia Web services considering the device exploited by the user. Three types of agents are proposed: one associated with each device; one for each user; and a recommender agent that collects information from the other agents to provide the user with recommendations. Finally, in [16], a mechanism for gathering QoS measurements from client and provider sides to support Web service recommendation is presented.

Existing approaches for QoS driven service selection have a lack of flexibility, since they rely on a fixed strategy to do the selection. Our goal in this work is not the competition against existing service selection approaches. Instead, we propose a framework to gather together different service selection approaches and take advantage of their multiple techniques with a minimal effort.

6 Conclusions

We presented a framework for transactional service selection based on voting services. Voting services are independently developed components which can join our system to contribute to the election of services. Each voting service ranks candidate services for selection according to their own criteria, and they do not have to know nor interact with each other; they only requirement is to rank a list of candidate services. Our approach relies on the crowdsourcing power by enabling service selection using crowds of voting services. Our future work concerns the analysis and evaluation of our approach using more realistic scenarios, and present in detail our management policies for voting services. These management policies comprise the criteria to accept joining voting services; the trust levels for voting services; and the exclusion of useless or harmful voting services. Finally, we plan to study and compare the result of using our framework with different voting systems.

References

1. Aznag, M., Quafafou, M., Durand, N., Jarir, Z.: Web services discovery and recommendation based on information extraction and symbolic reputation (2013). CoRR, abs/1304.3268
2. Cardinale, Y., El Haddad, J., Manouvrier, M., Rukoz, M.: Transactional-aware Web Service Composition: A Survey. IGI Global - Advances in Knowledge Management (AKM) Book Series, ch. 6, pp. 2–20 (2011)
3. Cardinale, Y., Rukoz, M.: Fault tolerant execution of transactional compositeweb services: an approach. In: The Fifth International Conference on Mobile Ubiquitous Computing, Systems, Services and Technologies, UBICOMM 2011, pp. 158–164 (2011)
4. Chan, N.N., Gaaloul, W., Tata, S.: A recommender system based on historical usage data for web service discovery. Serv. Oriented Comput. Appl. 6(1), 51–63 (2012)

5. Chen, L., Wu, J., Jian, H., Deng, H., Wu, Z.: Instant recommendation for web services composition. IEEE Transactions on Services Comp. **99**(PrePrints), 1 (2013)
6. Girbea, A., Suciu, C., Nechifor, S., Sisak, F.: Design and implementation of a service-oriented architecture for the optimization of industrial applications. IEEE Transactions on Industrial Informatics **10**(1), 185–196 (2014)
7. Hall, M., Frank, E., Holmes, G., Pfahringer, B., Reutemann, P., Witten, I.H.: The weka data mining software: An update. SIGKDD Explor. Newsl. **11**(1), 10–18 (2009)
8. Kang, G., Liu, J., Tang, M., et al.: Awsr: active web service recommendation based on usage history. In 2012 IEEE 19th Int. Conf. on Web Services (ICWS), pp. 186–193 (2012)
9. Klusch, M., Fries, B., Sycara, K.: Automated semantic web service discovery with OWLS-MX. In: Proceedings of the Fifth Int. Joint Conf. on Autonomous Agents and Multiagent Systems, AAMAS 2006, pp. 915–922. ACM, New York (2006)
10. Liu, L., Lecue, F., Mehandjiev, N.: Semantic content-based recommendation of software services using context. ACM Trans. Web **7**(3), 17:1–17:20 (2013)
11. Mattei, N.: Empirical evaluation of voting rules with strictly ordered preference data. In: Brafman, R. (ed.) ADT 2011. LNCS, vol. 6992, pp. 165–177. Springer, Heidelberg (2011)
12. Rosaci, D., Sarné, G.: Recommending multimedia web services in a multi-device environment. Information Systems **38**(2), 198–212 (2013)
13. Seber, G.A., Lee, A.J.: Linear regression analysis, vol. 936. John Wiley & Sons (2012)
14. Sharifi, M., Manaf, A., Memariani, A., Movahednejad, H., Md Sarkan, H., Dastjerdi, A.: Multi-criteria consensus-based service selection using crowdsourcing. In: 2014 28th Int. Conf. on Advanced Information Networking and Applications Workshops (WAINA), pp. 114–120, May 2014
15. Sheng, Q.Z., Qiao, X., Vasilakos, A.V., Szabo, C., Bourne, S., Xu, X.: Web services composition: A decades overview. Information Sciences **280**, 218–238 (2014)
16. Thio, N., Karunasekera, S.: Automatic measurement of a qos metric for web service recommendation. In: Proceedings of the 2005 Australian Soft. Eng. Conf., pp. 202–211, March 2005
17. Vu, L.-H., Hauswirth, M., Aberer, K.: QoS-based service selection and ranking with trust and reputation management. In: Meersman, R., Tari, Z. (eds.) OTM 2005. LNCS, vol. 3760, pp. 466–483. Springer, Heidelberg (2005)
18. Zheng, Z., Lyu, M.: Collaborative reliability prediction of service-oriented systems. In: 2010 ACM/IEEE 32nd Int. Conf. on Software Engineering, vol. 1, pp. 35–44 (2010)
19. Zheng, Z., Ma, H., Lyu, M.R., King, I.: Qos-aware web service recommendation by collaborative filtering. IEEE Transactions Services Comp. **4**(2), 140–152 (2011)

Mobile e-Services and Open Data in e-Government Processes - Concept and Design

Dan Johansson[1]([✉]), Josefin Lassinantti[2], and Mikael Wiberg[1]

[1] Umeå University, SE-901 87 Umeå, Sweden
{dan.johansson,mikael.wiberg}@informatik.umu.se
[2] Luleå University of Technology, SE-971 87 Luleå, Sweden
josefin.lassinantti@ltu.se
http://www.informatik.umu.se
http://www.ltu.se

Abstract. The traditional service life cycle starts with the formulation of required needs and ends with the adoption and ownership of the service. In an e-government context, this takes the form of citizens consuming services provided by the public sector bodies. We examine how a combination of mobile e-services and open data can extend and allow possible citizen-driven continuation of the service life cycle. The chosen method is a concept-driven approach, manifesting our concept in a digital prototype, which allows citizens to generate and acquire open data, as well as develop and publish their own e-services.

Keywords: Mobile e-services · Open data · e-Government

1 Introduction

An e-service is *"an act or performance that creates value and provides benefits for customers through a process that is stored as an algorithm and typically implemented by networked software"* [16], or, simplified, a service delivered over the Internet [35]. The mobility of an e-service can be measured in terms of portability, i.e the ability of the user to change location or device while actively using the service. The mobility is further enhanced, should the functionality be increased due to terminal and user mobility, if the e-service has cross-platform platform support, and if it supports offline usage. [21] Thus, a *mobile* e-service is more than just an e-service ported to a mobile device.

There are many stakeholders involved in the e-service area. For example, there are the service owners, the service innovators, and service developers, who may or may not belong to the same organizations. Further, there are integrators, maintainers, administrators, operators, and possibly even third-party e-service providers. [1] [25] One of the most important stakeholders is the e-service consumer. As the consumer contributes with information and perceptions of the service quality and value, his/her involvement and participation is desirable

© Springer International Publishing Switzerland 2015
M. Younas et al. (Eds.): MobiWis 2015, LNCS 9228, pp. 149–160, 2015.
DOI: 10.1007/978-3-319-23144-0_14

throughout the whole service process [13]. Mobile e-services rely on interaction and information exchange between the user and the service provider [21], and research points out that alongside enhanced adoption and increased availability, better and more innovative co-operation between stakeholders is an important element when trying to transform the opportunities for citizen's participation in public service processes [23].

Open data could play a role in supporting co-operation, as well as increasing availability. Open data is perceived as a new wave of transformative ICT, currently emerging to bring new innovations and new values. This transformation means that public sector data is now being made accessible on the Internet in digital formats [19], thus leveraging the previous public access by making specific requests and getting the data delivered on paper in accordance to freedom of information rights [15]. Putting the public data to use in new contexts and by other people than the original public sector employees performing the public task defines the re-use of public data [41]. Enabling citizen access to public data is seen to increase the citizens' opportunities to engage in public processes [11] [27], and thus become more engaged and helpful in e.g. fighting corruption [6] and interacting with decision makers in matters that pose as important [29].

This re-use of data by citizens and companies is believed to foster new creative and innovative impacts among member states in EU and is fueled by realisation of the European directive for Public Sector Information (PSI) which legislates the issues related to the opening up of data for public sector bodies [8]. Aiming for a new information market and addressing the knowledge society, as well as new ICT enabled products and services, and increased circulation of information, can be seen as important steps towards an open society. [37].

1.1 Purpose

This study sets out to explore a new ICT-platform, combining mobile e-services with open data and extending the traditional life cycle of citizen involvement in public sector service processes. The chosen method is a concept-driven approach, manifesting our concept in a digital prototype. By manifesting the concept in a concrete design, we can expose our thought platform to both theoretical and in use evaluation. As an example of our concept, we describe and apply a mobile e-service allowing road surface quality measurements of walkways and cycle paths. The data is automatically compiled and presented through a free of access municipal application directed towards citizens, who can use the information for route planning. The app is part of an open framework, allowing citizens to design their own mobile e-services and/or creating their own subset of available services choosing from a range of existing services provided by the municipality. Moreover, the road quality measurements are stored as open data, allowing people to include them in self-made services, mediated through the municipal application. Our hypothesis is that this concept can transform the opportunities for citizen's participation in public service processes and thereby increase our understanding of ICT as a driver for transformed relations between citizens and public sector, that are valuable not only to public sector but also to society through new services.

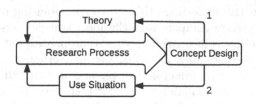

Fig. 1. Concept-driven design research [39]

1.2 Methodology

To advance the area of mobile e-services and open data, we chose a concept-driven approach [39], trying to manifest a theoretical concept in a concrete design. As figure 1 depicts, concept-driven design research can be used to both support the theoretical development (arrow 1), and the use situation (arrow 2). The idea is that the concrete manifestation – the artifact or prototype – should express a composition that incorporates the concept design as a "whole". The artifact thus becomes an object of study that say things about the concept and advances the area (at the same time enhancing the use situation). All in all, the artifact functions as a proof-of-concept.

The concept-driven approach consists of seven stages, being: 1) concept generation, 2) concept exploration, 3) internal concept critique, 4) design of artifacts, 5) external design critique, 6) concept revisited, and 7) concept contextualization. Concept generation and exploration is about defining the concept, its foundation and most important properties. The internal concept critique relates the design and its underlying concepts to the established theoretical foundation. The concept is then manifested within a concrete design, that undergoes external design critique (i.e. tests and evaluation).This serves as a basis for theory development, used for revising and refining the concept. Finally, concept contextualization is about relating and valuing this new concept against the current body of concepts and theory in the field. The disposition of our paper follows the chronology of the chosen method, where we carry out the first four steps from concept generation to artifact design.

2   Conceptualization

Citizens and companies are pictured as the target group for a new information market. Citizens are seen as not only consumers of public information, but also as future developers of new digital services, and the public sector as its provider of raw material. As Don Tapscott describes the transformation: *"government becomes a platform for the creation of public value and social innovation.*

It provides resources, sets rules, and mediates disputes, but it allows citizens,
non-profits, and the private sector to do most of the heavy lifting" [27]. The
European Commission [10] underlined this viewpoint, pointing out Public Sector Body (PSB) and private companies as the ideal stakeholders for providing
open data, excluding citizens in providing other than private data.

Data about various topics such as maps, weather, crime rates, traffic, and
infrastructure, budgets, environmental ratings, and census studies are being
released in open and machine readable formats. It is suggested that open government, and in particular its key pillar, i.e. open data, has greatly influenced the
way the public sector interacts with citizens, the way innovation is created, and
by whom services is created [27]. In this sense, open data as a concept contains
strong influences from other crowd-based open movements such as open source
and open access [42].

However, both practice and theory about managing these transformations
remains scarce and current discourse is mainly targeting the challenges concerning publication of data rather than the challenges of obtaining value from
innovative use of the data [4] [20]. In particular, understanding how new forms of
relations between citizens and public sector organizations can enable citizens in
participating in public processes is being neglected in many open data initiatives
[11]; [38]. Not only does this pose as a problem for the future potential of regarding citizens as a source of knowledge for rationalize public sector processes and
increase democratic processes, it also becomes a hinder for seeing the citizens'
possible participation in new value creating services [7] [11].

In terms of e-services targeting citizen involvement and participation, much
work has been directed towards social networking: the Wave platform [28] utilizes a combination of argument visualization, social networking and modern
web technology to enhance debates in community environments; the Initiative
Mapper [26] helps immigrants communicate and collaborate through the social
web; and [34] examines the support for e-participation and e-governance through
social media channels such as Facebook and Twitter. Social software allows quick
access to information and easy means of networking. On the other hand, its laden
with barriers such as redundancy with regard to other systems, a loss of control
over one's data and knowledge, and its also somewhat time-consuming. [33] E-
participation through social networking typically allows participation through
service consumption and data generation, not through service development. In
many cases (e.g. [14]) social networking services only offer one-way information.

While open data is increasingly published using cloud storage technology,
access and provision of the same data is to a large extent provided through
apps, often compiled as service content [7]. This implies that when examining
citizen involvement in innovative open data use, one cannot neglect the media-
tor of this data; the mobile device connects the user to the open data through
the mobile app and service. This is also substantiated by research that points
out the mobile device as a driver for open data, superseding web solutions targeted for laptops and stationary computers [27]. Thus, mobility and the mobile

e-service has the potential to play a key part in transforming citizen involvement in e-government processes.

One way to describe the service process is through the Customer Service Life Cycle (CSLC) [18]. The CSLC represents an established way to depict a typical transaction between a customer and a service emitter. It consists of four main phases, being requirements, acquisition, ownership, and retirement. Within e-government processes, requirements, acquisition, and ownership are the most germane [40], and as e-services emitted by governmental instances most often is free of charge, the term ownership will be replaced by service consumption in our argumentation. *Requirements* is about assisting citizens in choosing the e-services most suitable for their needs. *[Service] acquisition* deals with helping the citizens obtain the desired transactional outcomes. The *service consumption* phase denotes when the citizen, more or less autonomously, uses the service. Activities like service development and data generation is not part of the traditional CSLS. Today, these pre-CSLS phases are almost exclusively managed by PSB or third party developers. As a recent report from the European Public Sector Information Platform (EPSI) [3] points out, this also causes problems for the PSB to foresee how citizen value different types of offered data.

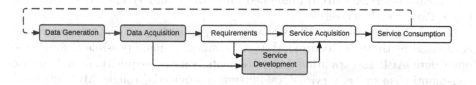

Fig. 2. Our concept; our CSLC extension marked with gray background/dotted line

Our concept is built around the combination of mobile e-services and open data, applied in the e-government service process context. The novel components, besides the actual combination of the two technology areas, are 1) the addition of data generation, data acquisition, and service development into the CSLS, and 2) the possible citizen-driven continuation of the CSLC, during or after the service consumption phase. As shown before, e-services are mediated through transmission over computer networks, and therefore have a digital nature. Data becomes the atomic unit of these services, and thus has to be generated in some way for the service to exist. This data generation is carried out in the *data generation* phase, and in our concept we allow the generation to be conducted by either government or citizens, or preferably both. In our conceptual model, data is made publicly available through an open data API. This allows *data acquisition* which may or may not be linked to the rest of the CSLC, and again offered to both government and citizens. Given an open and easy-to-use framework for service design, once again we extend the CSLC to include citizens in the e-service process, in this phase by allowing citizens to compose the actual service (*service development*). Although uncommon, there are some related projects where the provision of citizen service development has been targeted. IFTTT [17] is an online service connecting different e-services through triggers and actions. This allows users to create composite services, i.e. having Dropbox react upon the user's Instagram activity. On a municipal level, there is the "My Skellefteå" framework [22], providing templates and API:s for HTML5 and JavaScript based e-service development and distribution, open for public use. Another example is SATIN [5], a toolkit targeting non-programmers, allowing citizens to develop mobile services through a drag-and-drop editor. However, these earlier projects do not combine service development with the generation or acquisition of open data. Figure 2 depicts our concept.

3   Results

Following the concept-driven design approach we created a concrete prototype manifesting our concept. The target was to incorporate the concept design as a "whole", making it possible for us to expose the concept to evaluation both in theory and (in our forthcoming work) in a use situation. The prototype consisted of four major connected modules, being 1) Roadroid, a tablet and an app used for road surface quality measurements; 2) An open data API; 3) "My Skellefteå", a municipal e-service platform intended for citizens; and 4) The "Walkways and Cycle Paths" mobile e-service.

The design incorporates all six phases of our extended CSLC. Data generation is carried out through Roadroid; data acquisition is made possible through the open data API; the traditional requirements, service acquisition, and service consumption, as well as service development, is provided through "My Skellefteå" and the "Walkways and Cycle Paths" mobile e-service.

3.1   Data Generation: Roadroid

Road quality decreases over time. Climate and traffic effects the road system (normally consisting of pavement, subterranean layers, and drainage) and wears it down [2]. Meanwhile, road maintenance costs grows almost exponentially, along with increased travel times, logistic problems, and injury risks. Road quality can be measured using a roughness measurement system, e.g. the International Roughness Index (IRI) [36], developed by the World Bank and adopted as the standard measurement system in many countries. IRI is a calculation of the vertical acceleration through the distance covered. Today it is the most commonly used index for evaluating road systems in the world.

Roadroid [12] is a service providing road quality measurements through an app installed on a regular smartphone. The smartphone is calibrated and positioned in a vehicle. The accelerometer analyzes 100 vibrations per second (i.e. a 100 Hz signal) and calculates one IRI value per second. Experiments [24] show that the precision of Roadroid correlates to laser measurement systems with a degree of 81%. Roadroid measurements are always accompanied by timestamps

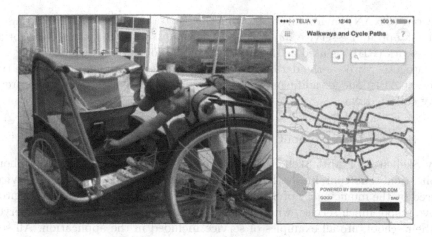

Fig. 3. Left: Roadroid installation; Right: Walkways and Cycle Paths Mobile e-Service

and GPS data, making it possible to export road quality information that is both location-based and temporal.

In our concept manifestation, the Roadroid app was installed on a pre-calibrated Samsung GT-P1000 running an Android 2.2 OS, and then mounted on an approved bicycle trailer, using a dedicated fastener to fixate its position. The trailer was also equipped with 10 kg of ballast, as per recommendation from the Roadroid manufacturer. Tires were controlled to have an air pressure of 1.8 bar (matching the recommended span of 1.5-2.0 bar). The initial data collection was carried out during a two month period during summer. Six people were taking turns in using a bicycle and the attached Roadroid-equipped trailer to cover a total of 70,9 km of walkways and bicycle paths. Before each round of tests, air pressure and tablet fixation was checked. Anomalies during test rounds were noted in a dedicated form, along with other observations such as weather conditions and visual inspections of the bicycle paths.

Roadroid stands as an example of a data generation system, that could be provided to citizens in different ways, e.g. by municipal libraries, lending them out in the same way as they currently do with books, tablets and other media.

3.2   Data Acquisition: The Open Data API

When allowing citizens to access and use raw open data, this activity is added to the CSLC. In our extended CSLC, data acquisition connects data generation to both requirements and service development. When data is communally collected, it needs to be transferred to the open data repository in a pre-defined way in order to map the data already in storage. Meeting this requirement, our design is influenced by standards for open APIs aiming to transfer open data in a structured form, commonly used for services like "Fix my street" [32]. In addition to this, data acquisition also includes an open API for citizens to retrieve stored data [9]. Our proposed design uses a scripted Comprehensive Knowledge Archive

Network (CKAN) environment, allowing open data download and providing an API for app and e-service integration. The open source Resource Description Framework (RDF) is used as the standard model for data interchange. [31]

Altogether, we see the data acquisition phase as being constructed with two different APIs; one for adding structured data, and one for retrieving the previously collected data.

3.3   Service Development

"My Skellefteå" ("Mitt Skellefteå", in Swedish) is a free of charge smartphone application that contains both public information and many of the services offered by the municipality of Skellefteå. Recycling, opening hours, and an interactive school lunch service, where pupils can rate the food that they are served at their school, are all examples of service included in the application. All services are developed using HTML5, and thus the application (which is available for both Android and iOS) functions as an enhanced web browser – a dedicated mobile e-service container. Most services are developed by Skellefteå municipality, but one of the services is a meta-service, allowing anyone to develop HTML5-based services and then run these through the "My Skellefteå" application. In that way, everyone with rudimentary web programming knowledge can contribute to the service development within the municipality. The application is part of a larger framework, offering back-end services such as database and server-side script support, a service library containing information about both services and devices, and both internal and external API:s for hardware access, geographical positioning, and enhanced communication. Templates help preserve a uniform look and feel of all services included in the "My Skellefteå" framework. As services are HTML5-based, they can often be accessed through an ordinary web browser as well, and thus not exclusively bound to the "My Skellefteå" framework, although the framework typically enhances the services. In summary, the "My Skellefteå" framework acts as a e-service marketplace, e-service development platform, and e-service container in one. [22]

The "Walkways and Cycle Paths" mobile e-service was implemented as a service within the "My Skellefteå" framework. As mobile e-services have been proven qualitatively different from traditional e-services [21], we followed existing guidelines for mobile e-services in our design. First, the mobile e-service was designed with full service mobility in mind. It should be reachable regardless of device, network, or location. The Android and iOS "My Skellefteå" "container applications" makes the service available on the two largest mobile platforms today, the app is easy to find in both Google Play and App Store. The service can also be accessed through an ordinary web browser, although this would be postulated by the user being aware of the actual "Walkways and Cycle Paths" service URL. The service is user-centered as it allows users to participate in development, usage, and upkeep of the service, although it also has the potential to aggregate measurement data from many sources, capitalizing on the co-operative features of joint creation. Direct two-way communication is also implemented through a basic service already included in the "My Skellefteå" platform allowing the user to contact the municipality making a direct phone call or through multimedia messages, and through a default contact-form embedded in all e-services offered through the framework (the "Walkways and Cycle Paths" being no exception to this). E-service UI design is accomplished using the "My Skellefteå" HTML5 and CSS3 templates, giving a uniform look-and-feel to all the mobile e-services within the framework. This also helps in achieving the goal of platform independence. As for the usefulness of the mobile e-service, this will be evaluated as part of future work, using real users as test subjects.

4 Conclusions

In this paper we have presented a mobile e-service and open data concept. The novel components in our concept, besides the actual combination of mobile e-services and open data, are 1) the addition of data generation, data acquisition, and service development into the service life cycle, and 2) the possible citizen-driven continuation of the service life cycle, during or after the service consumption phase. We allow the data generation to be conducted by either government or citizens, or preferably both. In our conceptual model, data is made publicly available through an open data API. This allows data acquisition which may or may not be linked to the rest of the service life cycle, and again offered to both government and citizens. Given an open and easy-to-use framework for service design, once again we extend the service life cycle to include citizens in the e-service process, in this phase by allowing citizens to compose the actual service (service development).

We have demonstrated how our concept could work in the context of e-government to support citizen involvement through the development of a concept design. Further, we have developed and evaluated our concept design according to the first four steps in the method of concept-driven design, being *concept generation, concept exploration, internal concept critique,* and *design of artifacts.*

Future work will include the last three steps of the conceptual design approach, being *external design critique, concept revisited,* and *concept contextualization.* We intend to include our design, based on our extended CSLC, in a focus group study, producing concentrated data about this certain phenomena in a relatively accessible way [30], which is very suitable when working with concept-driven interaction design research. This will be important for revisiting the concept, finding support for our ideas and validating the prototype with its underlying concept. Our main purpose will be to continue the examination of the possible transformation of citizen involvement in e-service processes.

Acknowledgments. The work presented in this article was partially funded by the Sense Smart City project (sensesmartcity.org) supported by EU Structural Funds, Skellefteå Municipality and the Regional Council of Västerbotten. The authors would especially like to thank Elin Blom and her town hosts at the municipal Technical office for prototype data generation. Our thanks also goes to Lars Forslöf and Martin Snygg at Roadroid for valuable technology support.

References

1. Al-Dabbous, N., Al-Yatama, A., Saleh, K.: Assessment of the trustworthiness of e-service providers. In: Proceedings of the 2nd Kuwait Conference on e-Services and e-Systems, KCESS 2011, pp. 24:1–24:7. ACM, New York (2011)
2. Anyala, M., Odoki, J., Baker, C.: Hierarchical asphalt pavement deterioration model for climate impact studies. International Journal of Pavement Engineering 15(3), 251–266 (2014)
3. Bargiotti, L., De Keyzer, M., Goedertier, S., Loutas, N.: Value-based prioritisation of open government data investments (2014), european Public Sector Information Platform. Topic Report No. 2014/08
4. Bekkers, V., Homburg, V.: The myths of e-government: Looking beyond the assumptions of a new and better government. The Information Society 23(5), 373–382 (2007)
5. Bergvall-Kåreborn, B., Broberg, A., Lassinantti, J., Davoli, L., Kuenen, S., Palmquist, L., Parnes, P., Ståhlbröst, A., Synnes, K., Wennberg, P.: User toolkits for citizen-centric mobile service innovation. In: eChallenges e-2012 Conference Proceedings. IIMC International Information Management Corporation Ltd. (2012)
6. Bertot, J.C., Jaeger, P.T., Grimes, J.M.: Using icts to create a culture of transparency: E-government and social media as openness and anti-corruption tools for societies. Government Information Quarterly 27(3), 264–271 (2010)
7. Conradie, P., Mulder, I., Choenni, S.: Rotterdam open data: exploring the release of public sector information through co-creation. In: 2012 18th International ICE Conference on Engineering, Technology and Innovation (ICE), pp. 1–10 (2012)
8. Cox, P., Alemanno, G.: Directive 2003/98/ec of the european parliament and of the council of 17 november 2003 on the re-use of public sector information. Official Journal of the European Union, Brussels (2003)
9. Ding, L., Lebo, T., Erickson, J.S., DiFranzo, D., Williams, G.T., Li, X., Michaelis, J., Graves, A., Zheng, J.G., Shangguan, Z., Flores, J., McGuinness, D.L., Hendler, J.A.: {TWC} logd: A portal for linked open government data ecosystems. Web Semantics: Science, Services and Agents on the World Wide Web 9(3), 325–333 (2011). semantic Web Dynamics Semantic Web Challenge, 2010
10. European Commission. DG CONNECT: A european strategy on the data value chain (2014). http://ec.europa.eu/information_society/newsroom/cf/dae/document.cfm?doc_id=3488
11. Evans, A.M., Campos, A.: Open government initiatives: Challenges of citizen participation. Journal of Policy Analysis and Management 32(1), 172–185 (2013)
12. Forslöf, L.: Roadroid: continuous road condition monitoring with smart phones. In: 17th IRF World Meeting (2013)
13. Grönroos, C., Heinonen, F., Isoniemi, K., Lindholm, M.: The netoffer model: a case example from the virtual marketspace. Management Decision 38(4), 243–252 (2000)
14. Harris, C.S., Winter, J.S.: An exploratory study of social networking services as a potential vehicle for e-participation in the city and county of honolulu. Int. J. Electron. Gov. Res. 9(2), 63–84 (2013)
15. Hazell, R., Worthy, B.: Assessing the performance of freedom of information. Government Information Quarterly 27(4), 352–359 (2010)
16. Hofacker, C.F., Goldsmith, R.E., Bridges, E., Swilley, E.: E-services: a synthesis and research agenda. In: E-Services, DUV, pp. 13–44 (2007)
17. IFTTT: Put the internet to work for you. - ifttt (2014). https://ifttt.com

18. Ives, B., Learmonth, G.P.: The information system as a competitive weapon. Commun. ACM **27**(12), 1193–1201 (1984)
19. Janssen, K.: The influence of the psi directive on open government data: An overview of recent developments. Government Information Quarterly **28**(4), 446–456 (2011)
20. Janssen, M., Charalabidis, Y., Zuiderwijk, A.: Benefits, adoption barriers and myths of open data and open government. Information Systems Management **29**(4), 258–268 (2012)
21. Johansson, D., Andersson, K.: 4th Generation e-services: requirements for the development of mobile e-services. In: eChallenges e-2013 Conference Proceedings. IIMC International Information Management Corporation Ltd. (2013)
22. Johansson, D., Andersson, K.: A cross-platform application framework for html5-based e-services. In: Proceedings of the 11th Annual IEEE Consumer Communications & Networking Conference: 5th IEEE CCNC International Workshop on Mobility Management in the Networks of the Future World, MobiWorld 2014, pp. 396–400 (2014)
23. Johansson, D., Andersson, K.: Mobile e-services: State of the art and focus areas for research. International Journal of e-Services and Mobile Applications (2014)
24. Johnston, M.: Using cell-phones to monitor road roughness. Tech. rep., University of Auckland, Auckland, New Zealand (2013)
25. Kamal, M.M., Weerakkody, V.: Examining the role of stakeholder's in adopting enterprise application integration technologies in local government domain. International Journal of E-Services and Mobile Applications (IJESMA) **2**(4), 42–59 (2010)
26. Laanpere, M., Tammsaar, K., Sousa, S.: A case study on using social media for e-participation: design of initiative mapper web service. In: Proceedings of the 5th International Conference on Theory and Practice of Electronic Governance, ICEGOV 2011, pp. 289–292 (2011)
27. Lathrop, D., Ruma, L.: Open government : [collaboration, transparency, and participation in practice]. O'Reilly, Sebastopol (2010)
28. Lee, D., Menda, Y.P., Peristeras, V., Price, D.: The wave platform: Utilising argument visualisation, social networking and web 2.0 technologies for eparticipation. International Journal of E-Services and Mobile Applications (IJESMA) **3**(3), 69–85 (2011)
29. Meijer, A.J., Curtin, D., Hillebrandt, M.: Open government: connecting vision and voice. International Review of Administrative Sciences **78**(1), 10–29 (2012)
30. Morgan, D.L.: Focus groups as qualitative research, 2nd edn. Sage, Thousand Oaks (1997)
31. OpenNorth: Opennorth - open data in the north of sweden (2014). http://www.opennorth.se/
32. OpenPlans: Open311 - a collaborative model and open standard for civic issue tracking (2014). http://www.open311.org/
33. Pellegrini, T.: Semantic web awareness 2009. a comparative study on approaches to social software and the semantic web. Tech. rep., Semantic Web Company, Vienna, Italy (2009)
34. Rojas, J.M., Ruiz, C.J., Farfán, C.: e-participation and e-governance at web 2.0 in local governments of colombia. In: Proceedings of the 5th International Conference on Theory and Practice of Electronic Governance, ICEGOV 2011, pp. 301–304 (2011)
35. Rowley, J.: An analysis of the e-service literature: towards a research agenda. Internet Research **16**(3), 339–359 (2006)

36. Sayers, M.W., Gillespie, T.D., Queiroz, A.: The international road roughness experiment. establishing correlation and a calibration standard for measurements. Tech. Rep. 45, World Bank (1986)

37. Schultz, M., Shatter, A.: Directive 2013/37/eu of the european parliament and of the council of 26 June 2013 amending directive 2003/98/ec on the re-use of public sector information. Official Journal of the European Union, Brussels (2013)

38. Shane, P.M.: Online consultation and political communication in the era of obama: an introduction. In: Connecting Democracy: Online Consultation and the Flow of Political Communication, pp. 1–20. MIT Press, Cambridge (2012)

39. Stolterman, E., Wiberg, M.: Concept-driven interaction design research. Human-Computer Interaction 25(2), 95–118 (2010)

40. Tan, C.W., Benbasat, I., Cenfetelli, R.T.: It-mediated customer service content and delivery in electronic governments: An empirical investigation of the antecedents of service quality. MIS Q. 37(1), 77–109 (2013)

41. de Vries, M.: Charging for psi re-use - a snap shot of the state of affairs in europe (2012). http://epsiplatform.eu/topicreports, topic Report. European Public Sector Information Platform (retrieved from)

42. Yu, H., Robinson, D.G.: The new ambiguity of "open government". UCLA Law Review Disclosure 59, 178–208 (2012)

Data Analysis as a Service: An Infrastructure for Storing and Analyzing the Internet of Things

Martin Lehmann[2], Andreas Biørn-Hansen[2], Gheorghita Ghinea[1,2],
Tor-Morten Grønli[2(✉)], and Muhammad Younas[3]

[1] Brunel University, London, UK
George.ghinea@brunel.ac.uk
[2] Westerdals Oslo ACT, Faculty of Technology, Oslo, Norway
{martin,tmg}@westerdals.no, andreasb.nor@gmail.com
[3] Oxford Brookes University, Oxford, UK
m.younas@brookes.ac.uk

Abstract. As the Internet of Things (IoT) is becoming an increasingly trendy topic both for individuals, businesses and governments, the need for academically reviewed and developed prototypes focusing on certain aspects of IoT are increasing as well. Throughout this paper we propose an architecture and a technology stack for creating real-time applications focusing on time-series data generated by IoT devices. The architecture and technology stack are then implemented through a proof-of-concept prototype named Office Analysis as a Service, DaaS, a data-centric web application developed using Meteor.js and MongoDB. We also propose a data structure for storing time-series data in a MongoDB document for optimal query performance of large datasets. One common research challenge in the IoT, *security*, is considered only briefly, and is of utmost importance in future research.

Keywords: Internet of things · Mongodb · Data analysis as a protocol · Meteor · Restful services · Reactive visualisation

1 Introduction

The Internet of Things (IoT) is perhaps the fastest emerging technology trend of the present time. The IoT technologies and applications are still in their infancy [6], and so the academic community must thoroughly address the area. Although 'IoT' was initially meant to describe a network of RadioFrequency ID-enabled devices, it has since been expanded to the following widely accepted definition [6]:

> *a dynamic global network infrastructure with self-configuring capabilities based on standard and interoperable communication protocols where physical and virtual Things have identities, physical attributes, and virtual personalities and use intelligent interfaces, and are seamlessly integrated into the information network* (Kranenburg, 2007 cited in [6]).

M. Younas et al. (Eds.): MobiWis 2015, LNCS 9228, pp. 161–169, 2015.
DOI: 10.1007/978-3-319-23144-0_15

It becomes clear that the Internet of Things indeed encompasses all devices with a sensor, but there is also a second implication: the huge number of data points that will inevitably be collected is of no use to anyone unless it is processed. The definition also presents us with several implicit challenges, backed by Xu et al. [6] and Palattella et al. [4]. These include, but are not limited to, privacy, distribution and maintenance, and security concerns in the distributed system that is the IoT. These are all important areas to explore, but outside the scope of this paper.

Also important to mention is the Web of Things (WoT) [1]: the software layer on top of the Internet of Things. This paper mainly focuses on the programming model side of an IoT application, and is thus mostly concerned with the WoT. Furthermore, standards are a real concern. This is described in Palattella et al. [4], which emphasises emerging industry alliances and IEEE/IETF working groups as the key to success. Finally, the pre-eminent concern of this paper is the gap of knowledge with regard to modelling and implementing complete IoT-oriented applications, as described by Paganelli, Turchi and Giuli [3].

This paper first revisits the current state of research on the fields of the Internet and Web of Things, respectively. It then presents an architectural model and proof-of-concept implementation of a full-stack IoT-oriented application which accepts, stores, and provides access to the data in addition to subscription to real-time feeds for new data points. Third, it compares the experiences from modelling and developing the application to the existing research. Lastly, the most important lessons are highlighted and briefly discussed.

2   Related Work

In this section we consider relevant literature and related work within the field. Xu et al. [6] contribute a major review of the current research on the Internet of Things (IoT). A very recent survey paper [6] identifies several key gaps in the current knowledge body regarding the Internet of Things. The main points - cost, security, standardisation, and technology – are all areas that will need to be explored further, but only standardisation and technology are considered in this paper. Additionally, they propose a service-oriented architecture (SOA) style approach to the Web of Things. This approach is not considered by this paper. As mentioned in the introduction, Paganelli et al. [3] describes a lack of actually modelled and implemented applications as a major hole in the current research body. This paper also refers to a relatively large number of other papers proposing middleware and frameworks for designing applications in the Web of Things. However, Palattella et al. [4] claim that what may have previously seemed impossible given the restrictions of the Internet of Things in terms of building a standards-compliant stack may indeed become a reality. They propose a highly technical communication stack for an entire application, but have not actually considered implementing a system. It is worth noting that their stack includes IETF's RFC 7252 - the Constrained Application Protocol (COAP) (2014) for application layer communication.

Xu et al. [6] also mention context awareness as an important factor in the Internet of Things, as millions and billions of sensors will be connected, collectively producing extreme amounts of data. While not considered by this paper, using context awareness and artificial intelligence to filter out meaningful, important data will be a great tool as we begin to find more and more use cases for the Internet and Web of Things.

It seems that there is no lack of proposed frameworks, protocols, and standards for connecting things to the internet and making them part of the web. There is no shortage of frameworks for the actual communication between devices and servers, either, and we have quite a few contributions regarding storage of very large numbers of data points. We also have much research on analysing the data on the field of Big Data, but that is outside the scope of this paper.

Disregarding cost, privacy, and security, the main problem of the current Web of Things research body seems to arise only when committing to building a complete full-stack application: there is no standard, proven, manufacturer-independent way to implement a complete application for gathering and analysing data from a custom Internet of Things system. Indeed, as Xu et al. [6] put it: the Internet of Things is still in its infancy.

3   Data Analysis as a Service (DSaaS)

A clear gap identified in the previous section is the lack of sample implementations of full-stack applications where communication, storage, analysis opportunities, and availability are all thoroughly discussed and actually implemented. DSaaS is an attempt to start bridging this gap, but will naturally only provide the perspective of one domain, one technology stack, and one use case. Very briefly, DSaaS accepts and stores data from providers (sensors), pushes the new data to a very simple customisable dashboard, and provides (optionally real-time) access to the data sets. Security is not considered in the prototype. It was implemented with the sole goal of building a complete application designed to handle data from the Internet and Web of things.

The current architecture and technology stack is the result of several iterations in which we experimented and prototyped in order to find the most well-fitting combination for our paper. We initially laid out a few requirements for the architecture and stack to support. Examples of such include the ability to rapidly prototype the artifact, support real-time data synchronization at some level, and it should fit into previously discovered challenges related to the IoT.

The DSaaS core is a central server written in Meteor[1] providing access to both storing and retrieving data. It also provides the option of subscribing to a change feed for a specific resource to receive updates to the dataset in real-time. DSaaS also provides a very simple real-time dashboard (Fig. 1) for monitoring incoming data. Finally, it provides a management interface for customizing the dashboard and defining the *integrations* that can be displayed in the dashboard.

---

[1] https://www.meteor.com

Fig. 1. The simple dashboard with two integrations

Fig. 2. Sample integrations

An integration is a data provider of any kind that will upload data to the service. An integration is expected to be a single sensor whose data is sent to the Internet - typically via an Internet-enabled microcontroller - although it is possible to get creative. As seen in Fig. 2, creating an integration automatically generates a unique ID, which must be included in requests to upload data as identification. In addition to endpoints for storing data, DSaaS provides two different types of endpoints for accessing the stored data. The simplest of these is a traditional REST endpoint that exposes data from each sensor as a resource with a unique URI: an HTTP GET request fetches data from the present day. Of course, applying filters to fetch for example all stored data, data from the present week, or data from the last ten days, would be helpful, but this was outside the scope of the prototype.

The second data access endpoint provides a real-time change feed that sends all new relevant data points to the consumer as it is stored in the database. The protocol for real-time data updates is Meteor's Distributed Data Protocol (DDP)[2], which is based on WebSockets. Because DDP's publish and subscribe-pattern (pub-sub) is agnostic [2] and not coupled with Meteor.js, DDP can be used to communicate between server-to-client, machine-to-machine, etc. This goes back to the interoperability aspect identified in several reviewed paper. It could naturally be possible to define a custom protocol with plain WebSockets, and that would enable building real-time graphs or custom dashboards for the data, or real-time analysis with for instance Apache Storm[3].

The prototype also includes three sample integrations/data providers (a Spark Core microcontroller[4], a native Android application listening for light values in the room using the light sensor on the mobile device, and a simple Ionic[5] cross-platform application for mobile and web for registering a single value. Finally, the prototype includes one external real-time consumer written in JavaScript, which is a proof-of-concept real-time graph for a single sensor.

4   Implemented Prototype Artefact

Our prototype, named Office Analysis as a Service (DaaS) consists of a web application where users can sign up and log in to the service, register new integrations (their own sensors), edit their dashboard, and view the dashboard to be displayed at a monitor or similar. The initial idea was to provide offices and workplaces with the ability to monitor their environments, and act on the resulting data. The end-product became rather general as it stores data from any source, being sensors or similar, as long as the data is in a given format, so the DaaS name is merely a thing of the past

There are various databases, like InfluxDB, KDB+ and KairosDB, exclusively developed to handle such data structures, but MongoDB comes bundled with Meteor.js, and is currently the only database fully supported by the Meteor Development Group. Because of the tight coupling, it was decided to implement a time-series data structure into MongoDB instead of writing an adapter for Meteor.js to talk to InfluxDB or some other time-series-only database. Because MongoDB is a document database, we store data in *documents* and *collections* instead of rows and tables like in a traditional SQL database. For instance, we have implemented a collection named IntegrationData, where a document has the following properties:

---

[2] https://www.meteor.com/ddp
[3] https://storm.apache.org
[4] https://store.spark.io/?product=spark-core
[5] http://ionicframework.com/

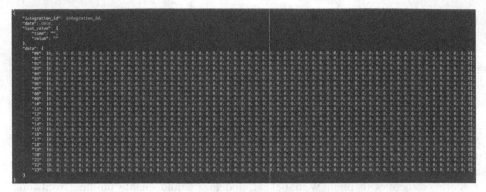

Fig. 3. A document data structure for time-series data in MongoDB.

Table 1. Properties of a time-series data document

integration_ID	The ID of an integration (physical sensor) to distinguish one sensor from another.
date	The date a given day in a given format.
last_value	A JavaScript object holding the latest value inserted into the document:
-time	the hour and minute (HH:MM) of an inserted value
-value	the value (numeric, string, bool)
data	A JavaScript object holding 24 arrays, one for each hour in a day. Each array has 60 indexes, one for each minute in that given hour.

This structure (Table 1) enables the client to quickly request the current data (last_value property) for real-time-display purposes, as well as for external services to integrate into DaaS to get time-series data (data property) for each day for each integration (integration_id property). Additionally, the size of the document is kept reasonable compared to the maximum size of 16 megabytes per document [2]. The main limitation with this approach is that one can only store one value per minute, else the previous value is overwritten, and if an integration's microcontroller halts and stops the data sending, the value for those minutes within the halted time frame will stay at 0. It is still the most optimal way we found to adapt parts of MongoDB's own advice on time-series storage into our service MongoDB based on read and write time, document size limitations and query optimization.

In order to prove parts of our current architecture, we developed an external (non-Meteor.js) example application connecting to our Meteor.js server instance through the DDP protocol. The example is a single HTML page graphing history data levering JavaScript, the D3 graph library, and the JavaScript library Asteroid for simple DDP connectivity. The DDP connection and MongoDB collection subscription (getIntegrationDataForDDP) with a parameter (integration_id) is configured like this

```
var asteroid = new Asteroid('oaaas.meteor.com');

asteroid.on('connected', function ()
{
    console.log('asteroid connected');
});

asteroid.subscribe('getIntegrationDataForDDP', 'HNcHW7wRKiw6MBEvE');

var lightCollection = asteroid.getCollection('IntegrationData');

var reactiveQuery = lightCollection.reactiveQuery({});
```

Fig. 4. Connecting to a Meteor.js instance with the Asteroid DDP connector

On change-events, an `asteroid.on('change', {})` event will fire, similar to the `asteroid.on('connected', {})` event, and serve the example application new, real-time data from the subscribed integration/sensor. This is in practice how the service, architecture and technology stack enables 3rd party developers, external services and more to integrate into our prototype and real-time aggregate on the time-series information we store. The prototype also provides RESTful non-real-time end-points for externals to hook onto and use for more static purposes, like weekly Excel reports or similar. The implementation of this is based on Paganelli et al.'s [3] idea of treating each integration as a web resource and builds further on how to handle persisting time-series data in a document-database like MongoDB.

5   Discussion: Experiences from Developing DAaaS

Unsurprisingly, many design decisions had to be made as we applied the Internet and Web of Things to a real-world application with a clearly defined use case such as Data Analysis as a Service (DAaaS). While frameworks for connecting things to the internet, machine to machine communication, data storage, and data analysis as plentiful, it proved impossible to apply these frameworks and protocol stacks to the application without modifications. In short, the development time can be greatly reduced by utilising tools which almost fit the use case, and customize what already exists. This experience differs from the main proposition in Palattella et al. [4], whose introduced IoT protocol stack should have been the best fit.

A key experience from the development process is that development time can be greatly reduced by using tools that already exists - in DAaaS's case, Meteor with MongoDB for storage, and REST and DDP as communication protocols or styles proved to be very effective tools for rapid prototyping. It should be noted that only REST was used for providing data to the application, as per Uckelmann, Harrison and Michahelles [5]. The prototype did not require two-way machine-to-machine communication, so COaP was not relevant to this system.

An obvious downside of this approach is that a framework (like Meteor) may impose requirements to other dependencies in the application. In DAaaS, the main issue was that Meteor only supports the document database MongoDB [6] out of the box. There are several other stores (I.e. TempoIQ and InuxDB) better suited than

---

[6] https://www.mongodb.org/

MongoDB to store timeseries data, which was expected to be stored in DSaaS. Being required to use MongoDB for storage required a custom data structure to achieve acceptable performance.

Another important point to make about using established protocols, even if they (like Meteor's DDP) are not widely used outside of a small community, it may be easy to find third party libraries to help speed up development. For example, the real-time consumer graph used the library asteroid[7]. By defining a custom protocol with Web-Sockets, all communication must have been implemented by hand.

As long as there are not enough good all-purpose reference implementations with the proposed frameworks and protocol stacks, building something based on existing and well-defined protocols is easier. For rapid prototyping of a system, it seems best to prefer well-defined protocols and architectural styles like REST, and try to use existing frameworks for both client- and server-side applications. For commercial products, however, and especially if one aims to deliver several variations of the same product, service, or platform, exploring and using protocol stacks and frameworks developed specifically for the Internet of Things may be the best fit.

Several aspects of building a commercial application for actual use have been ignored in the development of DAaaS. Examples include security in both providing and consuming data; privacy, which has not been considered whatsoever (and rightfully so: the platform only stores and displays data in a custom fashion); and no error handling is implemented: if anything unexpected happens, the system will not do anything to restore state or shut down gracefully. These are all considerations to make which may differ from the regular Web application when introducing the aspect of Internet and Web of things.

While no actual (big data) analysis of the data was performed by the prototype, leaving potential issues with this type of data unexplored by this paper, the proof-of-concept shows that, in its current state, it can connect Internet-enabled devices to our service via REST interfaces, persist the time-series data in a query-optimized fashion, and both real-time (DDP) and statically (REST) integrate into external services.

Because of DDP's agnostic communication-approach, it could be of interest to research on the protocol's ability to handle real-time machine-to-machine communication in constrained environments. Overall, the DDP protocol has proven itself as a potential standard for real-time data synchronization between client and server, and the REST paradigm for sending data between constrained environments (sensors via microcontrollers) to RESTful endpoints at a server.

However, the possibly most important experience from developing the DSaaS application is that handling providers and consumers of the Internet and Web of Things just like any other type of client in the business logic of the application is tremendously helpful: if data from things needs to be transformed to fit a certain structure, then it should likely be transformed in the communication layer of the application before ever reaching the business logic.

---

[7] https://github.com/mondora/asteroid

As a final remark, HTTP/2[8] is on its way, and will certainly be an interesting player once released, allowing two-way communication and several asynchronous requests over the same connection. This may impact the need for COaP and WoT performance, create some disturbance in the effort to standardize WoT protocols, and certainly improve performance on the Web in general.

6   Conclusion

We have seen that the current body of research on the Internet and Web of Things agrees that standardization, full-stack research-oriented implementations, technology, and security are among the most important areas to look into in the future. Data Analysis as a Service attempts to address the first two of these issues, and is a small step on the way to bridging the gap. More focus must be directed at full-stack implementations of Internet and Web of Things-oriented applications, with special regard to separate use cases and domains. In particular, it should be interesting to see what matters in development of commercial products.

Utilising existing Web standards instead of developing the Internet and Web of Things as its own technology is going to be an important part of the process of simplifying the Internet of Things. We will probably require some new protocols as well - CoAP is a great example of this - but developing the WoT with the Web and upcoming technology advancements like HTTP/2 in mind will be crucial. At present, business needs and proposed technology, frameworks, and protocols are in conflict - but as more example implementations become available, this will hopefully change. Standardizing protocols instead of having manufacturers implement custom means of communication is key to simplifying the Internet and Web of Things.

Security, privacy, cost, and maintenance of a distributed network such as the Internet of Things are still major considerations to make, and are certainly directions in which the academic community should go in the near future.

References

1. Duquennoy, S., Grimaud, G. and Vandewalle, J.-J.: The Web of Things: Interconnecting Devices with High Usability and Performance (2009)
2. Meteor: DDP Meteor.com. (2015). https://www.meteor.com/ddp
3. Paganelli, F., Turchi, S., Giuli, D.: A web of things framework for restful applications and its experimentation in a smart city. IEEE Systems Journal, 1–12 (2014)
4. Palattella, M.R., Accettura, N., Vilajosana, X., Watteyne, T., Grieco, L.A., Boggia, G., Dohler, M.: Standardized protocol stack for the internet of (important) things. IEEE Communications Surveys & Tutorials (2013)
5. Uckelmann, D., Harrison, M., Michahelles, F.: Architecting the internet of things. Springer, New York (2011)
6. Xu, L.D., He, W., Li, S.: Internet of things in industries: a survey. IEEE Transactions on Industrial Informatics, 2233–2243 (2014)

---

[8] https://tools.ietf.org/html/draft-ietf-httpbis-http2-17

Storage and Processing of Data and Software Outside the Company in Cloud Computing Model

Aneta Poniszewska-Maranda[✉] and Michal Grzywacz

Institute of Information Technology, Lodz University of Technology, Łódź, Poland
aneta.poniszewska-maranda@p.lodz.pl

Abstract. In the modern world there exists many solutions for storing and processing of data outside the company. However, despite the fast development of many outsourcing technologies, especially cloud computing, still there are many problems and barriers connected with provisioning of data storage and processing to the third parties. The paper presents Extendable Software as a Service (ESaaS) cloud solution to allow customer to store and process data and their software using external provider, with keeping control over the algorithms and methods used for processing this data.

1 Introduction

In modern world a great development of mobile solutions can be observed. With introducing variety of mobile devices such as smartphones, tablets or smart watches, a new problems and barriers raised. The biggest issue had vastly became a problem of data synchronization and its availability. In order to efficiently and effectively manage this situation a new approach in data processing was introduced – a cloud computing. This revolutionary idea of storing and processing data in one place brought a new quality to the IT market. It allowed not only to easily overcome problem of data availability, but with appearance of specialized cloud computing providers it also introduced a great costs savings for the customers. Nowadays there exist numerous professional cloud computing providers, offering variety of cloud services. Despite that, due to complexity of the market and moving companies focus onto cloud computing there still exists a place for a new, more specialized cloud computing solutions.

Cloud computing is a general term for everything that involves delivering hosted services over the Internet. In other words it is regarded as a "method of running application, software and storing the related data in provided computer systems and providing customers or other users the access to them through the Internet" [1,2]. Cloud computing is the use of computing resources (hardware and software) that are delivered as a service over a network (typically Internet).

The purpose of cloud computing is to provide easy, scalable access to computing resources and IT services. Currently, many types of development models of cloud computing can be found in the literature. The most popular ones are: Software as a Service (SaaS), Platform as a Service (PaaS) and Infrastructure

© Springer International Publishing Switzerland 2015
M. Younas et al. (Eds.): MobiWis 2015, LNCS 9228, pp. 170–181, 2015.
DOI: 10.1007/978-3-319-23144-0_16

as a Service (IaaS) [3–5]. *Software as a Service*, sometimes also referred as "on-demand software", is a software delivery model in which software and associated data are centrally hosted on the cloud. It is typically accessed by users using a thin client via a web browser. *Platform as a Service* is a category of cloud computing services that provide a computing platform and a solution stack as a service. In this model, the consumer creates the software using tools and/or libraries from the provider and controls software deployment and configuration settings. The provider provides the networks, servers, storage and other services. In *Infrastructure as a Service* the most basic cloud-service model, providers offer computers – physical or (more often) virtual machines and other resources.

However there are also a few issues connected with cloud computing. The major problem had vastly became a lack of law adjustment in many countries, which hardly follows the complexity and the size of the growing cloud computing market. Thus in many countries a problems with interpretation of data ownership and data protection had raised.

The problem presented in the paper concerns the storage and processing data and software outside the company in cloud computing model. It presents the solution, which is believed to be capable to solve the common cloud computing problems and is thought to be suitable for companies, which pays a great attention to the legal aspects of cloud computing. According to the legal definition: "data processing involves a system which processes information after it has been encoded into data, including performance of operations upon data such as handling, merging, sorting and computing" [6,7] data processing is an action taken on the data. It especially refers to the process of performing specific operations on a set of data or whole database.

In order to answer the needs of companies connected with external data and software storage and processing, a new Extendable Software as a Service (ESaaS), cloud solution was proposed. The goal of the ESaaS solution is to solve the problems seen by customers in currently existing cloud solutions like lack of control over core aspects of application, without removing most important benefits of cloud such as: consistency of resources, minimization of costs, constant availability and scalability. That is why the proposed ESaaS cloud assumes, that customer obtains from provider a base cloud application, which can be easily extended by client, using modules containing new functionalities (created by the client). Thus an Extendable Software as a Service can be understood as an intermediate solution between typical PaaS and SaaS clouds.

The presented paper is structured as follows: section 2 presents the issues of data storage and data processing outside the company such as their reasons, models and possible benefits of cloud usage for companies, while section 3 deals with description of Extendable Software as a Service cloud solution.

2   Data Storage and Data Processing Outside the Company

Data processing and data management are nowadays one of the most important aspects in almost every business organization. Moreover with the growth of the information technology and computer science the value of data possessed by a company had greatly increased [11]. With the development of mechanisms for data analysis and data mining it became possible to convert a pure data into valuable information. Thus a data can be understood as a set of raw facts such as name, surname or address [10]. An information can be produced from data and it is a collection of facts, gathered together in such a way that it has a more value beyond the facts themselves. For example, a database of customer names and purchases might provide an information on a company's market demographics, sales trends, and customer loyalty/turnover. However in case of computing a data can be also understood as an information translated into digital, binary form, which is more convenient to move and to process [12].

2.1 Reasons for Storing and Processing Data Outside the Company

Among past few years a great revolution in the IT market can be observed. With the development of Internet and increasing mobility and capabilities of computers and electronic devices the new opportunities arise for industries. It became easy for companies to gather, store and exchange a large amount of data, which nowadays is considered as the most valuable asset of every company [9]. Moreover emerging of Internet had its result also in the increase of the requests for both on-line and off-line data storages. However the rapid pace of change in technology started to cause a variety of problems for a company of any size. It became a great challenge for many of them to catch up with the IT infrastructure in order to keep it up to date and in appropriate size, which will allow to maintain a large amount of data [11,12].

Thus, a few reasons for moving storage and processing of data outside the company can be distinguished:

- Financial benefits – moving data storing and processing outside the company may bring cost reduction for this company independently from the used outsourcing model [1,8]. Unlike in the traditional in-house model, the company does not has to pay for setting the infrastructure and its maintenance (which in most cases is at the beginning partly used) – in most of the outsourcing models the costs are spread over time in form of monthly fees. However, in case of hosted model and cloud solutions, in long term period it may show up, that a sum of monthly fees could exceed the costs of in-house solution. Thus the financial benefits should be assessed individually for company depending on many variables [14].
- Availability of storage and space – development of the technology (especially Internet and mobile devices) had caused for many companies the problems with ensuring appropriate amount of disk storage and space for servers [9]. Many industries search for big amount of data storage at elastic manner for their increasing amount of processed data [14].
- Easier maintenance – with evolving corporate IT into more distributed form and vastly changing business needs, there raised a need for data storage and back-ups to evolve [11]. This can be easily realized with moving data storage

and processing outside the company structure, where data is stored in one, common place. Moreover in case of outsourcing storage, the responsibility for updates of the infrastructure and software may be passed to service the provider side.

- Availability of processing resources – one of the most important reasons leading companies to move the processing of data outside the company is the increasing amount of data to be processed. Nowadays an increasing need to shorten the time of searching through the growing amount of data can be observed [14].
- Availability of data – nowadays one of the biggest challenge for most of the companies is how to ensure a constant access to their services through variety of devices. With moving data storage and processing to the external servers it became easier to ensure a constant access to the resources and applications [14].

2.2 Data Storage and Data Processing Models Outside the Company

Among the past few years, with increasing need in companies for easily accessed and processed data a few external data storage and processing models were developed.

Collocation – one of the most basic and simple form of storing data outside the company. In this model company buys from third-party an access to the shared datacenter facility over which may store its IT equipment [2,6]. In other words a collocation can be understood as rental of place, Internet connection bandwidth, air-conditioning and power supplies for keeping customer-owned servers in good shape, at secure place and constantly connected to the Internet.

Hosted Model – an extended form of collocation, in modern sense well known from the 1990s. Hosting supplier provides not only the facility as in collocation but also ensures IT equipment. In its essentials hosted model means, that customer buys from host vendor a solution which is installed in datacenter or 'hosting center', where either physical or virtualized servers that he owns/leases/finances are setup. The owner of the software is customer, who buys an indefinite license for it, and pays monthly fees for its maintenance. If the customer stops paying for maintenance the software will continue to work at a last paid version. In its most developed form this model can resemble the low end cloud solution [6,7,11].

Cloud Computing – one of the newest approach in outsourcing, very similar to the most developed hosted models. However unlike in hosted model the customer has almost no knowledge about physical placement of the servers and technical details of the solution. The customer pays vendor monthly fees, according to the actual usage of the data storage and processing resources (or in its highest form for a whole application). Data storage services, processing resources or end-solution runs on a distributed network using virtualized servers. The resources provided by vendor are accessed using well-known Internet protocols with a typical web-browser. All costs connected with initial setting hardware and software are moved to the vendor and spread over time. Moreover cloud computing model provides high elasticity in availability of resources whenever customer will request them. The root idea of cloud computing is to provide to client a high-end solution, ready to use, which incorporates all components requested by a customer. Such solution may be composed of servers, database engines, network connections, monitoring tools, collaboration applications, objects storage and processing resources [1–3,8].

The cloud computing as a model provides many useful features for a client. Despite many specific implementations, the general and the most important advantages of cloud computing are [6,14]:

- elasticity and scalability of resources – provided resources can be easily adjusted to the needs of a client; available resources are almost unlimited,
- reduction of costs – by introducing of monthly fees and reduction of infrastructure, client can gain wide costs savings,
- easy access to data – data stored and processed in one place can be easily accessed through the Internet connection.

To sum up, there are several reasons, which may drive company to move data storage and data processing outside its structures. The main factors, which are considered before introducing external data storage and processing are: reduction of costs, pursuing for gaining efficient resources, which may be easily extended and obtaining easier maintenance of the infrastructure. Moreover one of the factor may be also lack of space for keeping appropriate servers inside the company. In order to achieve these goals a client can consider many options. The most popular models are collocation, hosted model and cloud computing. Out of these three models the newest and thus the most popular model is cloud computing, which is flexible and can easily answer to most of the needs of the single client and can provide a great help in storing and processing of data outside the company. In contrary the collocation requires from the customer many investments, which does not guarantee great boosting of the effectiveness, but provides the highest (especially from the legal point of view) control over data storage and processing resources, because the owner of them remains the customer.

2.3   Possible Benefits of Cloud Usage for Companies

The most clear and important benefits of introducing the cloud into company corresponds to the companies' expectations, however it holds much more values to the companies than their managers used to think. For instance the cloud computing can not only reduce costs up to 15% of IT budget [13], but it also provides a great possibility to obtain a better control over them. The typical payment system for the cloud usage – "pay-as-you-go" basis allows to manage the costs and fit usage of cloud to the current needs of company [8].

Next benefits brought by cloud computing can be found in technical aspects of IT in company. As it is expected by most of companies the cloud computing can give company a superior IT performance and great scalability. This can be considered not only as single adjustment of resources in order to maintain the proper level of access to the services. It can be also seen as a scheduled, frequent changing of scale of demanded resources – even on a daily basis. Cloud providers can give a possibility to enhance resources in a daily schedule for some applications which need extended resources for couple of hours (usually for tasks performed at night, e.g. reporting services or newsletters) in order to perform their tasks and then return to the standby mode [12,14]. Free for the rest of a day resources can be then allocated to the other services, giving more rational resources usage and reducing the probability of oversizing IT infrastructure.

Cloud computing can bring to the IT infrastructure a great opportunity to have an access to the newest technologies. The cloud computing allows for easier implementation of changes into outsourced hardware and software, which reduces necessary of buying multiple licenses for new software and replacement of the multiple similar server units. For instance in case of the PaaS solutions an update of the development environment has to be done only on one outsourced machine, which is then accessed by many users. However in order to get that benefit a proper regulations have to be included in agreements with provider, which should be responsible for upgrading of physical resources and their software.

Reduction of IT hardware resources and moving the responsibility for companies' maintenance and upgrading allows to enhance flexibility and opening to introduce the new solutions. According to the study conducted by IDC, cloud computing allows to simplify and fasten a process of application deployment at time rate about 75% [13]. Moreover, a cloud computing can also ease an access to the services and applications. The web based character of cloud services and access through the Internet connections allows to simplify the process of data access from any place in the world using tablets, smartphones, laptops, PCs [8].

3   Extendable Software as a Service Solution

Many of the customers search for flexible solution, well-tailored to their needs, for a low price. What is more many of them want to keep control over core aspects of their business, which in some cases may be hardly reachable in terms of the newest outsourcing model – cloud computing model. Furthermore, there exist many threats preventing companies from outsourcing their data storage and processing to the external firms. The top threats seen by companies are: security issues, losing control over data and application, legal aspects of cloud computing. Finally, in case of customers whose trade area is specific or hermetic environment, or demands very specific knowledge and years of experience in business it may be very hard for the customer to find a proper cloud solution. This derives from the fact, that in such situation it is also hard for provider to offer a high quality, robust solution, which will fully satisfy the needs of such customer.

The answer for the situation described above may be presented in **Extendable Software as a Service (ESaaS)** solution. The core assumption of the proposed solution is to allow customer to store and process data using external provider, with keeping control over the algorithms and methods used for processing this data. Moreover, in order to maximize the benefits for customer, it is assumed that ESaaS should incorporate benefits of cloud computing model, especially: minimization of costs, scalability, availability, consistency of resources and ease in development. That is why, the base idea of ESaaS solution is to supply customer with a basic cloud solution (fulfilling the most common needs of the companies), which functionality can be enhanced by customer. Thus, Extendable Software as a Service can be understood as an intermediate solution, between typical PaaS and SaaS cloud models.

The base idea of ESaaS is to allow the customer to extend the functionality of base web application by loading into it an additional modules developed by him (Fig. 1). Such module is in essentials a package with a code (Java classes), which would be dynamically loaded to the base ESaaS web application. This approach has its reflection in the "world" of desktop programs, where user installs some application and after that he is able to add on-demand the new functionalities. In the ESaaS solution this additional, on-demand functionalities are brought to the world of web applications, which should be constantly accessible.

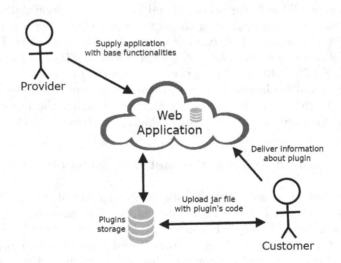

Fig. 1. General scheme of ESaaS solution idea

Figure 1 describes the general idea of ESaaS cloud solution. According to this figure there are a few constraints, which should be fulfilled:

- The base application should be ensured by provider. The role of a vendor is to create a web application, which will act as a basis for adding extensions and will consist of some basic set of features and functionalities.
- Base application should be able to load Java classes encapsulated in form of *jar* package.

- Loading of plugin to ESaaS application should not interrupt its operation and force disruption in usage for a user. In other words, user should be able to use loaded plugin just after adding it to the application or in short period after that.
- Each plugin should be validated in order to allow to load only such plugins, which are delivered by trusted suppliers (customers).
- Customer may store plugins on his file server, which allows to give him a better control over delivered plugins.

To sum up the constraints listed above the base assumption of Extendable Software as a Service cloud is that this cloud is provided by vendor, who allows customer to add valid plugins to it, which are basically Java classes packed in JAR file. However, provided cloud application should allow to add the additional functionalities in real time manner, so the user could use them immediately. At the end the customer should have the ability to add plugins, which are stored at his place, not in the place strictly defined by vendor. That is why, the process of adding plugin to the application consists of two steps:

1. Uploading plugin to the plugin's storage server.
2. Adding information about plugin to the web application's database.

However, such approach of ESaaS cloud may cause many security threats. Thus in order to minimize such concerns and maintain a high level of security only selected users should be able to add plugins to the application. The control over addition of plugins should be provided only to the administrator (Fig. 2), who should be able to expose additional functionality only to the given group of users (or all users). Thus only users with given permission to use plugin are able to use this plugin. The administrator should be a person delegated from the customer's side, but it may be also one designated by the provider. He has to take care of access permissions because the plugin has to be developed taking care of this issue. Such approach allows to easily control the access to the plugins and ease maintenance of the application.

To conclude Extendable Software as a Service solution is an intermediate solution between PaaS and SaaS cloud models. The main goal of ESaaS is to answer the needs of customers, who want to keep benefits of cloud computing and in the same time have much more control over algorithms and methods used for processing of data stored and processed beyond company's structure. Moreover Extendable Software as a Service can provide many advantages for both customer and provider. Developing by provider only base web application allows him to broaden his target group of customers. What is more he can also minimize the costs of developing ESaaS application. In the other hand with ability to enhance the functionality of ESaaS cloud the customer gains a possibility to obtain a "tool" which fully satisfies his needs. Thanks to basing ESaaS on the cloud model, the customer gains an easily accessible application over the Internet. With a possibility to scale resources, the client can adjust amount of storage and processing resources to the actual supply. Moreover, resources obtained from provider are consistent, so the problem of mismatches between

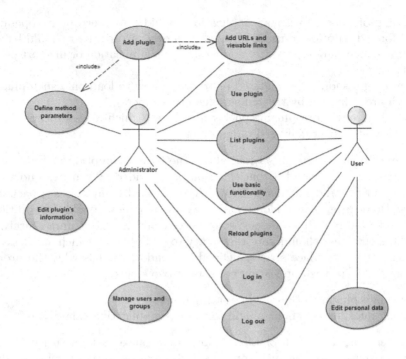

Fig. 2. Use case diagram of basic ESaaS cloud

different branches of company is minimized. Finally, the last benefit for customer is derived from the possibility to store plugins on his file server. This allows to reduce the problem of ownership or copy rights, because the most important for customer functionalities remains at place owned by him, not by vendor of ESaaS cloud. Thus the provider has no legal rights to the plugin, because it is not stored with ESaaS base cloud application.

Described base idea of ESaaS prerequisites connected with maintenance and usage of application became the basis for design of prototype of base ESaaS cloud, called *PlugCloud*. Moreover the necessity of solving the problem of easy and effective development of base application and its plugins had also played a significant role in design of exemplary *PlugCloud* solution.

Generally, the working ESaaS solution should consists of file server for storing plugins and application server, over which the base application and its database are installed (Fig. 3). The access to the application for client is realized through the Internet using a standard web browser. The process of adding plugin to the application consist of two activities, which have to be successfully processed:

1. Creation of valid plugin, according to the defined requirements using appropriate components of base application.
2. Adding information about plugin – its class name, URL address, author, users group, visibility, paths to methods and parameters used by them.

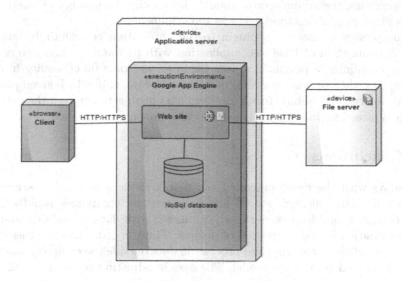

Fig. 3. Infrastructure diagram of exemplary ESaaS solution

The first step in extending functionality of base ESaaS cloud is to create a valid plugin by a customer, using appropriate components of base application. During this stage of adding plugin to the ESaaS application, the main activities are connected, with the plugin development and uploading it to the chosen files server. When the customer finishes the development of plugin's code, he is obliged to export it to the form of Java package. Then he has to upload this package to the chosen files server, in order to obtain URL of the uploaded file. Next, having obtained the path to plugin, the customer should add information about plugin to base application database (or send this information to the administrator responsible for such task). In this place a next stage of plugin loading start.

The main goal of second step in extending functionality is to provide base application with all information necessary to process correctly the plugin. The role of an administrator is to add the information about plugin to the base web application database, which allows to keep plugin code separated from the base application. The basic information about each plugin component should be filled-in including: full class name, URL path to plugin file, author of the plugin (it may be a person or a company), target user group (the group, which can use functions and visibility of plugin – if it is an active plugin). The next step is to add paths to the plugin's functionalities. The design of the ESaaS assumes, that the access to the appropriate plugin's functions will be realized using calling URL link to the given method. Thus administrator has to add the information about URL path to the given method and text, which will be displayed in GUI in order to allow a user to access that URL. Moreover in order to enable inputs for the functionalities, the administrator should also specify the number of parameters, which given plugin's method takes as the arguments.

The process of loading a plugin to the application is essentially based on the communication of base web application with its database and external file storage containing a plugin. If a user wants to use some functionality from the plugin, then the application connects to the file storage, in which given plugin is placed. Information about storage of the given plugin is taken from the database, which is placed within the application's environment.

4   Conclusions

Nowadays with the development of the mobile devices and web platforms an amount of data collected, stored and processed by companies rapidly grows. Moreover, new problems were raised, connected with data availability and data synchronization between varieties of devices. Thus, in order to solve these problems a new model for storing and processing data outside the company was introduced – a cloud computing model. The ease in adjusting resources to the need of the company, attractive pricing options, possibility of fitting costs to incomes and variety of cloud types had rapidly made this model the most popular one in many industries. However, despite many advantages some of the companies are still not fully convinced about moving their data to the cloud computing. The major factors, which prevent them from introducing cloud computing are:

- unclear and outdated law regulations in many countries, especially the one connected with definition of owner of data stored in cloud model,
- lack of consistency in law regulations between different legal systems,
- security concerns – for most of the companies the main area of concern is losing control over the core resources and applications outsourced to the cloud computing.

In order to overcome problems listed above, the Extendable Software as a Service cloud solution was proposed. Compared to the currently known cloud computing models an ESaaS cloud puts emphasis on giving control over outsourced resources to the customer, forcing cooperation between the provider and the customer. The main advantages of ESaaS, over other cloud models are:

- giving customer a possibility to fully fit the application to his needs by providing a possibility to supply an application with functionalities created by customer (not given by existing cloud models),
- overcoming the problem of ownership, by allowing the customer to store his plugins in external server,
- keeping control by customer over functionalities important for his business more than in other cloud models,
- reducing costs of developing ESaaS solution by limiting the amount of functionalities to be implemented,
- introducing a possibility for vendor to extend a target group of his product by offering many customers the same base cloud solution for adding plugins.

To sum up, based on the conducted researches it can be clearly stated that the biggest potential in storing and outsourcing data outside the company is in the cloud computing model. Despite described drawbacks and problems connected with known cloud computing solutions their advantages made cloud computing the best of the known answers for growing amount of data to be processed by the companies. By incorporating the best features of the known cloud solutions, and introducing new approach into management of cloud application functionalities, the ESaaS cloud may provide a great aid for many companies to overcome their concerns about lack of security in cloud computing and losing control over the core aspects of their business. It is supposed, that allowing customers to adjust their cloud application to their needs on their own, may help many of them to take a decision about moving the data storage and data processing to the outside of the company, into cloud computing model. In the end an ESaaS solution may help to develop a general cloud computing model and introduce a new quality into it, by forcing the cooperation of provider and customer in order to obtain a high quality, complete solution.

References

1. Mell, P., Grance, T.: The NIST Definition of Cloud Computing. Recommendation of NIST (2011)
2. Subashini, S., Kavitha, V.: A survey on security issues in service delivery models of cloud computing. Journal of Network and Computer Applications **34**, 1–11 (2011)
3. Armbrust, M., Fox, A., Griffith, R., Joseph, A.D., Katz, R., Konwinski, A., Lee, G., Patterson, D., Rabkin, A., Stoica, I., Zaharia, M.: A View of Cloud Computing. Communications of the ACM **53**(4), 50–58 (2010)
4. Velte, T., Velte, A., Elsenpeter, R.: Cloud Computing, A Practical Approach. McGraw-Hill, Inc., New York (2010)
5. Poniszewska-Maranda, A.: Selected aspects of security mechanisms for cloud computing - current solutions and development perspectives. Journal of Theoretical and Applied Computer Science **8**(1), 35–49 (2014)
6. Wang, Q., Wang, C., Li, J., Ren, K., Lou, W.: Enabling public verifiability and data dynamics for storage security in cloud computing. In: Backes, M., Ning, P. (eds.) ESORICS 2009. LNCS, vol. 5789, pp. 355–370. Springer, Heidelberg (2009)
7. Zissis, D., Lekkas, D.: Addressing cloud computing security issues. Future Generation Computer Systems **28**(3), 583–592 (2012)
8. Sosinsky, B.: Cloud computing Bible. Wiley Publishing Inc. (2011)
9. Hayes, J.: Storage outsourcing renaissance. Engineering and Technology Magazine, October 2009
10. Ahson, S.A., Ilyas, M.: Cloud Computing and Software Services. Theory and Techniques. CRC Press (2011)
11. Ring, K.: Time to outsource data storage. ComputerWeekly.com
12. Hausman, K., Cook, S.L., Sampaio, T.: Cloud Essentials. John Wiley and Sons (2013)
13. Perry, R., Hatcher, Mahowald, R.P., Hendrick, S.D.: Force.com Cloud Platform Drives Huge Time to Market and Cost Savings, IDC (2009)
14. Shroff, G.: Enterprise Cloud Computing. Technology, Architecture, Applications. Cambridge University Press, Cambridge (2012)

Smart Phones and Mobile Commerce Applications

Mobile Payments in Austria – Is Mobile Banking Paving the Way for Mobile Payments?

Katerina Markoska[1], Irene Ivanochko[1,2(✉)], and Michal Greguš[3]

[1] School of Business, Economics and Statistics,
University of Vienna, Oskar-Morgenstern-Platz 1, 1090 Vienna, Austria
markoska@gmx.at, irene.ivanochko@gmail.com
[2] Secure Business Austria (SBA),
Sommerpalais Harrach, Favoritenstrasse 16, 1040 Vienna, Austria
[3] Department of Information Systems, Faculty of Management,
Comenius University in Bratislava, Odbojárov 10, 820 05 Bratislava 25, Slovakia
michal.gregusml@fm.uniba.sk

Abstract. The paper comprises three aspects of our contemporary society: the importance of the tertiary sector of the economy - services in the developed countries, the development of new (mobile) technologies and the high penetration rate as well as an acceptance of "the device" in contemporary history - smartphone. The aim of this work is to translate these three aspects into the banking service sector in Austria with a focus on the payments. Due to the fact that banks are much impacted by developments in new ICT technologies, and they are among the heaviest investors in IT, this paper attempts to provide an insight of how the banks implement or could implement new (mobile) technologies and end-devices such as the smartphones, and how it can influence banking services in general.

Keywords: Smartphone · Mobility · Mobile payments · Technology · Mobile banking services

1 Introduction

"The Internet and the commercial development of the World Wide Web" [1], have an enormous impact on the behavior of the people and companies, delivering goods and services. Furthermore, empowered with "the device" of the contemporary history, the smartphone, it has become even easier to purchase goods or services being just a fingertip away of it [1, 48, 52].

Banking is "a major service category" [2] of the financial services family, dealing with payments and accounts as one of its core business activities. Though it seems rather conservative industry, banks are very much impacted by the developments in technologies. And over the years they have adopted a vast amount of different technologies – from ATM to Internet banking to mobile banking. But, what is next?

© Springer International Publishing Switzerland 2015
M. Younas et al. (Eds.): MobiWis 2015, LNCS 9228, pp. 185–197, 2015.
DOI: 10.1007/978-3-319-23144-0_17

The latest trend in the banking industry is the mobile banking, as a complementary service distribution channel to the online and offline (bricks-and-mortar) banking and as a way of improving the value proposition to the customers. On the other hand, in a world "where money is increasingly more digitized" [3] there is a great plenty of other players (non-banking institutions) directly competing with the banks "on multiple fronts for the ownership of the customer transaction, customer relationship and customer experience" (ibid). And yet there is no bank playing the same game. Is mobile banking paving the way for successful mobile payment service offered by the banks? Are banks waiting to catch the right wave?

Due to high data sensitivity and an anticipated little chance of big banks revealing their strategy, this work represents the current occurrences in the banking industry based on a numerous scientific papers as well as case studies and reports, published by prestigious consulting companies [2, 3, 49, 53]. The focus is set on Austria, for couple of reasons; it is a developed country with a relative conservative banking culture and a birthplace of innovative phenomenons. We attempt to conclude and to suggest whether mobile banking is paving the way for a mobile payment service and whether banks in this way are going to extend and defend their role in the payment industry.

2   The Power of the Letter "m"

The advancement in the information technologies (IT) have resulted in significant progress towards strategies, requirements, and development of e-commerce applications [4, 50]. The Internet itself has transformed the way people interact with each other, the way they search for information, how they acquire products and services and so on. In addition to that, "the wide-ranging economic developments, e.g. the integration of world economies, have made a significant impact towards increasing the mobility of the people" [5, 54].

The next new and big thing in the eCommerce is the mCommerce. Tiwari et al. refer to it as "an extension of Electronic Commerce to wireless mediums" (ibid) [5]. In its broadest sense mCommerce includes "any transaction with a monetary value – either direct or indirect – that is conducted via a wireless telecommunication network" [6]. The cornerstone of the mCommerce is the proliferation of the smartphones (not long ago). Smartphones are becoming an indispensable part of our everyday lives. The telephone itself has long ago exceeded its function of being a device for making a simple phone call. Nowadays, when speaking about phones, we think of a device which can literally replace our PC & camera; capable of multitasking; able to connect to the Internet; sending e-mails etc. Thus, smartphones can literally replace the computers and laptops and "open lucrative opportunities to merchants and service providers" [7, 51].

"Going "mobile" can be considered as one of the main global trends of the 21st century" [8]. Rapid advance in technology is undoubtedly making businesses dependent today on technological advances only made available just years ago. This notion of inter dependency between business and technology is stirring up an essential need to always stay vigilant of new things. Hence, the financial industry is not exclusion and as the other industries it is affected by as well and cannot remain immune of it. "Mobile Commerce services in the financial sector are generally known as mobile financial services (MFS) and they comprise of two applications, "Mobile Payment" and "Mobile Banking" [5].

2.1   Mobile Banking

The banking industry as one of the heaviest investors in information technology has been over the decades using the benefits of the IT, "not only to run the internal business activities and to promote products, but also to dematerialize the customer relationships" [9]. On top of it, banks are cutting down on operating expenses and can "act and fight" on different fronts serving and reaching different customer segments through diverse distribution channels. New distribution channels, "such as telephone banking, ATMs, Internet, and mobile phones have become more firmly established" [10]. And exactly distribution channels and customer interfaces are on the agenda of many bank executives from US and Europe as the main focus areas for innovation [11].

Advancement of the ICT; mobility as one of the main global trends of the 21st century; high penetration rate and acceptance of the smartphones; mixed altogether they trigger the digital mobility as "the next logical stage in the evolution of the World Wide Web" [12]. "Technological developments especially in the field of telecommunication have made it possible to offer innovative, location-sensitive services on ubiquitous ("anytime, anywhere") basis to customers on the move" [5]. The mobile technology has enriched the *anytime, anywhere* paradigm and *on any device* moment has been added to it.

"Mobile Banking refers to provision and availment of banking and financial services with the help of mobile telecommunication devices. The scope of offered services may include facilities to conduct bank and stock market transactions, to administer accounts and to access customized information" [5].

mBanking is being usually offered in form of an mobile application downloadable in the App Stores available for different operating systems (e.g. Andorid or iOS). In Austria all of the established and well-known banks (UniCredit Bank Austria, Erste Bank, Raiffeisen Bank, BAWAG etc.) have their own mobile banking application. As it is consumed and configured, it is being perceived as an additional channel of providing the usual services offered in online banking and is adding value to the service delivery process.

"The term of mobile banking usually refers to the following three basic applications: mobile account, mobile brokerage (purchase and sale of securities) and mobile financial information services (account balance, securities deposit account, current stock prices, stock alerts, etc.)" [13]. According to the latest ING International Survey (2014) [14] on how people in Europe are using mobile banking, Austria counts among the top 5 countries (Turkey, Netherlands, Poland and Spain) with the highest mobile banking usage (43% (2014)) and shows a positive tendency in this regard compared to previous year (see Fig. 1). Among the Austrians the most used mobile banking service is checking account balance (see Fig. 2) [15].

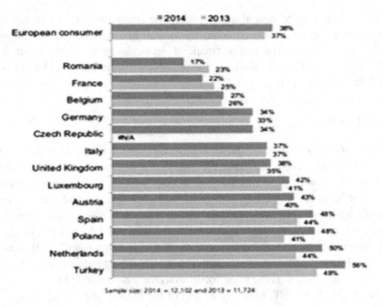

Fig. 1. Do you use mobile banking? [14].

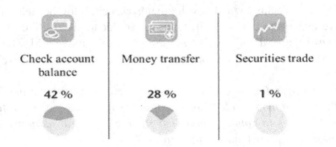

Fig. 2. Mobile banking - usage purposes [15].

Due to the high penetration rate and acceptance of the smartphones, banks can use their potential and "retain existing banking users in providing a new system (mobile banking) into the existing systems and have an opportunity to convert cell phone users into banking users" [16]. It is inevitable to state that the "digital technology and rapid-fire changes in customer preferences are threatening to weigh down those full-service banks that limit themselves to products and services that get primarily distributed through physical channels" (i.e. branches) [17].

2.2   Mobile Payments

Accounts and payments as part of the retail banking services "are positively correlated because they often serve as anchor product and there is cross-selling potential" [18]. In Austria according to figures of OeNB from April 2014 there were 8.2 million transferable overnight deposit accounts, whereas "almost 90% of the Austrian citizens (from the age 15 up) have payment cards" [19]. Retail payment services are perceived as "stable sources of income, contributing with the fees from payment services (or bank account management) to the non-interest income and helping to attract deposits (and thereby add to interest income)" [12].

In the course of time, with the commercialization of the Internet (eCommerce; recently mCommerce as well) not only the way of how we buy has changed, but along with that (mutually dependent) the way of how we pay has also changed. The cashless market opens space for new entrants and financial cards (as mostly accepted payment method) will fight on the same front with new competitors – electronic and mobile (e-/m-)payments. With the increase in popularity of mCommerce, "m-payment will continue to facilitate secure electronic commercial transactions between organizations or individuals" [20].

"M-payments are payments for which the payment data and the payment instruction are initiated, transmitted or confirmed via a mobile phone or device. This can apply to online or offline purchases of services, digital or physical goods. Mobile payments can be classified into two main categories (see Figure 3):

1. *Remote m-payments mostly take place through internet/WAP or through premium SMS services which are billed to the payer through the Mobile Network Operator (MNO). Most remote m-payments through the Internet are currently based on card payment schemes. Other solutions, based on credit transfers or direct debits, are technically feasible and possibly as secure, efficient and competitive, but seem to have difficulties entering the market.*
2. *Proximity payments generally take place directly at the point of sale. Using Near Field Communication (NFC), the leading proximity technology at this stage, payments require specifically equipped phones which can be recognised when put near a reader module at the point of sale (e.g. stores, public transport, parking spaces)" [21].*

In Figure 4 two categories have been differentiated – bank and non-bank providers. Exactly this captures the essential difference between mBanking and m-payment (both as sub-groups of the MFS), due to the fact that "(m-) payment constitutes an independent business field that does not necessarily involve banks" [5].

"Mobile banking services are based on banks' own legacy systems and offered for the banks' own customers" [24]. "Mobile payments, on the other hand, are offered as a new payment service to a retail market, which is characterized by 1) a multitude of competing providers such as banks and telecom operators, 2) two different and demanding groups of adopters; consumers and merchants, and 3) challenges regarding standardization and compatibility of different payment systems" (ibid).

The definition and classification of mobile payments show the complex nature of the mobile payments ecosystem, containing various m-payment market participants (such as "mobile network operators (MNOs), financial institutions, handset manufacturers or technology providers) providing the payment service through numerous enabling technologies (such as SMS or Unstructured Supplementary Service Data (USSD), NFC, and mobile Internet") depending on "the distance and relation between buyers" [22].

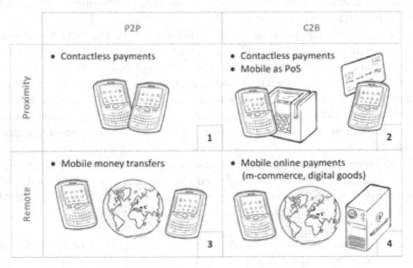

Fig. 3. Mobile payment categories [22]

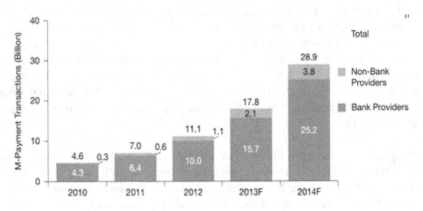

Fig. 4. Number of Global M-Payments Transactions (Billion), 2010–2014F [23].

"The proliferation of smartphones, which enable both connection to the Internet and the installation of third-party apps to access new content and services" [10] is opening two horizons for the mBanking; one as a new banking channel and the other as a direct payment method. Mobile payment is an area with high potential and growth. The emergence of new players in the payment market is shaking the ground and at the same time is threatening the banks on their core financial services.

3   Alternative Payment Methods

"Payments fall broadly into two categories; payments for purchases and payments of bills/invoices" [20]. This categorization further on suggests if alternative payments act as a complementary to or compete on the same fronts with already established payment methods. In this chapter couple of alternative (cashless) payment methods will be presented. Methods, which by their existence, improve the quality of the payment process and establish new innovative ways of making payments and are becoming serious threat to the conventional payment services offered by financial institution.

3.1   Focus: Austria

According to World Payments Report 2013, Austria counts among the top ten European non-cash payments markets [23]. In Austria there are two examples of alternative payment methods that are worthwhile mentioning; namely paybox and VeroPay. At the same time they are both representatives of the group of m-payments; paybox belonging to remote, while VeroPay to proximity payments.

A decade and a half ago, in 2000, "paybox introduced the first mobile service worldwide for a simple, user-friendly and safe payment via a mobile phone" [25]. "From its outset paybox was designed as an open payment platform and regardless of its ownership structure its service is available for the customers of all Austrian mobile network operators (MNOs)" (ibid). The crucial element in the payment process is the phone number. After entering/specifying the mobile number the user get an automatic call (PIN Call) and he/she is being required to enter a 4-digit PIN and press the # key on the keyboard of the phone. Subsequently, the amount for the purchased product or service will be directly debited from the user's bank account [26].

"Over the years through the cooperation with attractive partners of the domestic economy (such as the municipality of Vienna, ÖBB, ASFINAG, Austrian lotteries, large retail chains etc.), paybox could achieve high market penetration within a few years and with that could expand its offer introducing innovative services"[25]. paybox customers could pay in online shops, in stores, in taxi and even at the vending machine purchasing parking tickets, tickets for the public transport and for concerts and other events, snacks and drinks, lotto tips and books using their mobile phones [27].

Paybox austria as a pioneer paved the way for mobile payments in Austria. And better later than never, in September 2012 SECURE PAYMENT TECHNOLOGIES GmbH (founded in 2011) introduced an App, called VeroPay, for mobile payment [28]. The App allows payments at POS scanner using Blue Code technology on the smartphone. The Blue Code is actually generated by the App in form of a barcode after entering a PIN code, which is defined by the user itself for accessing the App. The Blue Code does not contain sensitive and personal data. At the POS "the Blue Code is being scanned and then transferred from the supermarket to the Secure

Shopping datacenter" [29]. "Subsequently, the bank transfers the amount from the checking account of the customer to the merchant" (ibid).

VeroPay was initially being offered for customers which have a bank account at Hypo Tirol Bank and buy in the supermarket chain MPREIS, both from the federal province of Tyrol. A year later, after its success at local level, VeroPay was available for customers of any Austrian bank. Following the example of paybox, VeroPay started cooperation with prominent retail chains, such as Billa, Merkur and Hartlauer [30]. Depending on the provider, a VeroPay user can make purchases of up to 150 euros per day [31].

3.2   Near Field Communication - The Promising Technology

"The innovation within m-payment has grown rapidly over the last decade with the introduction of various payment methods such as Wireless Application Protocol (WAP), Unstructured Supplementary Service Data, SMS, and General Packet Radio Service (GPRS)" [32]. In the course of time, "with the advancement in short-range wireless technologies such as Near Field Communication (NFC), Bluetooth, Infrared Data Association (IrDA) and Radio Frequency Identification (RFID)" [33] and the looking for a more flexible, more convenient and more user-friendly payment method, brought all the technologies together and integrate into the mobile phones. In this way, it is easier to facilitate the uptake of m-payment due to the fact that they are already "installed in the current customer base" [34] and they can be used promptly by the users themselves.

"Payments via NFC are an increasingly important area of m-payments" [35]. "Totally unknown just a few years ago, NFC is now increasingly establishing itself as one of the most promising forward- looking technologies for wireless data exchange over short distances"[36]. "NFC technology enables simple and safe two-way interactions between electronic devices (usually at a distance of 4 cm or less), allowing consumers to perform contactless transactions, access digital content, and connect electronic devices with a single touch" [37]. A contactless payment transaction "does not require a physical connection between the consumer payment device and the POS terminal" [38]. "Contactless payment was firstly developed on credit cards and an important implementation of that type of contactless payment is the PayPass program of VISA and MasterCard" (ibid).

"NFC's "birthplace" is in Austria (in the town of Gratkorn near Graz) and it is being invented by chip manufacturers NXP Semiconductors and Sony in 2002" [36]. After several pilot projects, the extensive market introduction of contactless payment in Austria happened mid-2013 [39] and ever since then several large Austrian banks (in chronological order: Erste Bank und Sparkasse, Volksbank, Raiffeisen Bank, UniCredit Bank Austria and BAWAG (upon customer request)) [40] issue debit cards in the wake of the general exchange cards with contactless technology. "At the same time began the roll-out of the corresponding terminals at major retail chains" [39]. Exactly this moment, "the infrastructure constraints in terms of handset and acceptance, have kept developments slow" [41]. "Domestic banks in Austria want to make more and more use of the NFC enabled cards and thus plan to introduce NFC-ATM for more convenient and faster cash withdrawal" [42].

NFC enabled card are a fast and convenient way of payment for purchases below certain amount (up to 25 euros) without any authorization requirements (PIN code or card holder's signature), whereas for all other payments exceeding the certain amount an authorization is required   [38]. According to the latest OeNB's survey about the means of payment in Austria from the 3rd quarter in 2013 [19], it has been shown that 58% from the respondents do not know about the NFC function. The information asymmetry increases with age and the level of education (ibid).

The potential of the NFC technology is being recognized by the big players in the payment industry in Austria. On the one side, "in September 2013 companies such as Austria Card, Card Complete, Drei, Erste Bank und Sparkassen, First Data Austria, MasterCard, Nexperts, PayLife Bank, T-Mobile and Visa with joint forces have created the "Mobile Wallet Initiative Austria" [43]. Though coming from different industries, initiative's common goal is to create "an open nationwide standard for NFC mobile wallets" [44].

"The combination between the global popularity of mobile devices and the speed and ease of NFC applications (whether they are used for payments, transit or access control) has the potential to significantly expand the already wide range handsets' capabilities" [22]. "Growing numbers of manufacturers are starting to produce NFC-enabled phones, and major NFC payments propositions - such as Google Wallet – are being introduced" [35]. The fusion of the ubiquitous character of the mobile phone, its wide acceptance and the convenience of the NFC technology making possible offering "additional features, such as loyalty programs, couponing and targeted marketing" [22], could bring bright future for making payments using the NFC technology.

4   Conclusions

In this paper, it was mainly discussed how banks' core business segments, payments and accounts, are being put under pressure due to coincidence of factors. The advances of (mobile) technologies and the loosen entry boundaries in the banking industry has opened possibilities for non-financial service providers to fight on the same front (payments) with the banks and with it the position of the banks on the payment market is threatened. Although payment service providers other than banks are still "unable to compete with banks on an equal basis as they are obliged to use the services of a bank to settle payments" [21], "profit opportunities are shifting to value-added services allowing nonbanks to provide payment solutions" [45].

The evolution of the mobile channel contributes in the enhancement of the customer experience. In order to sustain their competitive advantage and enhance service quality and with it the customer experience, banks in Austria should consider providing mobile payment services. The terrain is prepared. Although, the cash is still the most preferable means of payment among the Austrians, we saw that there is positive tendency and consumers' willingness to use mobile banking functionalities. Policymakers are creating the laws in favor of cashless payments and big players in Austria (such as Austria Card, Card Complete, Drei, Erste Bank und Sparkassen, First Data Austria, MasterCard, Nexperts, PayLife Bank, T-Mobile and Visa) have recognized the potential of the technologies that enable m-payments. Moreover, the smartphone acceptance in Austria is high (96% worldwide; 82% in Austria [46]). By going this way, banks should truly consider to extend the horizon of perceiving the smartphones as just another service distribution channel (as Gupta [47] suggests) and properly make use of its potential.

References

1. Hilton, T., Hughes, T., Little, E., Marandi, E.: Adopting self-service technology to do more with less. Journal of Services Marketing **27**(1), 3–12 (2013)
2. Fasnacht, D.: Open Innovation in the Financial Services. Springer, Heidelberg (2009)
3. Oliveira, P., von Hippel, E.: Users as service innovators: The case of banking services. Research Policy **40**(6), 806–818 (2011)
4. Lukies, A.: Separating Hype from Reality in the World of Mobile Money. How Companies can Win the Battle Against Disintermediation. n>Genuity, Fall 2012 **5**(4), 39–43 (2012)
5. Varshney, U., Vetter, R.: Mobile commerce: framework, applications and networking support [Abstract]. Mobile networks and Applications **7**(3), 185–198 (2002)
6. Tiwari, R., Buse, S., Herstatt, C.: Mobile services in banking sector: the role of innovative business solutions in generating competitive advantage. Technology and Innovation Managment Working Paper, (48) (2007)
7. Barnes, S.J.: The mobile commerce value chain: analysis and future developments. International Journal of Information Management **22**(2), 91–108 (2002)
8. Dahlberg, T., Mallat, N., Ondrus, J., Zmijewska, A.: Past, present and future of mobile payments research: A literature review. Electronic Commerce Research and Applications **7**(2), 165–181 (2008)
9. Höhler, G.: Mobile Money - The future of the payments market. BearingPoint, 1–55 (2012).   http://www.bearingpoint.com/en-uk/7-5317/mobile-money-the-future-of-the-payments-market-white-paper/ (accessed April 24, 2015)
10. Martins, C., Oliveira, T., Popovič, A.: Understanding the Internet banking adoption: A unified theory of acceptance and use of technology and perceived risk application. International Journal of Information Management **34**(1), 1–13 (2014)
11. Arguedas, R., Pra, I., Reina, M.D.: Mobile banking: challenges and opportunities for the financial sector. In: Liébana-Cabanillas, F., Muñoz-Leiva, F., Sánchez-Fernández, J., Martínez-Fiestas, M. (eds.) Electronic Payment Systems for Competitive Advantage in E-Commerce, pp. 164–185. Business Science, Hershey (2014)
12. Sullivan, B., Garvey, J., Alcocer, J., Eldridge, A.: Retail Banking 2020. Evolution or Revolution?   PWC,   1–41   (2014).   http://www.pwc.com/en_GX/gx/banking-capital-markets/banking-2020/assets/pwc-retail-banking-2020-evolution-or-revolution.pdf (accessed April 24, 2015)

13. Dapp, T.F.: Pay Wars –Attack of the internet giants. Deutsche Bank DB Research, 1–3 (2013). http://www.dbresearch.com/PROD/DBR_INTERNET_EN-PROD/PROD00000 00000301712/Pay+Wars+%E2%80%93+Attack+of+the+internet+giants.PDF (accessed April 23, 2015)
14. Lerner, T.: Mobile Payment. Springer (2013)
15. ING International Survey: Cash no longer king! Mobile banking still rising (May 2014). http://www.ing.com/Newsroom/All-news/NW/Cash-no-longer-king-Mobile-banking-still-rising.htm
16. ING International Survey: Digitales Banking verdrängt Filialen. ING DiBa Austria (September 2013). https://www.ing-diba.at/ueber-ingdiba/presse/pressemeldungen/2013/ digitales-banking-verdraengt-filialen (accessed April 07, 2015)
17. Gu, J.C., Lee, S.C., Suh, Y.H.: Determinants of behavioral intention to mobile banking. Expert Systems with Applications 36(9), 11605–11616 (2009)
18. Accenture: Banking 2020. As the storm abates, North American banks must chart a new course to capture emerging opportunities. October 2013, 1–15. http://www.accenture.com/SiteCollectionDocuments/PDF/Accenture-Banking-2020-POV.pdf (accessed April 09, 2015)
19. Dapp, T.F.: The Future of (mobile) payments. New (online) players competing with banks. Deutsche Bank DB Research, 1–32 (2012)
20. OeNB: Ergebnisse der OeNB Zahlungsmittelumfrage. OeNB-Zahlungsmittelumfrage – 3, 1–4 (2013). http://www.oenb.at/Publikationen/Zahlungsverkehr/Zahlungsmittelumfrage. html (accessed April 09, 2015)
21. Kim, C., Mirusmonov, M., Lee, I.: An empirical examination of factors influencing the intention to use mobile payment. Computers in Human Behavior 26(3), 310–322 (2010)
22. European Commission: Green paper. Towards an integrated European market for card, internet and mobile payments. Brussels, 1–25 (2012). http://eur-lex.europa.eu/legal-content/EN/TXT/PDF/?uri=CELEX:52011DC0941&from=EN (accessed April 09, 2015)
23. de Bel, J., Gaza, M.: Mobile payments 2012 – My mobile, my wallet? Innopay, pp. 1–100 (September 2011). http://www.mobiltarca.com/media/documents/mobey-forum-mobile-payments-2012-innopay-2011.pdf (accessed April 08, 2015)
24. Capgemini and The Royal Bank of Scotland (RBS): World Payments Report (WPR) (2013). http://www.capgemini.com/wpr13 (accessed March 28, 2015)
25. Mallat, N.: Exploring consumer adoption of mobile payments – a qualitative study. In: Proceedings of Helsinki Mobility Roundtable. Working Papers on Information Systems, Sprouts, vol. 6, no. 44, pp. 1–16 (2006)
26. Punzet, J.: Paybox austria – eine M-Payment Erfolgsgeschichte. In: Handbuch E-Money, E-Payment & M-Payment, pp. 221–247. Physica-Verlag HD (2006)
27. Paybox: Zahl's mit dem Handy. - So bezahlen Sie mit paybox. https://www.paybox.at/6192/Privat/Bezahlen/Wie-bezahlen (accessed March 28, 2015)
28. Paybox: Zahl's mit dem Handy. - paybox macht Ihr Handy zur Geldbörse. http://www.paybox.at/6193/Privat/Bezahlen/Was-ist-paybox (accessed March 28, 2015)
29. VeroPay - Über uns. http://veropay.com/submenu/ueber_uns.html (accessed May 14, 2015)
30. VeroPay - Presse Archiv 1. http://veropay.com/submenu/Presse_archiv_1.html (accessed May 14, 2015)
31. VeroPay - Händler. http://veropay.com/mainmenu/akzeptanzstellen.html (accessed May 14, 2015)

32. VeroPay: Bezahl-App aus Tirol startet in ganz Österreich - futurezone.at. http://futurezone.at/b2b/veropay-bezahl-app-aus-tirol-startet-in-ganz-oesterreich/33.188.020 (accessed May 14, 2015)
33. Tan, G.W.H., Ooi, K.B., Chong, S.C., Hew, T.S.: NFC mobile credit card: the next frontier of mobile payment? Telematics and Informatics **31**(2), 292–307 (2014)
34. Leong, L.Y., Hew, T.S., Tan, G.W.H., Ooi, K.B.: Predicting the determinants of the NFC-enabled mobile credit card acceptance: a neural networks approach. Expert Systems with Applications **40**(14), 5604–5620 (2013)
35. Ondrus, J., Pigneur, Y.: An assessment of NFC for future mobile payment systems. Management of Mobile Business, International Conference on the ICMB **2007**, 43 (2007)
36. Accenture: Accenture Payment Services for Financial Institutions. Bridging communities, enabling commerce, 1–26 (2012)
37. Lamedschwandner, K., Bammer, M.: NFC-Aktivitäten in Österreich. e & i. Elektrotechnik und Informationstechnik **130**(7), 189–190 (2013)
38. About the Technology | NFC Forum. http://nfc-forum.org/what-is-nfc/about-the-technology/ (accessed May 11, 2015)
39. Pasquet, M., Reynaud, J., Rosenberger, C.: Secure payment with NFC mobile phone in the SmartTouch project. In: International Symposium on Collaborative Technologies and Systems, 2008. CTS 2008, pp. 121–126 (2008)
40. Card Payments - Current-Trends - Oesterreichische Nationalbank (OeNB). http://oenb.at/en/Payment-Processing/Card-Payments/Current-Trends.html (accessed May 12, 2015)
41. Kontaktloses Zahlen: Banken starten NFC Bankomatkarten - Telekom - derStandard.at > Web. http://derstandard.at/1363708001840/Kontaktloses-Zahlen-Banken-starten-NFC-Bankomatkarten (accessed May 11, 2015)
42. Pratz, A., Bloos, J.W., Engebretsen, O., Gawinecki, M.: Winning the Growth Challenge in Payments. European Payments Strategy Report. A. T. Kearney, pp. 1–16 (2013)
43. Banken planen Einführung von NFC-Bankomaten - Innovationen - derStandard.at > Web. http://derstandard.at/2000003524352/Banken-planen-Einfuehrung-von-NFC-Bankomaten (accessed May 11, 2015)
44. Startschuss für nationale NFC-Initiative - futurezone.at. (http://futurezone.at/b2b/startschuss-fuer-nationale-nfc-initiative/27.090.230 (accessed May 17, 2015)
45. Austrian companies plan national NFC wallet standard - NFC World. http://www.nfcworld.com/2013/09/18/325959/austrian-companies-plan-national-nfc-wallet-standard/ (accessed May 16, 2015)
46. Chakravorti, S., Kobor, E.: Why invest in payment innovations. J. Payment Sys. L. **1**, 331 (2005)
47. Mobile Marketing Association Austria: Mobile Communications Report 2014, pp. 1–146 (June 2014). http://www.mmaaustria.at/html/img/pool/Mobile_Communications_Report _2014.pdf (accessed May 12, 2015)
48. Gupta, S.: The Mobile Banking and Payment Revolution. European Financial Review, pp. 3–6 (2013)
49. van Thanh, D., Hallingby, H.S., Khuong, L.H., Kryvinska, N.: A disruption analysis of mobile communication services using Business Ecosystem concept, Inderscience Publishers. International Journal of Services, Economics and Management (IJSEM) **6**(3), 248–262 (2014)
50. Weber, M., Denk, M., Oberecker, K., Strauss, C., Stummer, C.: Panel Surveys go Mobile. International Journal of Mobile Communications **6**(1), 88–107 (2008)

51. Becker, A., Mladenow, A., Kryvinska, N., Strauss, C.: Aggregated survey of sustainable business models for agile mobile service delivery platforms. Journal of Service Science Research, Springer 4(1), 97–121 (2012)
52. Bashah, N.S.K., Kryvinska, N., Van Do, T.: Quality-driven service discovery techniques for open mobile environments and their business applications. Journal of Service Science Research 4(1), 71–96 (2012). Springer
53. Kryvinska, N., Strauss, C., Collini-Nocker, B., Zinterhof, P.: Enterprise Network Maintaining Mobility - Architectural Model of Services Delivery. Int. Journal of Pervasive Computing and Communications (IJPCC) 7(2), 114–131 (2011)
54. Strauss, C.: Informatik-Sicherheitsmanagement - Eine Herausforderung für die Unternehmensführung, Vieweg+Teubner Verlag, Stuttgart, ISBN: 978-3-519-02186-5 (1991)
55. Kryvinska, N. Auer, L. Zinterhof, P. Strauss, C.: Architectural Model of Enterprise Multiservice Network Maintaining Mobility. In: IEEE 13th International Telecommunications Network Strategy and Planning Symposium (NETWORKS 2008) - "Convergence in Progress", Budapest, Hungary, September 28–October 2, 2008

Impact of the Mobile Operating System on Smartphone Buying Decisions: A Conjoint-Based Empirical Analysis

Stephan Böhm[✉], Fabian Adam, and Wendy Colleen Farrell

Department of Design Computer Science Media,
RheinMain University of Applied Sciences, Wiesbaden, Germany
{stephan.boehm,wendycolleen.farrell}@hs-rm.de,
mail@fabianadam.info

Abstract. A key technical product feature of today's Smartphones is the mobile Operating System (OS). The choice in OS, not only commits consumers to essential technical features, but also has implications with regard to the user interface or availability of applications in the associated App Stores. In this context, this article examines the significance of the mobile operating systems with regards to the purchase decision. To this end, an empirical survey of Android and iOS buyers was carried out using a Choice Based Conjoint (CBC) analysis. In addition, the importance of various OS features as well as differences in personal attributes of Android and iOS users were analyzed. As a result, important differences are presented in terms of the attitudes and preferences of these groups of buyers with regard to mobile operating systems. In particular, it was found that the mobile OS plays the most important role in the purchase decision compared to brand, price, or design.

Keywords: Smartphone buying decision · Consumer behavior · Mobile operating system · Empirical study · Conjoint analysis

1 Introduction

The global market for smartphones has continued to grow in 2014 [1]. The majority of consumers planning to purchase a smartphone over the next year already own a smartphone [2]. When purchasing a device, consumers are faced with the task of choosing one from the ever growing variety of different device brands and models. One product feature is of essential significance for any smartphone – the mobile OS. The mobile OS is a piece of essential software for any smartphone and acts as an interface between hardware resources and applications. Deciding on a mobile OS therefore also determines essential aspects with regard to performance, security, and applications available to the user with respect to the smartphone. But, going beyond the technical features, the buyer also opts for the associated Mobile Ecosystem. This system is created by the available mobile applications and business models pursued to market this software.

© Springer International Publishing Switzerland 2015
M. Younas et al. (Eds.): MobiWis 2015, LNCS 9228, pp. 198–210, 2015.
DOI: 10.1007/978-3-319-23144-0_18

Globally, the mobile OS market is currently dominated by two companies: Google with Android and Apple with its competing product iOS. As a percentage of world-wide smartphone sales, Android achieved a market share of 84.4 percent in the third quarter of 2014 [1]. Apple's iOS, the second best-selling OS, only had a market share of about 11.7 percent. Other major operating systems include Windows Phone (2.9 percent) and BlackBerry OS (0.5 percent). These only play a minor role in terms of their market share, at least as far as new sales of smartphones are concerned. Thus smartphone buyers basically decide between devices using the mobile operating systems Android and iOS. The two mobile operating systems, iOS and Android, differ in many ways but also have various things in common. The differences are mainly due to the contrasting approaches that Apple and Google follow as a result of their different business models. Apple offers the end user the device and the OS from a single source. Google, on the other hand, has positioned its OS as open source software. The OS is thus installed on a wide range of device brands and models. Although the vast majority of mobile applications are now equally available for Android and iOS, the choice of the OS also affects the way the device is used. For example, the operating concepts and user interface designs differ in many ways as do the options for setting and configuring the OS. Moreover, a certain lock-in effect [3] arises for the buyer, as the mobile applications used for the device platform generally need to be reinstalled or even repurchased when switching operating systems. Thus, the impact of the choice of a particular mobile OS is complex and multifaceted. Particularly in the private end user customer segment, it can be expected that individual product features associated with the OS are not being compared with each other and thus have a relatively small impact on the ultimate device selection and purchase decision. Rather it is much more likely that the OS itself is a key factor in the purchase decision.

In light of the above, this study investigates the significance of the mobile OS for the smartphone purchase decision for private end users. In section 2 the current state of research is presented. The research approach chosen to analyze the importance of the mobile OS with regards to the smartphone purchase decision is then discussed in section 3. The discussion includes reasons for the application of Choice Based Conjoint (CBC) analysis. The empirical study and the main findings are subsequently described in section 4 before we discuss the implications for practice in section 5.

2   Research Background

Consumer buying behavior is a field of marketing research that looks at what factors influence consumers purchase decisions. In the behavioral research approach, cause-and-effect relationships between a stimulus that triggers purchase and the purchase itself, is regarded as being a reaction of the buyer [4, 5]. These stimulus response models, however, neglect to offer a more nuanced view of the purchase decision process itself and thus also provide no explanation of internal processes or buyer-related factors that influence the purchase decision. In contrast, the neo-behavioral Stimulus Organism Response (SOR) model also takes into account not directly observable factors such as perceptions, attitudes, and internal processes that occur during the purchasing decision [6]. It can be assumed that individual perceptions and attitudes with regards to a mobile OS (particularly for repeat and replacement purchases as mentioned above) have a significant impact on purchasing decisions. Understanding these individual perceptions and attitudes can improve the accuracy of explanations and predictions concerning smartphone buying behavior. Among other considerations, consumers make purchasing decisions by considering possible alternatives in terms of the expected benefits [7]. In general, utilities can be defined as the degree to which a customer's needs will be satisfied by the purchase or consumption of the product they have bought. The tangible benefits of a product depends on its features and its intended use.

When conducting consumer behavior research, it is difficult to ascertain the true value consumers place on certain characteristics. If asked about the certain characteristics, a consumer is likely to confirm it is important. The same response would be likely for other characteristics as well. One solution to this dilemma is the usage of preference models. We differentiate preference models between compositional and decomposition methods. In the decomposition method, no individual benefit dimensions are evaluated, but rather part-worth utilities are derived from an overall assessment. Here part-worth utility is a measurement of value per feature derived from the choices users made in trade off scenarios. The Conjoint Analysis, which will be discussed in section 3 in more detail, is one such method with which not only the part-worth utilities for each product feature can be determined, but also their relative importance within a set of stimuli [8]. Due to the market share distribution discussed above, observations will be confined to the two dominant mobile operating systems, Android and iOS. Within this context, this article aims to explore three research questions with respect to the impact of the mobile OS for the smartphone purchase decision:

- How do Android and iOS users differ in their attitudes (personal attributes, loyalty, and propensity to switch) to mobile operating systems?
- How do Android and iOS users differ in their perception of the relevance of various characteristics of mobile operating systems?
- How important is the mobile OS from the smartphone user's perspective in comparison to other product-related stimuli (brand, design, and price)?

Some groundwork and findings on various aspects of these research questions can already be found in scientific literature. Several academic studies have already explored the significance of various aspects of device design for conventional mobile phones (e.g. [4, 9]). Furthermore [10] found that both brand and price are also a significant factors in the selection of smartphones. Conjoint analysis (e.g. [11]) and other methods of user preferences analysis (e.g. [12]) have been carried out to determine the significance of various device functions. What all these early analyses have in common, however, is that the mobile OS was never comprehensively examined as a discrete preference forming feature in its own right. This is due to the fact that at this time, user devices were still mainly used for voice telephony and very little software-based personalization of the device could be carried out. More recent studies, however, also examine the influence of the mobile OS on the purchase decision.

In a study by Lay-Yee et al., 36 percent of the survey participants strongly agreed with the statement that they used their particular smartphone due to the mobile OS [10]. Other studies have examined the significance of the mobile OS as a determinant of smartphone purchase decisions in the context of factor analysis. In Sainy's study, the mobile OS as a decision criterion for the use or purchase of smartphones is included in the factor Product Features. However, it was identified as having a smaller influence [13] in comparison to other features such as smart phone design, number of apps, quality of available games and speed of Internet access, which were all included in this factor. Malviya et al. come to a similar conclusion in their factor analysis on smartphone purchase behavior. According to their findings, the mobile OS has "... a fairly good impact on the Brand Preference" [14]. Further studies have examined the influence of Android's and iOS's different OS features on the purchase decision [15] as well as on aspects of user propensity to switch between different mobile operating systems [16]. What all these studies have in common is that the selected research approach draws abstract conclusions, ignoring the actual purchase decision, and does not identify the relative importance of the mobile OS as a determinant of the decision to purchase. In addition, several of the studies focus on smartphone markets that are characterized by very specific environmental conditions and trajectories. Taking all these factors into consideration, and despite the groundwork available in scientific literature, there is a need for further research in order to answer the research questions formulated above.

3 Research Approach

To find answers to the research questions mentioned above, an empirical study was carried out. The focus of the study was to identify the relative importance of the mobile OS on the purchase decision based on a Conjoint Analysis (CA). CA is a multivariate analysis technique that looks at consumer preferences by taking a tradeoff approach when formulating the question. CA is also a decompositional approach, in which part-worth utilities are inferred from the participant's assessment of the "total" package or combination of attributes (Consider Jointly) through the application of statistical methods. For this purpose, it is generally assumed that the sum of all part-worth utilities corresponds to the total utility value. CA is one of the most frequently used methods to examine product preferences in market research [17]. By using CA, product manufacturers, for example, can find out how various individual product components contribute to the perceived total benefit. A CA is carried out in several stages [8]: In the first phase, a set of product relevant attributes is selected and the related attribute levels are defined. For this study, the smartphone was the product with the mobile OS being considered a product attribute. The two mobile operating systems, Android and iOS, were defined as possible levels or attribute levels of the product attribute OS. The next phase involves survey design followed by the actual data collection where participants rank the product attributes through a series of trade off scenarios. Finally, the part-worth utilities for each individual attribute level is assessed based on the data obtained, using statistical estimation methods.

The exact form of the survey design and the methods used to estimate the part-worth utilities vary according to the selected method variant. The rapid spread of CA in research and practice has produced numerous variants, of which the Choice-Based Conjoint Analysis (CBC) was selected as suitable for our purposes [18]. CBC is currently one of the most commonly used method variants and provides preference assessments in the form of trade off based selection decisions as opposed to rankings or rating scales. For this purpose, the participants must choose from a set of available product alternatives (Choice Set), once or repeatedly. With CBC, in contrast to other methods, a "none" choice option is also possible. CBC was used in our research because with this method, a high degree of realism can be achieved. This is due to the fact that on a survey, consumers will generally rate most product attributes as important, but when the decision to purchase comes, they often must make tradeoffs. Finally, CBC was chosen as implementation is simple through the use of computer software. On the basis of the previous literature analysis, four attributes were selected for the analysis: (1) device design, (2) device brand, (3) mobile OS, and (4) price. Thus, a simple and focused survey design was established in order to avoid a possible overload of the test subjects.

When determining the attribute levels, we can basically differentiate between symmetrical and asymmetrical designs [19]. With symmetrical designs, the number of attribute levels to be examined is equal for all product attributes being investigated. With asymmetrical designs, the number of levels varies, depending on the attribute. Generally, a symmetrical design is recommended, if possible, because otherwise attributes with a higher number of levels are often awarded higher significance by the test subjects [20]. Therefore, a symmetrical design with three levels for each of the attributes design, brand, OS, and price was applied. The full-profile method was used for the presentation of the stimuli with three product alternatives respectively plus a "None" option for each selection decision. The CA was carried out as an online questionnaire using the Sawtooth SSI Web 7 software package [21]. In addition to the conjoint-specific section, two further sections were added. In the first of these two sections, the test subjects were asked about certain personal attributes. In particular, questions were formulated to determine how design-oriented the test subjects are, their affinity for technology and security, trend and brand consciousness, as well as how open they are for new experiences. In the other section, the test subjects were asked to rank ten different attributes of mobile operating systems according to their subjectively perceived significance. Additional questions on smartphone and app usage, as well as demographic data, served to round out the survey.

4   Study Findings

The survey was conducted from the 22nd to the 31st of May 2014. A total of 149 test subjects participated in the online survey, of which 102 subjects completed the survey and are included in the subsequent analysis. The majority of the respondents that did not complete the survey quit on the title page. According to [22] the minimum sample size can be determined by the equation $n \cdot t \cdot a/c \geq 500$ where n is the number of respondents, t the number of tasks, a the number of alternatives presented per choice task, and c the largest number of levels for any attribute. Accordingly, taking the configuration of the present conjoint analysis into consideration ($t=5$; $a=3$; $c=3$), the minimum number of survey participants is 100. The number of participants in the study just fulfils this requirement. The average age of the survey participants was 28.8. The sample is well-balanced by gender, with 54 percent male and 46 percent female participants. The majority of the participants were employees (42 percent) and students (38 percent). For nearly 22 percent of the smartphone owners, the smartphone used at the time of the survey was a first-time purchase. Only one of the 102 participants did not own a smartphone. The mobile OS used by the smartphone owners was almost exclusively Android (47 percent) and iOS (52 percent). One test subject stated that he/she did not know which OS version was in use. Operating systems other than Android and iOS were not represented in the sample. Given the fact that iOS has less than 20 percent market share [23], the survey result is slightly biased in terms of OS usage, i.e., the share of iOS users is overrepresented. This is due to the survey environment and its focus. However, the results of the survey constitute a suitable basis for the proposed comparative analysis between Android and iOS users.

4.1   OS Usage and Loyalty

Initially, the survey participants were asked directly about the importance of the mobile OS when making a purchase decision. Approximately 76 percent of the participants rated the mobile OS as an important (31 percent) to very important (45 percent) criterion for smartphone purchase. Less than 2 percent of the participants stated that the mobile OS does not play an important role in the smartphone purchase decision.

Table 1. Mobile OS Usage and Loyalty

Study Items	Android User	iOS User
Previously used OS		
Android	46.8%	20.8%
iOS	4.3%	54.7%
Other OS	17.0%	11.3%
First smartphone	31.9%	13.2%
Loyalty toward current OS (on next smartphone)		
Not at all	2.1%	1.9%
Probably not	6.4%	0.0%
Maybe	25.5%	13.2%
Rather likely	46.8%	49.1%
Definitely	17.0%	35.8%
Do not know	2.1%	0.0%
Next OS (already decided users per OS)		
Android	27.7%	3.8%
iOS	2.1%	49.1%
Windows Phone	2.1%	0.0%
Blackberry OS	0.0%	0.0%

When comparing the Android and iOS users groups shown in Table 1, the first interesting factor to note is that the proportion of first-time smartphone buyers among Android users is much higher (32 percent) than among iOS users (13 percent). Furthermore, it can be seen that the percentage of Android users who previously used this OS is considerably lower (47 percent) than the proportion of continuous iOS users (55 percent).

The higher loyalty of iOS users to the currently used OS becomes apparent when asked directly about the probability of choosing the same OS for their next smartphone. Approximately half of the users of both groups considered it very likely that they would continue using the current OS. For those who are already very sure about their decision, however, the result is very different. While only 17 percent of Android users definitely want to continue to use the same OS, this proportion is more than twice as high for current iOS users, at almost 36 percent.

However, there is still room for uncertainty among smartphone users with respect to the OS purchase decision. This can be seen when they are asked, not about their loyalty, but about the likelihood of using Android, iOS, Windows Phone or BlackBerry operating systems in the future. The last section of Table 1 shows only the proportion of responses where participants stated that they would definitely use the current OS with their next smartphone. Here we see that almost 28 percent of Android users and over 49 percent of iOS users would choose the same OS again. This is another indication of the very strong loyalty of iOS users. Hardly any of the participants wanted to commit themselves to an alternative OS. This may also indicate that in addition to the respective groups of loyal OS users, there is also a large proportion of smart phone users who do not give much consideration to the various operating systems until faced with an actual or impending purchase decision.

4.2   Personal Attributes of OS Users

On the basis of the above explanations on smartphone users' OS loyalty, it can be assumed that these user groups differ in terms of their personal attributes. In this context, participants were asked to make an assessment on a four-point Likert scale of the degree or the existence of the personal attributes. The results are listed in Table 2.

Table 2. Empirical Results Personal Traits

Personal attributes	Median	Mean Rank	Mann-Withney U	p-Value (2-tailed)
	Android / iOS Users			
Design-oriented	2 / 1	57.88 / 42.88	851.5	0.005*
Technophile	2 / 2	54.40 / 46.02	1,015.0	0.124
Security-oriented	2 / 2	55.19 / 46.34	1,025.0	0.101
Trend-conscious	3 / 2	63.45 / 37.85	590.0	0.000**
Brand-conscious	3 / 2	63.15 / 38.58	614.0	0.000**
Experimental	3 / 3	45.31 / 51.31	1004.0	0.265

Median (Likert scale): 1 = fully applies, ... , 4 = does not apply at all
Significance levels: * p < 0.01, ** p < 0.001

On examination of the survey results, it is apparent that differences in terms of the median in design, trend and brand orientation can be observed. In each of these three categories, the iOS users rate themselves as having a higher affinity (lower median of Likert scores) than Android users. In order to examine the statistical significance of these differences in terms of the observed medians of these Likert-scaled questions, a Mann-Whitney's U-test was performed. As shown in Table 2, the differences between the groups are statistically significant with respect to design orientation ($p < 0.01$) as well as trend and brand consciousness ($p < 0.001$). On the other hand, a significant effect of membership of the group of either Android or iOS users cannot be established with respect to technology and security orientation and in terms of how experimental the participants see themselves to be. We can initially interpret these results as demonstrating that Apple, with its iOS operating system and its associated smartphone products, attracts especially design-oriented, trend-conscious, and brand-conscious buyers. The fact that this is less pronounced in terms of the Android operating system may also be related to the fact that Android is available on the market for various smartphone brands and designs and therefore addresses a less homogeneous buyer community.

4.3   Relevant OS Characteristics

Besides the differences in personal attributes, the importance of various OS characteristics from the perspective of Android and iOS users was examined. For this purpose, ten different characteristics were initially identified in discussions with experts. In addition to the OS supplier, these were the first characteristics most determined by smartphone technology and design: usability, functionality, performance, security, and configurability. For other features, expectations were reflected to the extent that the OS affects the usability of smartphones in connection with other devices (Device Compatibility) or the available options with respect to certain smart phone manufacturers (Brand Compatibility). Other features included were the total number of available apps in App Stores for the respective OS (Number of Apps) as well as the availability of certain preferred apps (Preferred Apps) for the respective OS platform. In order to obtain information on the relevance of these features for the groups of interviewed Android and iOS users, all participants were asked to rank these ten characteristics according to relevance, with rank one considered to be the most relevant from the perspective of each participant.

In Table 3, the results of this part of the survey are summarized. The table shows the averages of the assigned rankings for the respective characteristics with respect to the Android OS on the left and for the iOS users on the right side. Here we see that usability is ranked as being of the highest importance, followed by further technical OS characteristics and the OS supplier. Compatibility, configurability, and availability of apps, were ranked lower. This, however, does not mean that these features are of no importance to users, but rather we can assume that these features are taken for granted given the current level of development and thus no longer regarded as being distinguishing features. Despite the generally high levels of similarity of the rankings, differing degrees of the characteristics' importance can be observed if we directly compare them in detail. Although in both groups of users usability is ranked as being of the highest importance, it was awarded an average -0.73 lower ranking among iOS users, i.e., this OS characteristic was assessed as being relatively more important compared to the ranking by the Android users. Another major difference is the position of configurability. This OS characteristic was awarded much less importance by the iOS users compared to the ranking by the Android users (+0.72).

Table 3. OS Characteristics Ranking

Android Users			iOS Users		
Mobile OS Characteristics	Average Ranking	Standard Deviation	Mobile OS Characteristics	Average Ranking	Standard Deviation
Usability	3.62	3.05	Usability	2.89	2.40
Security	4.09	2.34	Functionality	3.77	2.33
Functionality	4.23	2.40	Performance	4.42	2.34
Performance	4.28	2.26	Security	4.60	2.45
OS Supplier	5.06	3.07	OS Supplier	5.25	2.93
Device Compatibility	6.00	2.32	Device Compatibility	5.85	2.44
Configurability	6.30	2.95	Preferred Apps	6.57	2.42
Preferred Apps	6.70	2.17	Number of Apps	6.94	2.73
Brand Compatibility	7.13	2.42	Configurability	7.02	2.45
Number of Apps	7.60	2.45	Brand Compatibility	7.70	2.19

With respect to the OS characteristics, we can therefore conclude that Android and iOS users classify the relevance of the characteristics examined here very similarly but, in comparison, iOS users attach particular importance to usability and Android users to configurability. In terms of the ascertained rankings, however, it must be noted that the ranking positions used do not allow conclusions to be drawn about varying distances with respect to the differences in importance of the individual characteristics.

4.4   Relative OS Importance

The final part of the research consisted of a conjoint analysis to determine the relative importance of the OS on the smartphone purchase decision. As previously mentioned, the investigation was confined here to the aspects of device design, device brand, OS, and price. In the questionnaire, each test subject was asked five times, i.e., was exposed to five choice tasks to make a choice decision between three smartphones configurations and a "none" option. The attribute levels selected were as realistic and as close to the market as possible. To present the device design, typical devices with their related user interface designs were visualized in the survey. A Windows Phone/Nokia configuration was also included in the analysis as a third option in addition to the typical Android and iOS attribute levels. Common smartphone profiles were also split and recombined, regardless of their availability on the market, and offered as alternatives to choose from. Before the stimuli were presented, the selection decision process was first presented to the survey participants. In addition, the participants were informed that products with combinations of features which are not available on the real market may also be offered for selection. In order to evaluate the data derived, an assessment of part-worth utilities was first carried out. On this basis, the relative importance of the individual attributes could then be determined.

Table 4 shows a summary of the results of the CBC analysis with regard to the investigated attributes and attribute levels. A first simple evaluation can be made using the relative frequencies which were determined. By calculating the frequency, the "winner" of each attribute level is derived. A high relative frequency of selection of an attribute level can thus be interpreted as the first indication of a presumably strong influence on the purchase decision. The part-worth utilities also shown in the table represent the contribution of each attribute level to the total benefit value of a stimulus. The part-worth utilities were calculated using the multinomial logit estimation provided by Sawtooth software for the CBC analysis. A Chi Square of 239.4 was reported for the model estimation. Considering 9 degrees of freedom (13 attribute levels and 4 attributes) the Chi Square is much larger than the required 21.7 for a 0.01 level, which would mean that the choices of the participants are significantly affected by the attribute composition [18]. The part-worth utilities shown in the table represent the contribution of each attribute level to the total benefit value of a stimulus. These values are standardized so that their sum per attribute adds up to zero. A higher number corresponds to a higher part-worth, which in turn means that these attribute levels are more preferred by the survey participants. Table 4 shows that for almost all the attributes, attribute levels typical for iOS versions were preferred (bold font) by the participants. It should be emphasized that in the context of conjoint analysis, a joint survey of Android and iOS users was carried out. This was done in the light of the fact that the overall relative importance of the OS was to be identified, independently of the particular user group.

Table 4. Summary of the Conjoint Analysis Results

Attributes and Attribute Levels		Counts (Prop. of "Wins")	Part-Worth Utilities
Design	**Form A (iPhone-style)**	**0.34**	**0.30768**
	Form B (Samsung S-style)	0.27	-0.03529
	Form C (Nokia Lumia-style)	0.22	-0.27239
Brand	Samsung	0.29	0.08496
	Apple	**0.36**	**0.37037**
	Nokia	0.18	-0.45533
Mobile OS	Google Android	0.27	0.10268
	Apple iOS	**0.43**	**0.65256**
	Windows Phone	0.13	-0.75524
Price	625 EUR	0.13	-0.77149
	350 EUR	0.33	0.28619
	270 EUR	**0.37**	**0.48529**
"None" Option	None	0.17	-0.15749

On the basis of the part-worth utilities of individual attribute levels, the relative importance of individual attributes can be determined. To calculate the relative importance, the range of the part-worth utilities for each attribute is divided by the sum of the ranges of all attributes. The values obtained are summarized in Table 5 and show that the OS with a relative attribute importance of 35 percent has the highest importance for the selection and purchasing decision. The second most important attribute is price, followed by the brand and the device design. The results of the conjoint analysis confirm the high relevance of the mobile OS for the purchase decision, which had already been identified by the direct question in the questionnaire.

Table 5. Relative Importance of Attributes

Attribute	Attribute Importance
Design	14%
Brand	20%
Operating System	35%
Price	31%
Total	**100%**

It is, however, interesting that even more importance is attached to this attribute than to the price of the smartphone. In particular the fact that the least importance is attached to design may at first appear surprising. It can be assumed that device design has become increasingly interchangeable from a customer perspective. Furthermore, it should be noted that the attribute "design" was reduced to the visualization of typical and presumably familiar design factors, similar to those presented in an online store.

5   Conclusions

As a result of this study, we can conclude that Android and iOS users differ considerably in terms of their loyalty to smartphone operating systems. The iOS users are more loyal to their OS and are characterized in terms of their personal attributes by a higher level of design, trend and brand orientation compared to Android users. When assessing the relevance of different OS features, the average rankings of the user groups were comparable. In both user groups, the most important feature was identified as being usability, which is accorded even higher priority among the iOS users when comparing the groups' average rankings for OS attributes. Contrastingly, the operating system's configuration options are particularly import to the Android users.

With regard to the importance of the OS for the smartphone purchase decision, both the direct question in the questionnaire and the conjoint analysis, indicated that the OS was a strong influencing factor. In the comparison between design, brand, and price, the OS is awarded the highest importance for the smartphone purchase decision. Another aspect of the results of the conjoint analysis that must be emphasized is that the highest part-worth utilities were calculated for the attribute levels of Apple/iOS smartphones – with the exception of price. These features may thus still be considered to be "best practice" in the marketplace. In view of the above, Google's strategy has also been proved to be effective by attacking Apple's market position. Google did this, not by focusing on its own product line, but by marketing a high-quality and technically advanced OS in a cooperative strategy and thus expanding into more price sensitive customer groups. It should be noted that the present analysis has only focused on partial aspects of marketing-relevant attributes of mobile operating systems. Aspects related to the wider adoption and diffusion of operating systems and the influences of network effects have not been dealt with here. In addition, the relatively small and non-representative sample as well as the pure online presentation of the stimuli may limit the generality of the findings.

References

1. IDC: Smartphone OS Market Share, Q2 (2014). http://www.idc.com/prodserv/smartphone-os-market-share.jsp
2. Accenture: Racing Toward a Complete Digital Lifestyle. Accenture Digital Consumer Tech Survey (2014). http://www.accenture.com/SiteCollectionDocuments/PDF/Accenture-Digital-Consumer-Tech-Survey-2014.pdf
3. Jelassi, T., Enders, A., Martínez-López, F.J.: Strategies for e-business. Creating value through electronic and mobile commerce; concept and cases. Pearson, Harlow (2014)
4. Chuang, M.C., Chang, C.C., Hsu, S.H.: Perceptual factors underlying user preferences toward product form of mobile phones. Int. J. of Industrial Ergonomics 27, 247–258 (2001)
5. Chiu, H.-C., Hsieh, Y.-C., Li, Y.-C., Lee, M.: Relationship marketing and consumer switching behavior. Journal of Business Research 58, 1681–1689 (2005)
6. Jacoby, J.: Stimulus-Organism-Response Reconsidered: An Evolutionary Step in Modeling (Consumer) Behavior. Journal of Consumer Psychology 12, 51–57 (2002)
7. Häubl, G., Trifts, V.: Consumer Decision Making in Online Shopping Environments: The Effects of Interactive Decision Aids. Marketing Science 19, 4–21 (2000)
8. Green, P.E., Srinivasan, V.: Conjoint analysis in consumer research: issues and outlook. Journal of consumer research, 103–123 (1978)
9. Yun, M.H., Han, S., Hong, S., Kim, J.: Incorporating user satisfaction into the look-and-feel of mobile phone design. Ergonomics 46, 1423–1440 (2003)
10. Lay-Yee, K.L., Kok-Siew, H., Yin-Fah, B.C.: Factors Affecting Smartphone Purchase Decision Among Malaysian Generation Y. Int. Journal of Asian Social Science 3, 2426–2440 (2013)
11. Kim, Y., Lee, J.-D., Koh, D.: Effects of consumer preferences on the convergence of mobile telecommunications devices. Applied Economics 37, 817–826 (2005)
12. Işıklar, G., Büyüközkan, G.: Using a multi-criteria decision making approach to evaluate mobile phone alternatives. Computer Standards & Interfaces 29, 265–274 (2007)
13. Sainy, M.: An Empirical Study On Factors Influencing The Buying Behavior of Smartphone Among B-school Students. BAUDDHIK J. of Management 5, 24–35 (2014)
14. Malviya, S., Saluja, M.S., Thakur, A.S.: A Study on the Factors Influencing Consumer's Purchase Decision Towards Smartphones in Indore. International Journal of Advance Research in Computer Science and Management Studies 1, 14–21 (2013)
15. Jain, V., Sharma, A.: The Consumer's Preferred Operating System: Android or iOS. International Journal of Business Management & Research 3, 29–40 (2013)

16. Wang, Y., Zang, H., Devineni, P., Faloutsos, M., Janakiraman, K., Motahari, S.: Which phone will you get next: observing trends and predicting the choice. In: 2014 IEEE/IFIP Network Operations and Management Symposium, NOMS 2014, pp. 1–7 (2014)
17. Green, P.E., Krieger, A.M., Wind, Y.: Thirty Years of Conjoint Analysis: Reflections and Prospects. Interfaces **31**, 56–73 (2001)
18. Sawtooth: The CBC System for Choice-Based Conjoint Analysis. https://sawtoothsoftware.com/download/techpap/cbctech.pdf
19. Sambandam, R.: Asymmetry analysis. Quirk's Marketing Res. Review **18**, 24–29 (2004)
20. Chrzan, K., Orme, B.: An overview and comparison of design strategies for choice-based conjoint analysis. Sawtooth software research paper series (2000)
21. Sawtooth Software: SSI Web Software. http://www.sawtoothsoftware.com/products/conjoint-choice-analysis
22. Orme, B.K.: Getting started with conjoint analysis. Strategies for product design and pricing research. Research Publishers, Madison (2010)
23. Gronli, T.-M., Hansen, J., Ghinea, G., Younas, M.: Mobile Application Platform Heterogeneity: Android vs Windows Phone vs iOS vs Firefox OS. In: 2014 IEEE 28th International Conference on Advanced Information Networking and Applications (AINA), pp. 635–641

SandMash: An Approach for Mashups Techniques on Smartphones

Raed Ali[✉] and Kalman Graffi

Technology of Social Networks Group, University of Düsseldorf, Düsseldorf, Germany
ali_raed@cs.uni-duesseldorf.de, graffi@cs.uni-duesseldorf.de
http://tsn.hhu.de

Abstract. Supporting Mashup on mobile devices allows supporting advanced use cases and thus to accelerate the creation and combination of smart mobile applications. In this paper, we evaluate the three client-side Mashups proposals JS.JS, OMash and SMash on mobile devices. Our evaluation on mobile devices shows that the SMash proposal by IBM is reasonably suited for mobile mashups development as it requires less amount of effort from developers and at the same time it has cross-mobile-browser compatibility. In order to address the security, we integrated a sandbox functionality. We have modified the OpenAjax JavaScript library proposed in SMash and have added support of HTML5 ⟨iframe⟩ tag's "sandbox" attribute to it. ⟨iframe⟩ "sandbox" attribute, mobile mashups developers can restrict the framed-content (which may not be trustworthy) in a low-privileged environment. We demonstrate our proposal on a mobile mashup application that integrates content from three different providers (i.e., News, Stock and Weather service).

Keywords: Mashup · Smartphones · Mobile services

1 Introduction

According to [8] mobile Internet and mobile devices will be available to 2 to 3 billion people over the next decade taking a huge impact on the media industry [7]. Nowadays, mobile phones have HTML and JavaScript compliant browsers. This makes mobile devices a potential and future venue for mashups like functionality. Mashups are web applications that combine data from different content providers at a single place i.e., web browser. The goal of mashups is to provide rich and better browsing experience to the users by taking advantage of client-side AJAX (Asynchronous JavaScript and XML). Third-party contents normally comes in the form of JavaScript code which may or may not be trustworthy. Third-party content, if malicious, may cause harm to the web application and its users. Researchers have proposed several solutions such as, JS.JS [14], OMash [2] and SMash [5], to confine third-party scripts. The motivation for this work is to evaluate client-side, web-based mashup solutions on mobiles which are nowadays essential part of our daily life.

© Springer International Publishing Switzerland 2015
M. Younas et al. (Eds.): MobiWis 2015, LNCS 9228, pp. 211–217, 2015.
DOI: 10.1007/978-3-319-23144-0_19

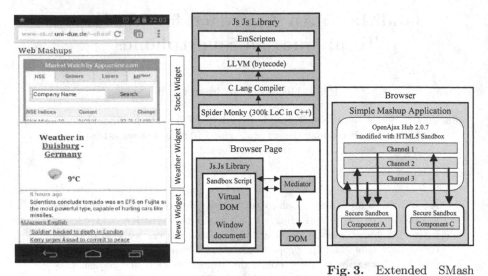

Fig. 1. Mobile Mashup Application

Fig. 2. JS.JS Architecture

Fig. 3. Extended SMash Architecture with Sandbox Support

In an earlier work [12], Philippe De Ryck et al. have identified the following Mashups requirements for building secure mashups: Separation, Interaction and Communication. *Separation* requires that the DOM tree of one mashup component should be completly separated from DOM tree of other mashup components. At the same time scripts belong to individual component and should not be regulated by other components' scripts. In the literature, we found several techniques proposed by researchers for "separation" requirement. The proposals listed in this umbrella are: JS.JS [14], HTML5 ⟨iframe⟩ sandbox attribute [13], Google Caja , AdSafe and AdSentry [3]. *Interaction* should be secured. In mashup applications, content from different providers often need to interact with other party's content and with the provider application. During the interaction the confidentiality and integrity of private information should remain intact. We refer to [12] for detailed discussions on these secure mashups requirements. We found the following techniques in this category: OMash [2], OMOS [16] and Post Message. Mashups should support same-origin and cross-origin *Communication*. SMash [5] and W3C CORS7 proposals fulfill this mashup requirement

In this paper, we have evaluated one client-side mashup technique from a set of requirements on mobiles. The main contribution of this paper is to evaluate Mashups technologies (i.e., SMash, OMash and JS.JS) on mobiles, see for that Section 2. In Section 3, we revisit SMash's implementation (i.e., OpenAjax JavaScript library) and add a support for ⟨iframe⟩ "sandbox" attribute. To the best of our knowledge, this paper presents the first evaluation of web-based mashups techniques on mobiles.

2   Evaluation of Web-Based Mashups for Mobiles

In this section, we discuss our evaluation of web-based mashups on mobile devices. During mashups evaluation on mobiles, we consider the following factors: 1) lightweight mobile applications, 2) cross-mobile-browser support, 3) amount of effort required from developers and 4) the developers' learning curve. Considering this, we evaluate SMash, OMash and JS.JS on mobiles using the following running example, which simulates the real-life mashup application. In our mobile mashup example, content and data is coming from three different service providers i.e., stock news, weather information and news information. Fig. 1 shows our mashup application that we used to evaluate the mashup techniques.

2.1   Evaluation of JavaScript in JavaScript (JS.JS)

Terrace et al. proposed in [14] a client-side mashup solution named JavaScript in JavaScript (JS.JS). The main goal of JS.JS is to sandox third-party scripts which may or may not be trustworthy. Working According to [4]: JS.JS is a JavaScript interpreter running in JavaScript that allows an application to execute a third-party script inside a completely isolated, sandboxed environment. JS.JS compiles the SpiderMonkey JavaScript interpreter to LLVM bytecode with the help of Clang compiler and then use Emscripten to translate the LLVM bytecode to JavaScript. SpiderMonkey is the JavaScript engine used in Firefox web browser. Emscripten is an LLVM-to-JavaScript compiler. Fig. 2) depicts the complete process of the JS.JS technique.

JS.JS is available in the form of gzipped JavaScript library with a size of 594KB. The original library has a size of around 14MB. The authors of [14] have also provided a wrapper API which consists of 1000 lines of code and noted in their work that JS.JS has performance issues due to its heavy-weight size [14] and its nature. Mobile applications are simple in nature and have less amount of code as compared to their desktop variants. The first challenge we faced during the implementation of our example mobile mashup application was performance. The execution time, i.e. setting up the environment of JS.JS on mobile devices, is much higher (around six times) as compared to the execution time on desktop machines (220ms). Considering the factors on which we have based our evaluation, we found JS.JS does not have cross-mobile browser support. At the time of writing, JS.JS is not compatible with Internet Explorer (IE) mobile browser as it IE does not support "typed arrays". The amount of effort developers have to put in is high as the JS.JS library does not provide string manipulation operations. Developers have to rewrite the code if they want to use these functions. The developers' learning curve is also high in JS.JS case.

We believe, it is reasonable to expect that if learning curve is high then there is a great chance that developers will not use the technology due to time constraints and business pressure. Our evaluation of JS.JS on mobile devices shows that JS.JS is not reasonably suited for mobile mashup applications development.

2.2   Evaluation of OMash

Crites et al. proposed in [2] OMash for secure web-based mashup application development. The authors have modified Mozilla Firefox 2.0 for proof-of-concept implementation of OMash proposal. OMash is an abstraction that treats web pages as objects and allows objects to communicate only via their declared public interfaces. Since OMash does not rely on the same-origin policy [11] for controlling DOM access or cross-domain data exchange, it does not suffer from the same-origin policy vulnerabilities. OMash leverages the idea of "object abstraction" from Java object model. In Java, object represents a principal and objects can communicate with other objects only via public interfaces. OMash considers every web page as principal. Contents belonging to the web page are private by default and other objects can access the content only via public methods.

OMash was available as an extenion of the Firefox 2.0 web browser. In order to demonstrate OMash, authors have to make some internal Firefox configuration settings in order to access the function "getPublicInterface" and to allow cross-domain communication. In the domain of *capability.policy.default* the three configurations to be set are *Window.getPublicInterface.get*(allAccess), *Window.getPublicInterface.set*(sameOrigin), *XMLHttpRequest.open*(allAccess). The current versions of the Firefox browser do not support these configuration values due to security concerns [9]. One alternative, we found is to reimplement the solution completely in JavaScript, but it is time consuming and will take a lot of time from developers. In JavaScript's implementation of OMash, the size of code will also grow as developers have to implement browser's security preferences explicitly in JavaScript which affects the performance of mobile mashup applications. Further, the learning curve is high and on mobile-side we do not see potential of OMash technique for mashup application development.

2.3   Evaluation of SMash

Yoshihama et al. have proposed SMash in [5]. It is a secure component model, supportingh the encapsulation of contents and data from different domains which may or may not be trustworthy. In SMash, components are linked together via communication abstraction and the ⟨iframe⟩ tag is used as a container. All mobile browsers also support the ⟨iframe⟩ tag. E.g. if a main mashup application wishes to integrate contents from three different domains, the application will use three ⟨iframe⟩ tags i.e., one for each domain. SMash is implemented in the form of an open-source JavaScript library named OpenAjax [10], which is browser independent. The model consists of components, with input/output ports, and an event hub, with mediated communication channels. A component contains contents from one domain. The event hub is a publish/subscribe system with many-to-many channels on which messages are published and distributed. Due to being open-source it is suitable for modifications and improvements.

3 SandMash: SMash with Iframe Sandbox Attribute

SMash's OpenAjax library does not support HTML5's ⟨iframe⟩ tag's "sandbox" attribute. We have added this feature to the OpenAjax library. The "sandbox" is a new attribute added to ⟨iframe⟩ tag in HTML5. It is based on a "principle of least privilege" [15]. It is now supported by major desktop browsers and according to [1], mobile browsers also support "sandbox" attribute. With the help of the ⟨iframe⟩ "sandbox" attribute, mobile mashups developers can restrict the framed-content (which may not be trustworthy) in a low-privileged environment. and they can also specify the security policy on the framed-content with the help of the following flags allow-same-origin, allow-scripts, allow-popups, allow-forms.

Fig. 3 shows our modified model of SMash. It includes support of the "sandbox" attribute as an additional layer of security on framed-content. In the Fig. 3, component A can publish to Channel 2 and 3 and is subscribed to Channel 1.

Listing 1.1. OpenAjax Library with "Sandbox" Support

```
var_d4=document.createElement("span");
_b7.IframeSandbox.parent.appendChild(_d4);
var_d5="<iframe_sandbox=
'allow-scripts_allow-same-origin_'
id=\""+_be+"\"_name=\""+_be+"\"
src=\"javascript:'<html>_</html>'\"";
var_d6="";
var_d7=_b7.IframeSandbox.iframeAttrs;
```

Fig. 4. Average Performance Timing for SMash and SandMash

Testing Type	SMash	Sand-Mash
connect	391 ms	41 ms
domContentLoadEvent	2 ms	1 ms
domainLookup	42 ms	23 ms
loadEvent	260 ms	305 ms
responseToRequest	91 ms	47 ms

3.1 Implementation

In this section, we discuss our implemention of proposed SMash model for mobile mashup application development. SMash's implementation is available in the form of open source, browser-independent library. For the implementation of SandMash, we have added support of the "sandbox" attribute in the library OpenAjax Hub 2.0.7 [10]. Listing 1.1 shows a code snippet from our modified OpenAjax library and how mobile mashup applications developers can set the security policy (e.g., allow-scripts, allow-same-origin) on individual components.

3.2 Evaluation

In this section, we discuss the evaluation of proposed SMash model on our running example (see Section 3.1) by keeping in mind the factors (see Section 1). The OpenAjax library is a lightweight JavaScript library. It is reasonably suited for mobile mashup application developement. We have already discussed that our modifications in the library are also not substancial. OpenAjax is also mobile-browser-independent library. The amount of effort required by the developers is low due to the use of ⟨iframe⟩ tag for content separation. Mostly developers are aware of ⟨iframe⟩ tag so the learning curve will also be low.

It may help in adoption of modified (added layer of security in the form of "sandbox" attribute) SMash technique on mobiles. As a part of performance evaluation, we have loaded the toy mobile mashup application with original SMash library and with our modified SMash library in mobile browser fifteen times as shown in the Figure 4 above. The average load time we experienced was 260 ms for original SMash library and 305 ms for our modified SMash library.

4   Conclusion

In this paper, we evaluated three client-side Mashups proposals (i.e., JS.JS [14], OMash [2] and SMash [5]) on mobile devices. Our evaluation on mobile devices shows that the SMash proposal by IBM is reasonably suited for mobile mashups development because it requires less amount of effort from developers and at the same time it has cross-mobile-browser compatibility. We have modified the OpenAjax JavaScript library [10] proposed in SMash and have added support of HTML5 ⟨iframe⟩ tag's "sandbox" attribute to it. With the help of ⟨iframe⟩ "sandbox" attribute, mobile mashups developers can restrict the framed-content (which may not be trustworthy) in a low-privileged environment. We demonstrated our proposal on a mobile mashup application that integrates content from three different providers (i.e., News, Stock and Weather service).

References

1. CanIUse?: Sandbox Attribute for iframes. http://caniuse.com#search=sandbox
2. Crites, S., Hsu, F., Chen, H.: OMash: enabling secure web mashups via object abstractions. In: Proc. of the ACM Conf. on Computer and Communications Security, (CCS 2008), pp. 99–108, October 2008
3. Dongy, X., Tranz, M., Liangy, Z., Jiangz., X.: Adsentry: Comprehensive and flexible confinement of javascript-based advertisements. In: Annual Computer Security Applications Conf., (ACSAC 2011), pp. 297–306 (2011)
4. JavaScriptinJavaScript(js.js): Sandboxing Third-Party Scripts, April 2012. http://sns.cs.princeton.edu/2012/04/javascript-in-javascript-js-js-sandboxing-third-5Cp-arty-scripts/
5. Keukelaere, F.D., Bhola, S., Steiner, M., Chari, S., Yoshihama, S.: SMash: secure component model for cross-domain mashups on unmodified browsers. In: Proc. of the Int. Conf. on World Wide Web (WWW 2008) 2008, pp. 535–544, April 2008
6. Kovacevic, A., Kaune, S., Heckel, H., Mink, A., Graffi, K., Heckmann, O., Steinmetz, R.: PeerfactSim.KOM - A Simulator for Large-Scale Peer-to-Peer Networks. Tech. Rep. Tr-2006-06, TU Darmstadt (2006)
7. Liebau, N., Pussep, K., Graffi, K., Kaune, S., Jahn, E., Beyer, A., Steinmetz, R.: The impact of the P2P paradigm on the new media industries. In: AMCIS 2007: Proceedings of Americas Conference on Information Systems (2007)
8. Manyika, J., Chui, M., Bughin, J., Dobbs, R., Bisson, P., Marrs, A.: Disruptive Technologies: Advances that will transform life, business, and the global economy, May 2013. http://www.mckinsey.com/insights/

9. Mozilla: Configurable Security Policies. http://www-archive.mozilla.org/projects/security/components/ConfigPolicy.html
10. OpenAjaxAlliance: Openajax alliance open source project at sourceforge. http://openajaxallianc.sourceforge.net/
11. Ruderman, J.: The same origin policy, August 2001. http://www.mozilla.org/projects/security/components/same-origin.html/
12. De Ryck, P., Decat, M., Desmet, L., Piessens, F., Joosen, W.: Security of web mashups: a survey. In: Aura, T., Järvinen, K., Nyberg, K. (eds.) NordSec 2010. LNCS, vol. 7127, pp. 223–238. Springer, Heidelberg (2012)
13. spec.whatwg: HTML-The Living Standard. https://html.spec.whatwg.org/multi-page/embedded-content.html#attr-iframe-sandbox
14. Terrace, J., Beard, S.R., Katta, N.P.K.: JavaScript in JavaScript (js.js): sandboxing third-party scripts. In: Proc. of the USENIX Conf. on Web Application Development (WebApps 2012), pp. 95–100 (2012)
15. West, M.: Play safely in sandboxed iframes, January 4, 2013. http://www.html5rocks.com/en/tutorials/security/sandboxed-iframes/
16. Zarandioon, S., Yao, D.D., Ganapathy, V.: OMOS: a framework for secure communication in mashup applications. In: Annual Computer Security Applications Conf., (ACSAC 2008), pp. 355–364 (2008)

In Need of a Domain-Specific Language Modeling Notation for Smartphone Applications with Portable Capability

Hamza Ghandorh[1]([✉]), Luiz Fernando Capretz[1], and Ali Bou Nassif[2]

[1] Department of Electrical and Computer Engineering,
Western University, London, ON, Canada
{hghandor,lcapretz}@uwo.ca
[2] Department of Electrical and Computer Engineering,
University of Sharjah, Sharjah, United Arab Emirates
abounassif@ieee.org

Abstract. The rapid growth of the smartphone market and its increasing revenue has motivated developers to target multiple platforms. Market leaders, such as Apple, Google, and Microsoft, develop their smartphone applications complying with their platform specifications. The specification of each platform makes a platform-dedicated application incompatible with other platforms due to the diversity of operating systems, programming languages, and design patterns. Conventional development methodologies are applied to smartphone applications, yet they perform less well. Smartphone applications have unique hardware and software requirements. All previous factors push smartphone developers to build less sophisticated and low-quality products when targeting multiple smartphone platforms. Model-driven development have been considered to generate smartphone applications from abstract models to alleviate smartphones platform fragmentation. Reusing these abstract models for other platforms was not considered because they do not fit new platforms requirements. It is possible that defining smartphone applications using a portability-driven modeling notation would facilitate smartphone developers to understand better their applications to be ported to other platforms. We call for a portability-driven modeling notation to be used within a smartphone development process. Our in-process research work will be manifested through the application of a domain-specific language complying with the three software portability principles and three design factors. This paper aims to highlight our research work, methodology and current statue.

Keywords: Smartphone apps · Model-driven development · Modeling · Portability · Modeling notation

1 Introduction

Smartphone applications[1] or apps become a vital part of our lives due to their contributions to achieve our daily and necessary tasks. The more smartphone

---

[1] Software or application terms will be used interchangeably.

© Springer International Publishing Switzerland 2015
M. Younas et al. (Eds.): MobiWis 2015, LNCS 9228, pp. 218–227, 2015.
DOI: 10.1007/978-3-319-23144-0_20

apps have become innovative, the more users see them as a desirable asset. This demand triggered an intense competition among leading smartphone companies, namely Apple, Google, and Microsoft, to provide more innovative apps. This competition not only had enabled a rapid growth in mobile market and the emergence of increasingly better features, but also was responsible for smartphone apps development complexity and smartphones platform fragmentation [1].

Similarly as other type of software, smartphone apps may need to migrate to a variety of platforms due to the growing diversity of computing environments over their lifetime and rapid changing users requirements [2]. For example, Android platform was the dominate platform for smartphone apps development where it held 71% of developers landscape in the end of 2014 [3]. Android was targeted, however, by only 40% of professional developers, where other platforms gained more priority, such as iOS for 37%, Windows Phone 7 and the mobile browser have 8% and 7% of the developers landscape, respectively [3]. Software developers agree that app portability is a desirable attribute for their projects due to durable cost-effectiveness and for a maximum of end-users. The primary goal of portability is to facilitate the activity of *porting* an application from an environment in which it currently operates to a new environment prior to allow reuse of complete existing codes in the new environment. Concerns in app portability include maintaining quality as well as saving time and money and leveraging an existing effort in the deployment of software design in new ways [2].

Smartphone apps are built through agile development methods, such as extreme programming (XP) [6], where they focus on incremental development steps and small and frequent systems releases. Agile development methods focus on apps design and implementation, and apps requirements are gathered through incremental development processes [4]. There are few smartphone development paradigms mentioned in the literature: 1) native software development kits (SDKs), 2) mobile web approach, and 3) hybrid approach [5]. Native smartphone apps are codes written to a specific platform with a particular programming language, such as Android Java or Objective-C. Smartphone apps developed by native SDKs ensure feel-and-look feature, and all smartphone devices hardware are accessible for their users. Native-SDKs apps are high-quality and ensure best user interface (UI) and user experience (UX) for their users, native-SDKs apps are very expensive to build and maintain for different smartphone platforms, though [6]. Mobile web apps are custom websites for small screen devices that use open web technologies, such as HTML5 or JavaScript. Mobile web apps run on smartphone web browsers, and mobile web apps support multiple screen sizes and different platforms. Mobile web apps are cheaper to build and capable of dynamic performance in terms of functionality and data updates, mobile web apps are slower, lack superior UX, and can not operate without an internet connection, though [7][8]. Hybrid apps are developed by cross-compatible web technologies and native platform code. Hybrid app are installed on smartphone devices and are easier to port to several platforms with few code adjustments. Hybrid apps allow for native-alike UX, hybrid apps are slow, suffer from low-performance, and their costs vary from a platform to another platform, though [8][6].

Several smartphone development tools used to target many different platforms: 1) cross-platforms tools, 2) runtime frameworks, and 3) cloud-based mobile web servers [9]. Cross-platforms tools, such as PhoneGap[2], develop hybrid apps and support developers to tolerate smartphone fragmentation. Cross-platforms tools neither ensure feel-and-look feature nor allow full use of device resources [9]. Runtime frameworks, such as Adobe Flash Lite[3], develop smartphone apps base on Flash technology to support apps with rich multimedia. Cloud-based mobile web servers, such as Altova MobileTogether Server[4], provide reusable services to facilitate integration with other back-end systems. Cloud-based mobile web apps are mobile web apps that uses cloud capabilities and do not target a specific smartphone device [10]. Although these tools support developers to tolerate smartphone fragmentation, these tools produce low-performance apps and no census exists to prefer a approach on another approach where they are still under research and development [1].

To ease the current highly fragmented world of smartphone platforms, model-driven development (MDD) concept have been investigated in the context of smartphone development. MDD advocates model transformations to produce executable code from abstract models [11]. MDD facilitates to raise abstraction level of development by hiding low-level specific platform details. Several programming methods exist to represent the concept of MDD, such as Domain-Specific Language (DSL)[12]. DSL is a programming language that specifies a software unit in a domain language considering the domain concepts and rules with a thorough understanding of the domain with best practices and expert knowledge. DSL automatically generates executable codes from abstract design models in a chosen programming language without afterward manual code modifications. DSL also aims to reduce manual code errors, to improve software quality, and to increase developers productivity [13].

This paper is organized as follows: Section 2 indicates our research problem, Section 3 describes relevant related work to our proposed solution, Section 4 highlights our proposed modeling notation and its components, and Section 5 concludes our paper.

2   Research Problem and Motivation

Each leading smartphone company, such as Apple, Google, and Microsoft, produces its smartphone apps complying with their own designing and implementation specifications by their specific tools. The specification of each platform makes developed apps for a given platform incompatible with other platforms. This lack of compatibility have smartphone developers to rewrite their apps for each one of the target platforms increasing the effort and the time to market of these apps. Hence, dedicated applications development for each platform is a

---

[2] PhoneGap site http://phonegap.com/

[3] Adobe Flash Lite site http://www.adobe.com/devnet/devices/flashlite.html

[4] Altova MobileTogether Server site http://www.altova.com/mobiletogether/server.html

non-trivial task for software engineers when considering labour and maintenance costs [6].

Software apps design seems independent of its implementation and it should be perfectly reused by definition, the chosen design method will have a major impact on smartphone apps portability and will direct software architecture, though [2]. Conventional software development methodologies are proven to be effective for desktop software products, and these methodologies are applied to smartphone apps. However, less quality appear on smartphone apps in terms of slow performance and less requirements [14]. Such phenomena occurred due to two perspectives: unique hardware and application requirements. Smartphone devices could be expanded to new and several type of hardware, and they could enable rich UI input which increases apps operability more then desktop devices [6]. Smartphone devices differentiate in screen size, input/output facilities, and their graphical user interface (GUI) which usually needs to be significantly adjusted. Smartphone apps require one-hand operation, and smartphone apps functionality and usability are impacted by inconsistent internet connections and current users contexts [6]. In addition, several special considerations need to be made for smartphone apps development. For example, smartphone apps is built in very short time with low prices, they operate on constantly event-driven, their life cycle is very limited, and their quality depends on their GUI responsiveness and its efficiently to save battery life [15]. All previous design requirements should be considered in the design phase and they impose own challenges against porting activity between different smartphone platforms. Another issue that negatively impact the quality of smartphone apps is that smartphone apps are designed with superficial or ad-hoc modeling approaches. Smartphone developers do not follow a systematic standard in designing their apps where they create mockups with simple and basic graphics and produce dummy version of their apps that include UI screens and their element interactions [16].

There is a gap in the smartphone literature about well-defined MDD methods complying with three key software portability principles [2]: to control interacting interfaces, to isolate external dependencies, and to design apps in a portable way. It is possible that defining smartphone applications considering app portability requirements by using abstract design models and automatically generating executable code from these models will contribute to alleviate smartphones platform fragmentation.

3   Related Work

General-purpose modeling notations (e.g. Unified Modeling Language (UML)[5]) were designed to be "one-size-fits-all". Smartphones are totally a different medium and their unique hardware capabilities, and their current context pose many constraints on their design [6]. To adapt to new smartphone modeling requirements, additional action languages, such as Object Constraint Language

---

[5] Unified Modeling Language site http://www.uml.org/

(OCL), are needed to be added to describe constraints about the model objects in the general-purpose modeling notations [13].

There are several efforts attempted to model smartphone apps by modifying general-purpose modeling notations. M-UML [17] and UML metamodel for Window Phone 7 (WP7) [18] are few examples. M-UML notation described all aspects of mobility for a mobile agent-based system to address inconsistent connectivity issues in their system. UML metamodel for WP7 notation described WP7 platform features by adding UML stereotypes to include UI elements and hardware resources of any WP7-based smartphone devices. These extended versions of UML will impact developers productivity with their long learning curve in a fast changing world of smartphone development. Another issue of using general-purpose modeling notations is that they do not represent final artifacts due to changing user requirements and agile-based development and maintenance tasks, and it is expensive to update these models to reflect the final artifacts [13].

Other efforts have used model-driven notations to generate executable code to various smartphone platforms. MobDSL [19] and X_{MOB} [20] are few examples. MobDSL notation defined a calculus language to produce mobile virtual apps to work on iPhone and Android smartphones and tablets. X_{MOB} notation defined a mobile dedicated language to produce native code through MDA model transformations. These modeling notations do not consider the possibility to reuse their models for different smartphone platforms. These modeling notations will need a considerable amount of changes if they want to consider different smartphone unique requirement and software portability key principles.

Our work is different where it concerns about providing a modeling notation that complies with common smartphone apps specifications in terms of UI/UX, architecture design rules and needed apps dependencies within given a smartphone platform.

4   Modeling Notation

We call for a DSL modeling notation to define smartphone applications using appropriate abstractions. We are going to maintain our version of DSL considering three design factors: 1) architecture design rules, 2) apps dependencies, and 3) UI/UX specifications in a given platform. Architecture design rules specify what kind of smartphone components to be put in different architecture levels and how these components supposed to be used in current infrastructures [21]. The notation should allow apps designers or developers to model their apps considering architecture design that entails direct interfaces (e.g. I/O storage and devices interfaces) and indirect interfaces (e.g.UI screens and their components). Apps dependencies are needed to be identified in terms of needed libraries and externals components. Also, UI/UX specifications are needed to be determined where different smartphone vendors set own best practices for their platforms. The model notation should aid app developers with a solid base to efficiently port their apps for a designated smartphone platform by visualizing smartphone apps components to be ported and reusing the resulted models for future porting.

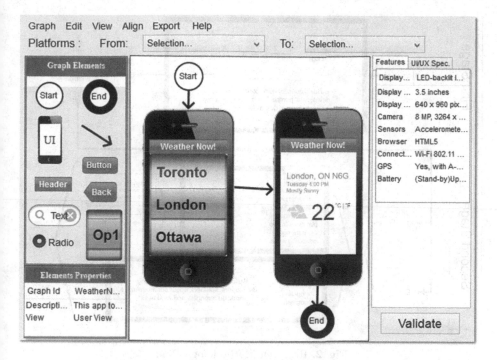

Fig. 1. SmartphoneML Tool

Fig 1 indicates our view of our tool (i.e. SmartphoneML tool) to use our modeling notation to draw the smartphone apps abstract models and their flows, to validate these models, and to generate executable code prior to be complied in a chosen smartphone platform. Fig 1 is inspired from open source MetaEdit+ tool[6] that concerns about maintaining a modeling notation for a specific domain [22].

We would like to investigate whether a portability-driven modeling notation could improve smartphone developers productivity during porting their smartphone apps. To achieve our goal, our research will undergo two stages as shown in Fig 2. First stage of our current research plan aims to maintain our modeling notation and its components: *smartphone ontology, smartphone domain model*, and *developers' perspective questionnaire*. The smartphone ontology[7] will be used to represent a set of concepts and relationships of smartphone domain. The smartphone domain model is responsible to bear domain elements (i.e. objects, relationships, roles, properties or other sub metamodels). Figure 3 illustrates a simple domain model diagram used to represent a simple family tree [13]. Figure 3 can be read as follows: *"a Person object (the blue rounded rectangle) can be in a Family relationship (the orange diamond) with other Person objects*

---

[6] MetaEdit+ tool site http://www.metacase.com/products.html

[7] Many efforts considered ontology-based approaches to handle smartphone app fragmentation, such as [23] or [24]. However, our work use ontology as a semantic knowledge base to unify varied terms used in the smartphone domain.

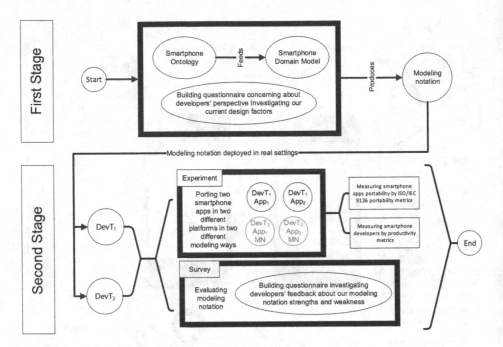

Fig. 2. Research Methodology Plan

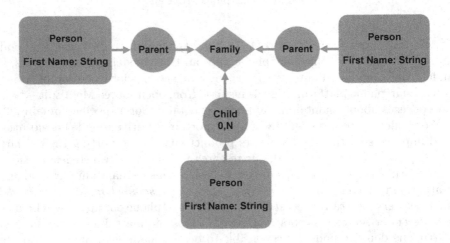

Fig. 3. Family Tree Domain Model Example [22]

and for each Family relationship there must be at least two Persons in Parent roles (the green circles). Optionally there can be more Persons participating in 0-N Child roles. Person objects also carry an identifying property called First Name" [22]. The smartphone domain model articulates the concepts of a language and their governing rules in the smartphone domain complying with our three design factors. Developers' perspective questionnaire will investigate our current design factors in terms of smartphone developers' perspective. Second stage of our current research plan aims to deploy our modeling notation in real settings through two development teams $DevT_1$ and $DevT_2$ in order to conduct *porting experiment* and *validation questionnaire*. The porting experiment concerns about letting each development team to port two smartphone apps twice by their preferred modeling approach ($DevT_1App_1$ and $DevT_1App_2$) and by our modeling notation ($DevT_2App_1MN$ and $DevT_2App_2MN$). The ported smartphone apps portability will be measured against ISO/IEC TR 9126 software portability metrics, such as porting user friendliness or installation effort [25]. In addition, the developers productivity is measured against a set of productivity metrics, such as function point development productivity $FDevP$ or code reuse CRe [26]. The validation questionnaire will investigate our modeling notation in terms of its strength and weakness.

5   Summary and Current Status

Many smartphone app requirements were not considered in their design phase, and these requirements impose own challenges against porting activities between different smartphone platforms. We found a research gap in smartphone literature about our portability-driven development methods concerning software portability key principles. We would like to investigate whether our modeling notation could improve smartphone developers productivity during porting their smartphone apps. We call for modeling DSL-based graphical notation complying with three design factors: 1) architecture design rules, 2) app dependencies, and 3) UI/UX guidelines in a given platform. Our modeling notation is meant to facilitate smartphone developers to understand their apps to port them to other platforms with a better process. This modeling notation should not only aid app developers with a solid base to efficiently port their apps for a designated smartphone platform by visualizing smartphone components to be ported but also allow developers to reuse the resulted models for future porting. Our modeling notation is in-progress work, and we are working on our model notation elements by building the smartphone ontology and gathering UI/UX guidelines for several smartphone platforms prior to maintaining the smartphone domain model.

Acknowledgments. The research for this paper was financially supported by the Ministry of Education of Saudi Arabia and King Abdullah Foreign Scholarship Program, and College of Computer Science and Engineering at Taibah University, Madinah, Saudi Arabia[8].

References

1. Wasserman, A.I.: Software engineering issues for mobile application development. In: Proceedings of the FSE/SDP Workshop on Future of Software Engineering Research, pp. 397–400. ACM, November 2010

---

[8] Taibah University site https://www.taibahu.edu.sa/Pages/AR/Home.aspx

2. Mooney, J.D.: Developing portable software. In: Reis, R. (ed.) Information Technology. IFIP, vol. 157, pp. 55–84. Springer, US (2004)
3. Economics, D.: Developer economics third quarter 2014 and first quarter 2015: state of the developer nation (2014–2015). (Online; accessed March-2015) https://www.developereconomics.com/reports/
4. Sommerville, I.: Software Engineering, 9th edn. Pearson (2010)
5. Gavalas, D., Economou, D.J.: Development platforms for mobile applications: Status and trends. IEEE Software **28**(1), 77–86 (2011)
6. Fling, B.: Mobile Design and Development: Practical concepts and techniques for creating mobile sites and web apps. O'Reilly Media, Inc. (2009)
7. Spriestersbach, A., Springer, T.: Quality attributes in mobile web application development. In: Bomarius, F., Iida, H. (eds.) PROFES 2004. LNCS, vol. 3009, pp. 120–130. Springer, Heidelberg (2004)
8. Heitkötter, H., Hanschke, S., Majchrzak, T.A.: Evaluating cross-platform development approaches for mobile applications. In: Cordeiro, J., Krempels, K.-H. (eds.) WEBIST 2012. LNBIP, vol. 140, pp. 120–138. Springer, Heidelberg (2013)
9. Ohrt, J., Turau, V.: Cross-platform development tools for smartphone applications. Computer **45**(9), 72–79 (2012)
10. Rodger, R.: Beginning Mobile Application Development in the Cloud, 1st edn. Wrox Press Ltd., November 2011
11. Beydeda, S., Book, M., Gruhn, V. (eds.): Model-Driven Software Development. Springer, Heidelberg (2005)
12. Fowler, M.: Domain Specific Languages, 1st edn. Addison-Wesley Professional, October 2010
13. Kelly, S., Tolvanen, J.P.: Domain-Specific Modeling: Enabling Full Code Generation. Wiley, March 2008
14. Inukollu, V.N., Keshamoni, D.D., Kang, T., Inukollu, M.: Factors influencing quality of mobile apps: Role of mobile app development life cycle. International Journal of Software Engineering & Applications **5**(5), 15–34 (2014)
15. Kraemer, F.A.: Engineering android applications based on UML activities. In: Whittle, J., Clark, T., Kühne, T. (eds.) MODELS 2011. LNCS, vol. 6981, pp. 183–197. Springer, Heidelberg (2011)
16. Ginsburg, S.: Designing the iPhone user experience: a user-centered approach to sketching and prototyping iPhone apps, 1st edn. Addison Wesley, August 2010
17. Saleh, K., El-Morr, C.: M-UML: an extension to UML for the modeling of mobile agent-based software systems. Information and Software Technology **46**(4), 219–227 (2004)
18. Min, B.K., Ko, M., Seo, Y., Kuk, S., Kim, H.S.: A UML metamodel for smart device application modeling based on Windows Phone 7 platform. In: Proceedings of the 2011 IEEE Region 10 Conference TENCON, pp. 201–205. IEEE, November 2011
19. Kramer, D., Clark, T., Oussena, S.: MobDSL: a domain specific language for multiple mobile platform deployment. In: Proceedings of the 2010 IEEE International Conference on Networked Embedded Systems for Enterprise Applications, pp. 1–7. ACM, November 2010
20. LeGoaer, O., Waltham, S.: Yet another DSL for cross-platforms mobile development. In: Proceedings of the First Workshop on the Globalization of Domain Specific Languages, pp. 28–33. ACM (2013)
21. Mattsson, A., Fitzgerald, B., Lundell, B., Lings, B.: An approach for modeling architectural design rules in UML and its application to embedded software. ACM Trans. Softw. Eng. Methodol. **21**(2), 10:1–10:29 (2012)

22. Kelly, S.: MetaEdit+- user's guides version 5.1., March 2015. (Online; accessed March-2015) http://www.metacase.com/support/51/manuals/
23. Agarwal, V., Goyal, S., Mittal, S., Mukherjea, S.: Mobivine: a middleware layer to handle fragmentation of platform interfaces for mobile applications. In: Companion Proceedings ninth International Middleware Conference, p. 24 (2009)
24. Stapić, Z.: Dealing with mobile platforms fragmentation problem: Ontology oriented approach (2013)
25. ISO/IEC: "software engineering - product quality - part 3: Internal metrics,". Technical report (ISO/IEC TR 9126-3, 2003). http://www.iso.org/iso/catalogue_detail. htm?csnumber=22891
26. Galin, D.: Software Quality Assurance: From Theory to Implementation, 1st edn. Alternative Etext Formats. Pearson/Addison Wesley (2004)

Author Index